ENDING CONGRESSIONAL GRIDLOCK MOVING TOWARD A MORE DEMOCRATIC AMERICA

Gary Y. Larsen

2012

First published in 2012 by
Boyd Street Press
Boonton, New Jersey 07005 USA
www.boydstreetpress.com

© Copyright Gary Y. Larsen, 2012

All Rights Reserved

Neither this book nor any part thereof may be reproduced or transmitted in any form or by any means, electronic or mechanical including photocopying, scanning, microfilming, and recording, or by any information storage and retrieval system without the express written permission from the author.

ISBN: 978-0-98506-160-9 (paperback)
ISBN: 978-0-98506-161-6 (e-book)

Cover design by Patricia Rasch: www.patriciarasch.com
Text design and typesetting: www.scholarlytype.com

Printed in the United States of America

CONTENTS

Preface... v
Acknowledgments...................................... viii
Introduction 1

I CREATING AN UNDEMOCRATIC GOVERNMENT

1 Economic and Political Precursors
  to the Constitution 11
2 Issues in the Construction of the Constitution 23
3 On Democracy....................................... 35
4 Modern Democracies 45

II PERPETUATING AN UNDEMOCRATIC GOVERNMENT

5 The Separation of Powers.............................. 61
6 Subordination of the House 73
7 The Executive: Master or Servant?....................... 85
8 Judicial Supremacy................................... 99
9 Anti-Party Politics................................... 113
10 Professionalization 129

III Congressional Gridlock

11 Compromising over Slavery 139
12 Slavery in All But Name. 149
13 Commerce and Credit 157

IV Imperial Presidents

14 Building a Nation. 179
15 Becoming a World Power. 191
16 War: Hot, Cold, and Forever 207

V Toward a More Complete Democracy

17 Structure of the U.S. Government 221
18 Changing the Government 233

Conclusion 245

Appendix: Greek Democracy 247
Notes. 250
Bibliography 260
Index 266

PREFACE

More than 300 years ago, 100 years before the United States even existed, the political system in England evolved from a feudal monarchy to a constitutional monarchy, in which Parliament runs the government. The change did not come easily. The issue was one of who was in charge, the executive (the King) or the legislature (Parliament).

The transition from feudalism to parliamentary government began in the 1640s, when Charles I wanted money to finance wars in Europe—wars that Parliament did not agree with. Parliament refused to appropriate the money. Charles' first response was to try to appropriate the money himself, by levying taxes that had not been approved by Parliament. Parliament, however, had enough authority in the population and in the government bureaucracy to prevent the King's efforts. The King was not able to make these taxes effective, but his fight with Parliament went on for years, creating a paralysis in government.

The end result, because Charles would not back down, was a civil war, which ended in 1649 with his execution. For a ten-year period, England was no longer a monarchy. Parliament ran the government under Cromwell. Parliament was never able to establish its ability to run the government on its own, however, and when Cromwell died in 1659, it allowed the restoration of the monarch, Charles II.

This restoration did not resolve the earlier issue of who was in charge, the King or Parliament. Conflict continued for another twenty-eight years, with the King trying to dissolve or prorogue Parliament (rule on his own without dissolving Parliament), while others developed plots to overthrow the King. It was during this period that Locke wrote his *Treatise on Government*, thus bequeathing to the revolutionaries in America his version of the ideal state, based on the conflicted failing state of his time.

It was not until 1688, the year of England's Glorious Revolution, that the conflicts between the King and Parliament were finally resolved. King James II abdicated the throne, and Parliament, meeting in an extraordinary session (essentially as a constitutional convention), accepted William of Orange as England's new King, *on the condition that he agree to rule only through, and with the consent of, Parliament.* The King's ministers, instead of following the King's wishes, became members and leaders of Parliament. The executive and the legislative functions were integrated.

This conditional, or constitutional, monarchy ended the continual debate over who was in charge of the government. From that point on, Parliament, and in particular the House of Commons, was clearly in charge—although in several ways it took at least another 100 years before this was clearly understood. The British government became the model for democratic governments around the world, even though it did not become fully representative until 1832.

The United States is in a position similar to that of England prior to their establishment of a constitutional monarchy. The essential issue of who is in charge of the government, the House or the President (and the Senate), means that we live with an ongoing conflict between the House of Representatives (the equivalent of the House of Commons in Britain) and the President (the King) over who can set policy and appropriate money for programs.

The Founders set up our government so that this conflict was a part of the process. They thought, relying on Locke and others, that government should involve struggle between bodies; indeed they believed it had to be this way, in large part because they feared majority rule. In this book I suggest that this is not the way it should be, or has to be. These conflicts have persisted for the last

200 or more years because of the idealistic American belief that the Founders were infallible, not because the U.S. government is a functional, effective, and efficient system. We can now see that we need not fear majority rule.

Over the course of U.S. history numerous situations have arisen—over slavery, civil rights, Vietnam, Medicare, health insurance—in which a pattern has repeated itself, a pattern in which a clear majority of Americans want something, but it is not successfully accomplished because of a determined minority who distort and derail the political process. It is only when a majority, frequently in extreme circumstances such as economic crises, wars, or following assassinations, overwhelms minority obstructionists that the government manages to enact the clear expression of the will of the majority.

The current situation can best be described as a dysfunctional government: one that is plagued by threats of government shutdowns, budget crises, party stalemates, and general paralysis. We are, perhaps, beginning to recognize the need to resolve this conflict and enact a system in which majority rule is the norm rather than the exception.

This book offers an extended explanation of why the government works the way it does, evidence of the consequences this system of government has had on U.S. history, and suggestions for how it might be changed to respond better to the will of the majority. Government needs to be more democratic, in the sense that it should operate by majority rule. If we want to continue as a democratic republic, we must give power to the House of Representatives, the one body that most accurately reflects the will of the majority of Americans, and by doing so, end this era of imperial presidents and congressional gridlock.

ACKNOWLEDGMENTS

I have benefited immeasurably from my readings of other authors who clearly know more about their subjects than I could ever hope to know. I take full responsibility for the ideas in the book and any mistakes I may have made. I would first like to thank Dr. Benjamin-Alvarado, a professor of political science at the University of Nebraska at Omaha for his early encouragement to continue with this project. I have benefited considerably from editorial comments from my editor Linda Bland and from Valerie Turner, who has also edited the manuscript, and more importantly has supported my efforts to complete the work. Muhammad Hozien has graciously contributed his skills to typesetting the book. Finally, I owe special thanks to my wife, Sharon, who continually forced me to clarify my thoughts and avoid excessive generalizations.

INTRODUCTION

Poll after poll in recent years has indicated that the people are not happy with the government in general, and the President and Congress in particular. Some people feel the government is not doing enough for the people, and others believe it is doing too much. Whatever the direction of the complaint, from the left or the right, the anger can be generalized into the feeling that the government is just not doing its job, that the government is only a tool of special interests, and does not express the will of the people. This is in contrast to the attitudes people have toward the *form* of our government.

Most Americans consider the form of our government enshrined in the Constitution as an ideal to which others should aspire. They believe that the Constitution is a sacred document that sets forth the most perfect form of government on earth. Abraham Lincoln in 1838 counseled that the Constitution and laws should "become the *political religion* of the nation."[1]

This sentiment is not limited to any particular group, but is most intensely felt among extreme right wing conservatives (the Tea Party). "Many Tea Partiers view the Constitution in much the same way that fundamentalists regard the Bible, a sacred text whose Language is the source of truth."[2] In spite of the continual criticism of what the government is doing or not doing, most Americans believe the fundamental form put forth in the Constitution guarantees the best, most democratic government in the world.

The proof of our excellence is that we have the most powerful and prosperous country in the world. Our power and prosperity must be the result of the form of our government. Most Americans would say other countries should copy our form of government, given how powerful and prosperous we have become. For many conservatives, the problems of today are only the result of the deviation from the form of government given in our sacred Constitution.

Much of what is written about the Constitution supports this view that the form of our government is nearly perfect and does not need changing. The 2007 book by Lane and Oreskes,[3] for example, is an unreservedly self-congratulatory account of the origins and development of the Constitution, replete with comments on how well-written, insightful, and nearly perfect the Constitution is, and how well it has done in surviving for 220 years without major changes.

This contrast between how people feel about the government, and how they feel about the form of our government must be examined. We need to consider that the structure of our government is not perfect. Our criticisms of what the government is or is not doing are as much criticisms of the structure of the government as they are of the particular issues involved.

The U.S. government was set up with the assumption that the President and Congress are separate and independent, but also with the expectation that they will cooperate in running the government. From the beginning, cooperation proved to be problematic and often difficult. Conflict between the parts of the government became the norm.

In 1790, when Secretary of the Treasury Hamilton tried to work too closely with Congress, to develop the budget for the government, Congress rejected his efforts, fearing the President and his cabinet would have too much control over Congress. From then until the twentieth century, when coordinating the budget became too complex for Congress to handle by itself, Congress jealously guarded its budgeting authority from incursions by the executive. Opposition between Congress and the President was just assumed.

Introduction

Tension between the President and Congress has existed from the beginning.

Meanwhile the Senate established itself, with unlimited debate and the filibuster, as the opposition to the House, and to national government action. It has been the source of congressional gridlock, able to delay, distort, or block the will of the majority in the House. This gridlock is the primary cause of the people's frustrations with Congress today. A common expression of this aggravation, dating back at least to the 1930s, even if said tongue in cheek, is "What we need is a good dictatorship!"[4]

Gridlock has been a perennial characteristic of our government, and is justified as the price we have to pay for democracy. We have accepted repeated gridlock, delay, and distortion of the will of the people. It is just the way politics work, we are told. These are the checks and balances we have been led to believe we need, even though the outcomes are most often gridlock and the frustration of the will of the people.

The ongoing battle between the President and Congress and between the House and the Senate has, at the least, wasted time and effort. Today their stalemate evokes disrespect from the general population. The conflict is basically one of power, of who is in charge. The legislature wants control over how the legislation it enacts is implemented, and so has tried to exert influence over the executive officers in charge of carrying out the legislation. At every point, though, and with increasing animosity, the President has resisted these efforts, claiming that only he controls the executive. The courts have largely upheld the President—encouraging and institutionalizing the continuation of the conflicts.

With the beginning of the twentieth century, the tension over who is in charge increased considerably, as the role of the federal government became much more complex and influential in the country. As federal agencies such as the Interstate Commerce Commission, the Bureau of the Budget, the Federal Reserve System, and the Federal Trade Commission were established to regulate national affairs, the issue of who is in charge of these agencies—the President, Congress, or the judiciary—became central. Fisher's book on the politics of shared power[5] documents these continual conflicts between the President and Congress, and the mountain of time and effort spent in their quarrels.

The continuing tensions built into our government have weakened and distracted governance throughout our history, and have contributed to the crises our country has endured, such as the Civil War and the Depression. A system in continual turmoil, as is the American government, tries to resolve the strain by clarifying and rationalizing the structure. It is natural to seek ways to reduce tension so governance can be more efficient and effective.

The predominant way to reduce these tensions, according to those who have written about how to develop better government, is to "get politics out of government," to remove the influence of parties and special interests in the operation of the government. Parties are seen as the sources of the failures of effective governance.[6] Removing such influences from government, however, gives more power to the President. Since 1900, giving more power to the President has been an explicit part of many recommendations for reform, starting with the Progressive movement in the early 1900s. These reform advocates have been successful: The President has become more powerful over the last century.

Corwin[7] demonstrated the "aggrandizement of power," of the presidency since Jefferson, and Schlesinger, in reaction to the Nixon era, updated this earlier account of the evolution of presidential power in *The Imperial Presidency*.[8] With the G. W. Bush administration we saw just another ratchet in the growth of presidential power.[9] Giving the President more power has been the path of least resistance for the United States in resolving problems of effectiveness and efficiency.

Increasing the influence of the President has a certain logic: The President is elected by all the people, and so represents all the people. He can be trusted to do what is best for the people. Besides, if he does not do a good job, he can be replaced after four years, or at most after eight years. For most people the really great presidents—Jackson, Lincoln, Teddy Roosevelt, and FDR—are great because they were strong and forceful leaders who got things done over the resistance of Congress.

The G. W. Bush administration, however, raised a basic question in this tendency to give the President more power: At what point in this accumulation of presidential power does the President have too much power? How should Congress act when the consensus is that the President has too much power? What does it take in our government for Congress to tell the President to stop doing what he is doing? At what point in the accumulation of presidential power would the President so blatantly and arrogantly claim so much power for himself that Congress would be forced to assert itself—or become irrelevant?

Is the ability of the President to get the United States involved in an immoral and unnecessary war, wasting billions of dollars, and losing the respect of the world, enough to motivate a reaction against presidential power? Are claims of executive privilege, claims of immunity from the Geneva Conventions and from anti-wiretapping laws, or refusal to testify before Congress, not enough to cause Congress to act? Apparently not.

If the President took on dictatorial powers, ignoring the ineffective Congress and the judiciary, what would the Congress do—or would it be too late? Will the President just gradually accumulate power until it is not possible to stop him? Are the Bush-Cheney administration challenges to democratic government now gone? Can we comfortably go back to our basic belief that the form of our government is the best in the world?

The logical endpoint of accumulation of presidential power is a presidential dictatorship, with Congress, mired in continual gridlock, having only a vestigial role to play. A forceful President is what we need to get things done in this country. Acceptance of more presidential power, however, contradicts the democratic principles on which our government supposedly operates.

Any contention that the government is still a democracy because the President is elected, is naïve. Many dictators throughout history have gained their power first through elections—Hitler among them. Unfortunately, both the advocates of increased presidential power and its critics offer no alternative solution to the problems that motivate the push for increased executive authority.

Most advocates of government reform do not question the basic structure of our government. Some authors[10] argue that we need a new constitutional convention to make it more representative, but they do not advocate any basic structural change. These scholars are content with minor adjustments around the edges—what could be called rearranging the deck chairs.

Others, such as Ackerman, try only to interpret the course of historical change.[11] He is not critical of the tendency toward more presidential power. For him the process of constitutional change has just shifted to a contest between the President and the Supreme Court—although much of the time the Supreme Court has supported the President. Congress has only a subsidiary, subordinate role in his discussion of constitutional change. The effects of the subordination of Congress are shown in Norman Ornstein and Thomas Mann's book, *The Broken Branch*,[12] which describes the deterioration of the legislative process in the House. What they describe may not just be a broken branch, but a branch that has become increasingly irrelevant to the operation of government.

Wolin[13] sounds the alarm about the conflicts between our image of ourselves as a democracy, and our image of ourselves as a superpower, but he does not consider structural change in the government a solution to the conflicts. The same could be said for James Dean's books,[14] and Charles Savage's account of Cheney's takeover of the presidency.[15]

None of these authors have any complaint about the form of our government. They implicitly accept we have the best possible governmental structure. They claim it is the *people* running the government who are at fault for our problems. They suggest only that citizens become more educated and involved in their government, and elect better people.

These critics lack imagination. They cannot envision our present government operating any differently. We alternate between strong imperial presidents, and gridlocked congresses where little is accomplished unless there is a crisis. The only solution proposed to the problems of delay and inefficiency is to further increase the power of the President. Little is said about changing Congress.

Abuses of past imperial presidents make it easier to accept the need to change our government, but now that we have an administration with more respect for Congress, it is easy to relax and believe that the abuses of executive power will never return. However, the 2008 election changed nothing about our government other than its personnel. The potential for the same assertions of presidential power—defiance of Congress and covert violations of the rights and privileges of individuals—remains. We have no assurance that our present President, or some future President, will not assert these powers again.

Our government is still in a state of debilitating tension between the President and Congress, leaving Congress either unable or unwilling to carry out its responsibilities. In such paralyzing circumstances it is not surprising that the President is encouraged to take on ever more power. President Obama may be more willing to cooperate with Congress than the previous administration but in crises like the credit crisis or the recent oil spill in the Gulf of Mexico we again cry out for strong, decisive leadership. In our present governmental structure, this means bestowing on the President even more authority. If the financial crisis we now seem to be recovering from were to worsen, we have no alternative. Crises always seem to require increased executive power.

To find alternatives to increasing presidential power, we must start by recognizing that our current government is not a fully democratic government. This is not even a point of controversy among students of American history and government. The constraints and restrictions, the "checks and balances" that have been built into our system make it less than fully democratic. The solution to inefficiency and ineffectiveness, to congressional gridlock and imperial presidents, is a more democratic government, one that eliminates those structures put in place because of the Founder's fear of the will of the majority.

We can complacently continue in our current direction and accept an eventual presidential dictatorship, or we can move toward a more truly democratic system—as have most other developed governments. Contrary to what most Americans hold dear, the British parliament, not the American government, is more democratic and is the model for most new governments.[16] It is now time for the U.S. government to complete its transition to a parliamentary government—just as the British government did over 300 years ago.

It is difficult for many Americans to comprehend the suggestion that we need to become more democratic. We have all been raised to learn and accept the principles and procedures of our government, and have seldom had occasion to question them. The ideas of the separation of powers, checks and balances, and the virtue of bipartisan consensus have been repeated over and over so much that for most people in the United States, "they must be true." This book questions all these concepts.

I

CREATING AN UNDEMOCRATIC GOVERNMENT

1

ECONOMIC AND POLITICAL PRECURSORS TO THE CONSTITUTION

Economic Pressures before the Revolution

The first step in understanding the present structure of U.S. government is to see better how we got the system we have. Many factors caused the American Revolution, including British intransigence, stubbornness, and shortsightedness.[1] The British made mistakes in dealing with the American colonies, and did not repeat their mistakes in dealing with their other possessions, such as Canada and Australia.

Other causes include a growing separateness and self-sufficiency of the colonies, and the growing rivalry in trade in the Caribbean between the British and the Americans. The ongoing conflict between France and Britain was another underlying influence on British-American relations.

The primary cause of the American Revolution, however, was economic. When the colonists complained about taxation without representation, their complaints were really economic. The problem was not so much that the taxes were unfair; this implies that if they were fairer they would pay them. The problem was rather that the colonists could not pay them; they simply did not have the money, in the form of hard currency, with which to pay. The problems went deeper than just taxes: The colonists had trouble paying *any* debts.

Almost a century ago, Beard[2] was the first to apply an economic perspective to the formation of the American government. He developed the argument that the Constitution was written in the context of an ideological war between capitalists and agrarians. His arguments were very controversial at the time, but have since been accepted as part of the account of American history of the eighteenth and nineteenth centuries.

Class and wealth conflicts have always been part of the formation of any government, and it was no different in 1787 when the Constitution was written.[3] The shift from an agrarian, feudal society to a commercial, credit-based, international, capitalistic economy had its impact on the colonies. The American Revolution was largely about how the colonies adjusted to this historical shift.

More recently, discussion of economic issues affecting the course of the American Revolution has been more concrete and less ideological. Bouton[4] and Holton[5] in their detailed descriptions of colonial experiences, especially Pennsylvania, provide an economic explanation for the revolution and the developments leading up to creation of the federal Constitution. Their accounts focus on the loss of hard money resulting from the end of the war between Britain and France in 1763.

With the end of this war, part of which was fought in the New World as the French and Indian Wars, Britain wanted to repair its financial affairs, and to do so it needed to increase its store of hard money: gold and silver. Although today effectively all money is paper, before the twentieth century there was a sharp distinction between "real" money, made out of gold and silver, and paper money, which relied only on a promise to redeem the paper with real money. One way to do this was to pass laws to force the colonies to pay their debts, and to buy merchandise with gold or silver coins.

The British banned the use of paper money in the colonies, a devastating edict for the colonists, but tending to the colonists' interests had a very low priority for the British government. It had much more pressing problems with its own money supply. The

British focus was on building up their supply of hard currency to prepare for the next war, and to project British power in other areas.

The requirement that debts and merchandise be paid in hard currency quickly depleted the colonies of what few coins they had, and left them unable to pay their debts at all. A chain reaction of demands to pay debts ensued: The British merchants needed coins to pay *their* debts and taxes to the crown, so they demanded that the colonial merchants pay up. The colonial merchants in turn had to demand payment from the small businessmen and farmers who had borrowed money to finance their businesses or to buy seed and equipment for the next harvest. At each link in the chain tremendous pressure developed to pay off debt.

Small businessmen and farmers had to sell whatever they had and often went out of business. Selling under such circumstances was itself very difficult because few had the hard currency to buy. Prices plummeted. Through the 1760s and 1770s, severe deflation occurred as money became increasingly valuable—and goods worth almost nothing.

In the end, everyone lost. Farmers and small businessmen went out of business, the merchants and shippers did not get paid, nor did the colonial or British governments increase their store of hard currency. Those at the lower end of the chain wanted to pay their debts, but with no hard currency, how could they? Ultimately they felt it was unfair to be asked to pay when they had no means to do so.

The only solution for creditors of the time was to try harder to collect the debts. Colonial governments were on their side in trying to force debtors to pay. For the governments and most of the wealthier merchants, the failure to pay debts and taxes was seen as a problem of enforcement against willful avoidance of the law and individual moral duty.

Even the individual farmers and businessmen often accepted this view of the problem. They were hard workers and wanted to pay their debts, but just could not. The inherent unfairness of being asked to pay debts without providing a means to do so was a major cause of the dissatisfaction leading to the American Revolution, and later to the Constitutional Convention.[6]

The colonists were especially upset that they were not allowed to produce and use paper money as a means to pay their debts to each other. Before the British made it illegal, the colonists had been using paper money based on loans to farmers, using the land as collateral. This had worked well, as it provided liquidity to their monetary system; from the British point of view, this method was just a way to avoid paying debts in hard currency.

Without paper money and with little hard currency, the colonists were subject to property auctions run by local sheriffs. There were no bankruptcy laws at the time; if debts could not be paid it ultimately meant jail. The lower and middle classes felt a great deal of sympathy for farmers and small businessmen, and systematic resistance to the efforts to enforce the law developed: Fellow farmers would refuse to bid on the property at auction. Much of the motivation and organization for the revolution derived from these efforts to support small farmers.

Responses to deflation and the lack of hard currency took two forms: Some, like Thomas Jefferson, made a virtue out of being self-sufficient and independent of the larger economic system. It helped that these individuals were relatively wealthy landowners. They allied themselves with the English landed aristocracy, who had enjoyed similar independence and self-sufficiency in the feudal system that was disappearing. Jefferson represented the agrarian point of view in Beard's terms: The farm and the extended family of those who worked on the farm were the central aspects of life, with trade and commerce unimportant, secondary contributors.

The other response, such as Alexander Hamilton's, was to accept the economic system as it was, and fight to become a part of that system. This was the commercial view of life, in which trade and commerce were central, and the farm was just another source of material for trade. Thus, for very different reasons, both groups were in favor of independence from Britain; after independence was achieved, their differences emerged.

Initial Attempts at Writing Constitutions

When the colonists were writing their first state constitutions prior to and following the Declaration of Independence in 1776, turmoil in the economic system continued. The general depression resulting from the absence of hard money persisted and worsened with the loss of trade with Britain. With no universally accepted monetary system, commerce between the individual states became even more difficult.

None of the individual states had a viable currency of its own, and hard currency was scarce for everyone. Paper money and bank notes were used, but without any real basis, they soon became worthless. Under these circumstances creditors had no choice but to continue to demand payment of debts, and debtors remained unable to repay their loans.

The states wrote their constitutions based on their experiences with colonial government and their readings in political theory. Some states, such as New York, and Massachusetts under the influence of John Adams, constructed governments that were direct copies of the colonial governments and the British system as it was presented in the writings of Locke, as interpreted by Montesquieu.[7] Adams saw the ideal government as one that balanced the three "branches" of government, as prescribed by Montesquieu. Montesquieu's theories were based, in turn, on Locke and others from the 1600s, writers who had wrestled with the turmoil of English politics at the time.

Some other states were more responsive to the theories of republicanism and democracy that the colonists had been reading about and discussing: the radical English writers of the 1600s.[8] Virginia, and in particular Pennsylvania, gave the legislature the dominant place in running the government, and made the executive subordinate to it. The governor had no veto, and the legislature appointed the governor and most other executive officers. Pennsylvania made the most determined attempt to reflect the changes that had taken place in Britain after 1688: Their new government was more parliamentary and gave more power to the legislature.

In America, state legislatures were much more representative than their British model at the time, and so were much more responsive to the will of the majority. They often acted in favor of the debtors, the large majority of the population, and tried to find ways to help them pay their debts. Pennsylvania, for instance, tried to reinstate the use of loans for land as a form of paper money. There were pressures in many other states to issue paper money, or somehow to forgive debts.

Creditors saw this as an intolerable situation, a reward to those who were lazy and immoral. They felt that the only way to preserve the existing economic structure was by doing what the British had been doing before the Revolution, demanding payment of debts in the form of hard currency. Creditors did appreciate the scarcity of hard currency, and the Bank of North America under the management of Robert Morris was chartered in Philadelphia to try to accumulate such currency.

Neither of these schemes—neither the state issuance of paper money, nor the establishment of a bank to accumulate hard currency—was successful. Both were undercapitalized and unable to resolve the problem of too little hard money. Many states could not pay even their own bills, much less pay the operating expenses of the national government that had been created by the Articles of Confederation.

The states remained under a great deal of pressure to relieve the debtors. The legislatures were reluctant to enact relief because they understood the need to maintain a sound credit system, but at the same time the legislators had to respond to the demands of their constituents, the majority of whom were debtors.

The scattered uprisings and rebellions, such as Shay's Rebellion in Massachusetts, made the state leaders apprehensive about the viability of the state governments. These fears fueled a pervasive feeling among the framers of the Federal Constitution that the state legislatures were subject to the "tyranny of the majority." The debtor majority could not pay their debts, but could "tyrannize" the legislatures into actions, such as forgiving debt, that were contrary to the interests of the minority of creditors, and perhaps even the general common good.[9]

The economic stresses of the times caused the failure of the more democratic state governments such as Pennsylvania. None of the state governments, regardless of their structure, could survive without a stable, secure monetary and credit system. The states with legislative dominance did not provide this stability. Under this tension, the state constitutions reverted to the familiar: governments with strong and independent executives that could restrain the perceived excesses of the legislatures.

The executive branch in state governments like Pennsylvania was nominally subordinate to the legislature, but past experience living under a monarchical system may have made it difficult for Americans to appreciate the importance of having a legislature with leaders who were more powerful than the executive branch; leaders who were powerful enough to control the executive. The legislature in Pennsylvania and similar states might have continued as only advisors to the executive, even when the executive was less powerful. Few may have understood or appreciated that the leader of the legislature could act with the authority of the prime minister and the king's cabinet in England, dominating even the King.

Final State Constitutions

In the twelve years between 1776 and 1788, after their first attempts to form governments similar to modern parliaments, Americans regressed. In part because of the continuing problems with the monetary system, by the 1790s all the states had reverted back to essentially the form of government the colonists had been familiar with before the revolution: a strong governor appointing the other executive officers and holding veto power over the legislature, and an additional upper house of the legislature.[12] Legislative dominance was tried but felt unnatural, and did not succeed. State constitutions were rewritten to provide a political solution for an economic problem. Government was designed to resolve conflicts between debtors and creditors. Rather than going forward toward a more parliamentary form of government, they adopted the more "traditional," feudal view of government: one that balanced the classical divisions of society into the monarch, the aristocrats, and the "demos," or the people.[10]

This tradition existed only in their colonial experience and in the writings of Locke, Harrington, and Montesquieu as a description of what was actually only a *transitional* form of government, the government that existed only between 1600 and 1688, during the transition from monarchical feudal government to parliamentary government. The balanced government described in Adams, Locke, and Montesquieu was an idealized government that was inherently unstable and in the process of disappearing in Europe, especially in Britain, just as the Founders were adopting it. It was never a stable, well functioning form worthy of emulation.

This "classical", balanced form of government may have corresponded roughly to the governments in the American colonies, but only because they were not independent, sovereign governments: they were subordinate to the government of the mother country, Britain.

The application of this traditional form is represented best in the governments of Massachusetts and New York. Adams wrote the Massachusetts constitution explicitly accepting the need for a mixed government,[11] one that combined aspects of monarchy, aristocracy, and democracy, with an independent governor as well as an upper house of the legislature.

For Adams and the writers of these state constitutions, there was a place for the House of Commons or House of Representatives; they agreed that the House should approve revenue measures. An equivalent to the House of Lords, our Senate, and a strong executive, an elected President, were felt to be necessary to restrain the expected excesses of the legislature, just as the colonial governor had restrained the colonial legislatures.

The newly independent American states modeled their governments on those that were familiar to them before the revolution. The colonists were used to having a governor and a legislature in principled opposition; the governor represented the owners of the colony (the king), and the legislature represented the colonists.

This opposition came to feel natural. The only problem was that in the newly independent states, the governor's role was no longer to act in opposition to the legislature.

The writers of some state constitutions initially solved this problem by making the governor subordinate to the legislature, but when they wanted the governor to restrain the legislature they had to justify having a governor in opposition to the legislature. Their solution was to declare that the governor was also a representative of the people. This was an almost inevitable adaptation if the colonists were to retain an equivalent to the governor or king.

Making the governor in some sense also a representative of the people blurred the meaning of representation, putting the governor as the representative of the people in opposition to the legislature as representative of the people. The legislature, the people's representatives, were in opposition to the governor, also the people's representative.

The new states also felt compelled to create a second, "upper" house that in some way represented the "better sort" of people, even though there were no credible aristocrats in the colonies. The governors in the colonies had seemed to need such a body, just as the British had their House of Lords. The existence of a second, superfluous house was justified by claims that this would give the people even more representation.

The Americans reproduced the structure of the governments they had been accustomed to. The state constitutions that developed after the Declaration of Independence resembled the colonial governments, and what Americans understood to be the English government. From their experience with the more democratic state governments like Pennsylvania, state constitution writers did not believe that a government dominated by the legislature would work.

Such governments were perceived as *too* responsive to the majority will, and not willing to take the stern measures necessary to make the new country viable. In revising their constitutions, the states accepted the need for a stable monetary system. Stability, for them, required restraints on majority will. This was not accidental or inadvertent. It was a reaction to the economic conditions. Unfortunately the economic problems continued.

The writers of the state constitutions were responding as well as they could at the time. They knew something had to be done. The economic crisis needed to be resolved in any way possible. In a crisis the natural human response is to revert to what is most familiar. The governments they created were no more than an adaptation of the governments they knew about from their experience with the colonies and governments in Europe.

It was natural, but perhaps ironic, that the former colonists did no more than restore many aspects of the very governments they had been fighting against, but with which they were familiar. The governments they created were not new and original: they made only minor adaptations to the past.

These experiments in the creation of governments occurred entirely within the individual states before the Constitutional Convention. Each state thought of itself as a sovereign nation, capable of surviving on its own. The Articles of Confederation, devised during the war with Britain, did not form a real government. Its Congress was more of an intergovernmental coordinating council than a true government.

It resembled more the modern Organization of American States, or the European Union in the 1950s. Each state sent delegates to the Congress, but it had no executive or judicial authority by which it could enforce decisions. Because decisions were made only with unanimous consent, it was an ineffective legislative body. The Congress survived only with contributions from the individual states, and after the war, in the middle of economic distress, these contributions disappeared.

The American states from 1776 to 1788 were without a national or federal government, open to influence from Britain, France or other major powers. No state, by itself, was economically viable. What government there was under the Articles of Confederation was bankrupt with no money coming in to support a federal government. A few individuals, such as Madison and Hamilton, recognized that the individual states could not survive without a larger, stronger federal government.

Their experience with the Articles of Confederation—where no executive existed at all—reinforced the idea that the states needed to create a federal executive that would act with respect to national issues, and, if necessary, in defiance of the individual states. They knew that a federal legislature by itself, without a federal executive, could not overcome the resistance of the individual states, and so they called for a new Constitutional Convention.

2

ISSUES IN THE CONSTRUCTION OF THE CONSTITUTION

The U.S. Constitution

The backlash against the more democratic measures of the initial phase of government formation in the 1770s meant that by the 1780s most state governments had revised their constitutions to make them less democratic, but supposedly more stable and orderly. They reinstated the executive veto, even though, as one commenter at the time remarked, even the English king had not used the veto for a century.[13] Executive officers were to be chosen by the governor, and a second house within the legislature was established to restrain the actions of the representative house. By the time the federal Constitution was written, the individual states had shown the way, and the federal Constitution simply followed them.

The United States claims to be a democratic republic, and such claims were certainly pervasive in the debates over the revolution and the Constitution. The common man saw democracy as the promise of a government for all the people. The more educated men, such as Madison and Hamilton, understood democracy as a degenerate form of a polity in which the poor majority attempted to take from the wealthier minority. The Founders distrusted majority rule and what they feared as the "tyranny of the majority."

The Founders had no faith that the popular majority would act in the interests of all the people. This reflected the Aristotelian sense that democracy meant the rule of mobs unfit to govern. The experience of governance in the states during economic distress only confirmed their fears.

The authors of the Constitution were familiar only with governments in Europe that were not very democratic in the modern sense of being representative and operating by majority rule. They were all monarchies, or at least aristocracies, and did not offer the Founders a model to use that trusted the people, the masses. Many of the Founders felt, as did Edmund Randolph, a member of the Constitutional Convention, that "Our chief danger arises from the democratic parts of our Constitutions. It is a maxim which I hold incontrovertible, that the powers of government exercised by the people swallows up the other branches. None of the Constitutions have provided sufficient checks against the democracy."[14]

Little controversy arose among the Americans about whether or not the government should be democratic in the sense of operating by majority rule. A well-run government, it was believed, needed to be run by an elite group of individuals, the "better sort of people." It was thus important to design the government so those elite people would actually run the government.

There was no confidence that the better sort of people would simply appear as a function of being elected to office. For the Founding Fathers, the better sort of people were born, not made, and had to be induced to govern. They did not understand or believe that those who govern, by virtue of governing, become "the better sort of people." Thus, the governments created after 1776 were designed deliberately to restrain the democratic expression of the majority of the population.

Holton[15] argues that if it were not that the Founders knew they would have to submit their efforts to ratification by the general population, the Constitution would have been even more restrictive and anti-democratic. As it was, the U.S. Constitution was more restrictive than the British government at the time. In the 1700s

Issues in the Construction of the Constitution

the British did not have a legislature that represented the general population, and so did not have to deal with issues of representation.

The framers of the American Constitution were faced with the reality that representation was going to be a central characteristic of their government. The Americans felt compelled to deliberately build in restrictions on the will of the majority. The British had these restrictions already: Voting was restricted to those who owned property, and candidates for election were limited to the wealthy.

The economic concerns behind these restrictions on the majority are shown in Section Ten of Article One of the Constitution: The states shall not "emit Bills of Credit; make any Thing but gold or silver Coin a Tender in Payments of Debt [nor] pass any. . . .Law impairing the Obligation of Contracts." This provision of the Constitution was deliberately designed to prevent any future possibility of the states or the federal government being too responsive to majority opinion, in particular any effort of the states to rescue debtors from their obligations by issuing paper money.

Although the American people have been taught that the Constitution is the epitome of a democratically designed government, serious students of the revolutionary period know that, on the contrary, the system of government was designed as an undemocratic oligarchy. Many modern authors have noted that the American government is not democratic,[16] but most have also described this, as the Founders did, as a virtue rather than a defect. The assumption, it would seem, is that it is sufficient that the government is representative. Further requirements that the government reflect *and* express the will of the majority of the people and be effective are not addressed.

It is interesting and dismaying to note that some of the measures the Founders used to restrain the legislature were measures the English had considered and rejected in their progress toward parliamentary sovereignty. The royal veto had not been used for over a century in England. Impeachment as a way of controlling executive officers was little used in England.

Prohibiting members of Congress from serving in the executive was an effort to prevent the President from unduly influencing the

Congress. It was a measure briefly promoted in Britain as a way of reducing the king's influence over parliament; but it became irrelevant after the 1688 Glorious Revolution that changed the relationship between the king and Parliament. After 1688 the king was forced to rule through Parliament, making Parliament the dominant power.

The idea of preventing members of parliament from becoming members of the executive was never again seriously considered, except as a tool with which the opposition in Britain criticized the ruling party. In the changing relationship between the king, his ministers, and Parliament, eventually all the ministers came from the House of Commons, and the ministers, not the king, controlled the government.

This prohibition on members of the legislature functions in the United States to keep the legislature and the executive separate, and ensure the subordinate status of the legislature. This separation of powers prevents our government from taking the next step in its evolution that the British took: integrating the executive and legislative into a single body.

The English government at the time was not representative of the people, and so had never had the kind of problems that the Americans were faced with: running a government without an aristocracy. Its Parliament had always been quite aristocratic: the House of Commons became more representative only long after the American Revolution.

The British government was democratic in the sense of being majoritarian, but it was not representative. The American government was fully representative for its time. Although there were some attempts to create property qualifications for voting in the American states, the ready availability of property in the United States made such qualifications meaningless. Ultimately every white adult male was able to vote.

Such universal representation had never occurred before in history, except possibly in the Athenian government in Greece 2500 years ago. The Founders' reading of their history of Greece and the Roman Republic made them suspicious and fearful of such complete representative democracy. The Founders felt they could not afford to make it also majoritarian.

The nature of the authority of individual states versus the authority of the federal government was a crucial issue in the formation of the new government. The Articles of Confederation failed because the states were unwilling to give up their executive authority to the national government. The states' jealousy of the national government continued into the debate at the Constitutional Convention.

The states recognized that they were going to have to give the national government some executive power, but they were determined to give as little as possible. As it turned out, the effort to restrict the power of the national government provided a principled and politically attractive basis for the creation of the aristocratic branch of the legislature: the Senate.

Writers of the federal Constitution knew that their work would not be accepted if the individual states rejected it. To placate the states, they formed the Senate into a body that represented each state equally. An upper house in the legislature was desired primarily to restrain the actions of the "lower" house; it also became convenient to argue that the Senate provided a way for individual states to retain their power over the national government. The result was a legislature in which the will of the people could be checked—and even overruled—by the will of the states. The states became the equivalent of the aristocracy in Britain.

The Founders wanted to restrain the people's representatives: they did this by giving the Senate the power to advise the House, and this became the power to block and subvert the decision making process carried out by the body representative of the people. Within each body, the process of decision-making may be democratic (although the Senate has allowed itself a number of procedures that limit majority rule); the interaction between the two bodies is less so.

Given the necessity for the concurrence of both bodies, the limitations on majority rule in the Senate, and possible disagreement between the two bodies, final decisions may not be democratic.

Conflicts between the two bodies may prevent the expression of the will of the majority. It is for precisely these reasons that the House of Commons in Britain has resisted suggestions that members of the House of Lords be elected.[17] They believe the will of the majority is best expressed through a single sovereign body.

Executive Powers

A more directly undemocratic aspect of the American government is the power given to the executive in the Constitution. The first and most obvious power is the President's authority to veto legislation, and thus require that legislation be passed by a supermajority. This enables a minority to prevent legislation, a result that is undemocratic. Defenders of the presidential veto say that this is good for the process of decision-making, since democracy, as the Founders believed, cannot be trusted.

Beyond the Founder's distrust of democracy, there are no principled, persuasive arguments or empirical evidence that being undemocratic improves the process of decision-making. In practice, the presidential veto became another way a minority of states, by gaining the support of the President, could further thwart the expression of the majority will.

Secondly, the Founders made the government less democratic when they gave final authority over implementation of decisions to the independent executive, weakening the authority of Congress. The legislature is thus emasculated and made to be dependent on the President to determine how and whether its decisions are implemented. After a decision is made, Congress is no longer responsible for how the decision is carried out.

Although a decision may be made democratically, the structure of our government allows Congress to make irresponsible decisions because they are not ultimately responsible for their implementation. Congress does have some degree of oversight and supervision of the executive, but the inherent conflict between the legislative and executive in our governmental structure weakens and attenuates the democratic character of our system.

This situation is not wholly a matter of the Constitution. The Constitution set up the President as executive officer of the government, and gave him certain powers—but specified little else about the executive or administrative part of the government. The Founders made clear that Congress should not make its own members part of the executive, but placed no other restrictions or specifications on how the executive offices were to be constituted.

The President was awarded the power to nominate and appoint the executive officers, but this was no more than a reproduction of the powers of the English king. In Britain the power to nominate and appoint ministers has become a pro forma power only, and it could easily have become so here also.

Ratification Issues

The anti-federalists were not opposed to the national government because it was undemocratic. Neither the federalists nor the anti-federalists wanted a government in which the majority of the people determined the policy of the government. The Founders were very much concerned about how representative the government would be, of both individuals and states, but majority rule was explicitly not accepted.

As Edling[18] argues, most of the debate over ratification of the Constitution related to two other issues: the right of the federal government to raise and maintain a standing army, and the right of the federal government to tax the people directly rather than through the individual states. The anti-federalists were afraid that the national government would dominate and oppress the people and state and local governments.

In the anti-federalist view, the national government threatened to overwhelm and eradicate the states, leaving only an oppressive, domineering national government that would then destroy individual liberties. Although the anti-federalists accepted that the state governments operated without threatening individual liberties, they did not believe that a national government could do so. Anti-federalists feared the federal government would be too distant and unfeeling to consider individual liberties.

These fears forced the federalists to craft a document that explicitly carved out a role for both the state and the national governments. The federalists, to reassure the people and the states, made strong efforts to ensure that the federal government was not seen as oppressive. In constructing the Constitution, however, the Founders went against the principles of democracy and freedom that they had claimed as the basis for the revolution, and had to create a smokescreen in their promotion of the Constitution in the Federalist Papers to hide what they had done.

Arguments for the new Constitution presented in the debate over ratification were never stated in terms of making the government *less* democratic. On the contrary, the arguments were all presented in terms of how democratic the Constitution was. Wood observes that

> Considering the Federalist desire for a high-toned government filled with better sorts of people, there is something decidedly disingenuous about the democratic radicalism of their arguments, their continual emphasis on the popular character of the Constitution, their manipulation of Whig maxims, their stressing of the representational nature of all parts of the government, including the greatly strengthened Executive and Senate. They appropriated and exploited the language that more rightfully belonged to their opponents. The result was the beginning of a hiatus in American politics between ideology and motives that was never again closed. By using the most popular and democratic rhetoric available to explain and justify their aristocratic system, the Federalists helped to foreclose the development of an American intellectual tradition in which differing ideas of politics would be intimately and genuinely related to differing social interests. In other words, the Federalists in 1787 hastened the destruction of whatever chance there was in America for the growth of an avowedly aristocratic conception of politics and thereby contributed to the real social antagonisms of American

politics. By attempting to confront and retard the thrust of the Revolution with the rhetoric of the Revolution, the Federalists fixed the terms for the future discussion of American politics. They thus brought the ideology of the Revolution to consummation and created a distinctly American political theory but only at the cost of eventually impoverishing later American political thought.[19]

The Founding Fathers quite deliberately misled the public, and probably themselves as well, about the state and federal constitutions, to promote a less than democratic form of government. Holton[20] observes that only the need to submit the Constitution to ratification prevented the framers from constructing an even more restrictive document.

Such deception has poisoned most subsequent discussions of political theory, and is one of the reasons we need to scrutinize more critically the ideas that came out of the American Revolution. It is perhaps partly because of the subsequent and ongoing confused notion of democracy that Edward Rubin[21] has argued that the term itself is not useful in describing modern government.

An example of the kind of arguments the Founders were making is clear in Madison's argument in Federalist paper no. 10.[22] This essay is "generally believed to epitomize Federalist ideas about representative government, [but it] failed to make much of an impression on contemporaries."[23] This was because its argument, that one virtue of a national government is that the power of factions would be neutralized when they are forced to compete with each other in a larger context, was precisely what the anti-Federalists feared about the national government. They were afraid the interests of individuals and the states would be submerged and ignored by the federal government.

Madison's argument was directed not at the anti-Federalists, but at the Federalists who feared the involvement of the people.[24] Its import was that it reduced the responsiveness of the federal government to local pressures.

Madison and his colleagues, echoing the views of many contemporary Englishmen, were adamantly against factions, believing they only served to subvert the process of governing. In England, since there was not yet any clear recognition of parties, factions were seen as being only in opposition to the government, interfering with its rule. In the American context, the reasons for opposition to factions are less clear.

Dahl provides a useful perspective on Madison's thinking in his statement that "When Madison explained how majorities could harm the rights of a minority, he invariably alluded, as did his allies and opponents, to the rights of property, specifically landed property."[25] Madison's distinction is between what were then termed freeholders, those who owned land and property, and those who did not. In these terms his objections were to "an interested and overbearing majority faction,"[26] of the poor and landless, those who were usually in debt. Madison was referring to those debtors, who, along with their sympathizers, may have made up a majority of the population.

Madison's support of property owners over those without property does not necessarily put him on the side of the creditors and advocates of the importance of hard money. Later, in the first Congress, Madison came out against measures to implement this hard money approach. In his world, money was only a medium of exchange, not a source of wealth and power itself. Banks, especially national, central banks, were new and not entirely welcome institutions for Madison and many of his fellow landholders; banks constituted a threat to the primacy of land as a source of wealth.

Wood[27] points out that Madison had a very different view of the world deriving from a pre-industrial age. He was trying to protect landed wealth not only from potential threats from an "interested majority" of landless peasants, but also from the wealth of traders. He was confident that at the state and local levels landed wealth would be secure; he and his audience could not be so sure about a national government. Federalist paper no. 10 was Madison's effort to reassure landholders that their rights to property would not be threatened.

The Constitutional Convention designed a government that required a consensus—just so the landholding minority could prevent any threat to its rights. This approach is just the opposite to that of the English at the time and thereafter. The English embraced national factions, developed parties, and used them to help govern, in part because trade was so much more a central and accepted part of English society. The British did not have to worry about the demands of the landless peasants; they were not represented even in the House of Commons.

Ultimately the writers of the Constitution succeeded in having the Constitution ratified—but not because the people approved of the structural details of the government it proposed. The Constitution was ratified because of a general recognition that something had to be done to preserve the Revolution. Assurances were given that the national government would not interfere with life in the individual states.

3

ON DEMOCRACY

In the modern world, democracy is held up as the ideal form of government, but the Founders were suspicious of rule by a simple democracy. If in the modern world, democracy is the ideal to which governments aspire, then we need to know what the term means, and how it has changed over the last 200 years.

Ancient Democracies

Any discussion of democracy has to start with Aristotle and the city-state of Athens; many scholars, such as Dahl, consider Athens the origin of democracy. Rubin[28] argues that democracy is not relevant to modern governments, but this is not quite fair to Aristotle. Aristotle posited three types of communities, depending on who is running the government: one man, a few men, or all men.

A government is a monarchy if one man rules wisely for the common good, and a tyranny if he rules selfishly. A government is an aristocracy if it is ruled by a virtuous few for the common good, and an oligarchy if the few are selfish and seek only their own wealth. A government is a polity if it is run by all the citizens, for the common good, and a democracy if the many become selfish and look after only their own interests. These categories still apply, though much of the discussion is now only about the third category.

Aristotle was not considering rule by all the people in his description of a polity/democracy. He was considering only the *citizens* of the community; these constituted a small minority of all the people in Athens. Citizens were only those men who owned land and property. Women, slaves, laborers, and artisans were all excluded from the group of citizens. From a modern perspective, such a government would be better described as an oligarchy, or rule by the few. Greek city-states were never governments of *all* the people. Every government was an oligarchy of some form, a government of the few who selected themselves to be involved in government.

In the modern world, the term "democracy" has replaced the Aristotelian term "polity" to refer to the ideal form of government. The modern world has transformed a concept Aristotle considered a degenerate polity, and raised it to the status of an ideal. The Athenian government as Aristotle described it has come to be considered the ideal democratic government.

This transformation of democracy from a defective form of government to an ideal government is a result of the misleading rhetoric first used by the writers of the American Constitution. This misuse affirmed itself through subsequent references in the French revolution, the European revolutions of 1848, the Russian revolution of 1917, and the many other revolutions since. Aristotle's use of the term democracy and the modern use of the term must be clearly distinguished. The Founders, in the late 1700s, were using democracy to describe Aristotle's defective form of government, not the modern concept of democracy as an ideal.

In Aristotle's definition, a democracy is rule by all members of the limited set of citizens, as opposed to only a few citizens, or only one citizen. As applied to Britain and its colonies in the late 1700s, this would mean only the landed aristocracy. Even within this restricted context, however, many of the eternal problems of government are the same.

Most of Aristotle's discussion focuses on the polity/democracy, where all the landowners are or can be involved in the operation of the government. Rule by all citizens almost always means the rule of the poorer citizens because they are almost always the majority.

The goal of a polity/democracy for Aristotle is liberty, or the absence of oppression of the poor by the wealthy and powerful. This goal has resonated through the ages, and continues to be a challenge today. Conflict between the rich and the poor is an eternal aspect of government. The issues Aristotle discusses are how to manage this conflict and ensure liberty.

The defect in Aristotle's polity/democracy becomes apparent if the poor citizens become selfish; in other words, if the polity descends into a democracy, the poor will try to take wealth away from the rich—not necessarily a good result for the whole community. Democracies in Aristotle's terms are vulnerable to demagogues, leading eventually to tyranny. Good government is government that serves the common good, which includes the rich.

The challenge is to find ways to ensure that the common good is served even when the poor dominate. Aristotle suggested that the laws and traditions of a polity prevent a descent into a democracy. In quite modern terms, Aristotle also suggested that the presence of a large middle class in a polity is vital to stabilizing and reducing the conflict between poor and rich.

These conclusions are what can be derived from Aristotle's writings about government, all of which were available to the writers of our Constitution. The Founders were justified in their suspicion of democracy; it was a degenerate form of government. The challenge for them, as for Aristotle, was to design a government that could avoid degeneration into democracy, in which the poor neglect the common good in favor of their own enrichment. The Constitution was the Founders' attempt to design such a government.

Athenian government was much more complicated than the simple notion of direct democracy, exemplified by New England town hall meetings, as shown in the appendix. The participatory democracy of Athens, where all landholding citizens were actively involved in not just making decisions, but in actually running the government, may have real applications to modern government, but since Athens no large, complex democracy has been participatory. Rather they have been hierarchical and representative.

The hierarchical, command-and-control structure of empires and nation-states has succeeded in a way the participatory democracy of

Athens could not. Athens did not develop its form of government beyond the small city-state. Thus its relevance to the design of a modern nation state is limited.

The Roman Republic was actually a much more relevant ancient model for the Founders. It was founded at about the same time as the Athenian city-state, around 506 BC. The Roman Republic government was not a democracy in the modern sense, but it did resemble the kind of balanced government espoused by John Adams and others. The Founders learned about the Roman Republic primarily from the writings of Cicero, who wrote at the end of the Roman Republic and the beginning of the Roman Empire.

At that time the Roman Republic consisted of an Assembly, a Senate, and two Consuls. The Roman Assembly represented the plebeians, those without property; and the Senate represented the patricians, old Roman families with property. Ownership of property was no longer a criterion for citizenship, and in fact Rome granted citizenship to every adult male they conquered. The Consuls, the executive officers, however, were elected from the members of the Senate, thus biasing the government toward the patricians.

The Roman Republic actually lasted longer (about 450 years) than the Athenian city-state, but was in a continual state of war both externally, against other groups, such as the Etruscans and Carthage, and internally, against the plebeians. Conflicts arose between patricians, who had property, and plebeians, who did not.

Eventually, as the plebeians gained influence in the government, the inability of the Republican form of government to incorporate the demands of the masses led to its transformation into a tyranny. The Republic failed when the plebeians became too numerous and powerful, and the government could not manage their demands.

The Roman government was more successful in expansion beyond its original community and absorption of foreign populations, including the Greeks; but it could not survive as a representative republic. Nevertheless, the Founders used the Roman Republic more than the Athenian government as their model.

Democracy as Representative Government

Athens made a serious attempt to involve every citizen in the process of governing. But even then, only a small portion of the citizenry was active in governing at any one time, and conceivably many did not really want to be involved at all. Since the end of the Athenian experience, democracy has existed within a variety of contexts, generally involving governance over large territories with diverse populations. The democratic part of government has had to be only a small part of a large, complex, hierarchical system. Any discussion of modern democracy must focus on this small part of a much larger system.

In any complex country larger than a city-state, the population can be divided into two parts: those who are and want to be actively involved in governing the city or country, and those who do not. In a large complex society there may be many gradations of involvement. The vast majority of the population in large countries is not directly involved in governing, other than perhaps by voting, and do not want to be more active in government.

There is nothing inherently wrong with this fact. For most of the people in any country their focus in life is on their own concerns, family, job, business, farm, or whatever is important for them. Governing the country is something they quite willingly leave to others, who make it their focus.

Those people who are actively involved in governing, solely by virtue of what they are doing, become an elite, privileged, powerful group. They have power over the rest of the society because of their involvement, and that power inevitably results in privileges and perquisites. This has been true throughout history. It is not that the elite run the government, but that those who determine the policies of the government become elite.

As an elite group, those who run the government inevitably tend to associate with those who have power in other ways, i.e., those who are wealthy, whether from land or business. This distinction between those who are and are not involved in governing does not depend on any particular characteristics of the members of the groups. Simply by becoming active in governing, no matter what one's previous status, one becomes a member of the elite.

At the margins in a complex society, membership of this elite group is fluid and changeable. Those who are already wealthy are more likely to choose to govern, because they have the leisure time, but this is not automatic. Others, who gain support, such as leaders of labor unions, are equally able to become part of the elite. Still others, who are wealthy or have other special skills, may not want to be involved in governing.

The crucial problem for the citizens in any country is how to ensure that those actively involved in a complex, hierarchical government will be responsible and responsive to the larger population, not just to themselves and their friends. In Aristotle's terms, how does one ensure that a government, however constituted, continues to be responsive to the common good, rather than to the selfish interests of the ruling group, and those it inevitably associates with?

The solution has been representation by election of the ruling body. Citizens in each political district elect the persons to be sent to the ruling body, making these persons responsible and responsive to the citizens of their districts. Such representative bodies have developed in many different contexts; the most important to understanding American democracy is its development in England as part of the evolution of its monarchy.

The value of having a representative body became more apparent as the House of Commons, the distinctively representative part of the government in England, gained power. In England, as in almost every other state, only citizens elected representatives, and citizenship depended on ownership of property, but within that restricted group, the members of the House of Commons were representative.

American colonial, state, and national governments initially assumed citizenship and eligibility to vote also depended on property ownership, but this requirement, with such easy availability of land, became so minimal that eventually it was replaced with only a requirement of residence, at least for adult white males. Some states tried to retain some property qualifications for the "upper" house of government, but eventually even these requirements were dropped.

At the beginning some doubts lingered that a government of all the people, or even only all the adult white males without further property qualifications, would be conducive to the common good. Remember that the Founder's understanding of democracy was not the modern understanding.

Following Aristotle, the Founders understood a democracy to be a defective, inferior form of government, and thus not something that should be adopted without restrictions. Nevertheless, the origin of the idea that citizenship was not necessarily tied to property ownership started in the American colonies, and has subsequently spread around the world.[29]

The development of democracy since about 1800[30] has been described as the expansion of the community from which representatives are chosen: from landed gentry to white men in general, to all men, and finally to both men and women. To accept the growth of democracy in these terms, however, is to tacitly concede that the basic structure of representative government, to which citizens freely and fairly elect representatives, is a given, something that does not need further refinement.

Edward Rubin is one of those for whom representation is sufficient for a government to be democratic, or in his terms, an interactive republic: "a government that has a well functioning system for the election of its decision makers."[31] By his definition, any government with a working electoral process is an "interactive republic."

Rubin is concerned only with the process by which the voter, the citizen of the country, decides who his representative will be. The implicit contract in this process is that the voter can express his preference for his representative, and in return he will accept the result of the election and consider it fair, even if his personal preference is not elected.

Dahl likewise considers representation sufficient to define democracy. Like Rubin, he wants to use a different term than 'democracy' for describing modern complex democratic governments, but the conclusions are the same. He labels modern states, usually described as democratic, as "stable polyarchies," where a minority or coalition of minorities actually govern. He concedes that representation is necessary for such governments but then, for that very reason, he considers them only an approximation to his ideal of democracy. Thus both Dahl and Rubin agree that representation is the only required characteristic of a modern democratic government.

Representation is an ambiguous notion, however. An elected President can claim to represent "all" the people, but how is he more or less representative than the House of Representatives, which as a body also claims to represent all the people? The British, to justify their unrepresentative government in the 1700s,[32] raised a distinction between collective or virtual representation and local representation.

Even now, the British tend to see their elected members of parliament as selected by a local community, but selected to represent the entire country. Americans, on the other hand, tend to think of their representatives as expressing the interests and issues of only the local community with a secondary responsibility to the entire country. Who can say which version of representation is more appropriate?

It is not sufficient to define a modern democratic state, Dahl's polyarchy, or Rubin's interactive republic, only in terms of whether it is representative. The process of selecting representatives is a process of voter decision-making. An equally critical feature of democratic government is how representatives make decisions in the legislative body. The decision-making rules for the representative body are at least as important for understanding democracy as the rules for the voter in choosing the representatives.

The implicit claim of writers about government is that the basic structure of democratic government has not changed since 1800, and the only differences among democratic governments are those involving the qualifications of the electorate. Focus then shifts from the form of the government to the rights of individuals to be represented.

The focus on ensuring the rights of individuals presumes a legal and procedural process for adjudicating between different rights—a governmental structure: to ignore this structure, and focus only on rights, suggests a complacency about government structure that could be dangerous. It allows the government to deflect criticisms of its functioning to the side issue of individual rights. A discussion of the rights of individuals in the larger society within which a representative government exists requires a discussion of the entire society. It diverts attention from the analysis of democratic government as a distinct element within the larger society.

4

MODERN DEMOCRACIES

Though all democratic states in the modern world are representative governments, this does not mean they are all the same. The particular forms and institutions of government vary widely. Fortunately, as Lijphart[33] points out, only two basic forms of democratic government prevail: the parliamentary form, based on the British government; and the presidential form, based on the U.S. government. Most European governments and governments of the former British Empire are parliamentary. Presidential governments are limited primarily to Latin American countries.

By far the majority of democratic countries in the world are parliamentary. Evidence suggests that parliamentary governments are more stable than presidential governments.[34] More importantly, there is evidence that parliamentary governments are more democratic than presidential governments. The American or presidential form of government, as discussed above, was not meant to be a fully democratic government. The modern British government has been accepted by most of the rest of the world as the standard and model for democratic governments.

Two primary and one secondary difference distinguish parliamentary governments from presidential government: Parliamentary governments operate entirely on the principle of majority rule in decision-making, and the executive and the legislative powers are integrated into a single body. Secondarily, well-organized national parties control the governments. A complete definition of democracy must go beyond representation and include these pivotal characteristics.

Majority Rule

In the modern world all complex governments are, in some sense, representative because the entire population does not run the government. Dahl, Rubin, and others do not consider, though, that the *process* by which the representatives make their decisions about policies and programs of the government might also contribute to an adequate description of a democratic government.

Both Dahl and Rubin seem to assume that with an effective electoral process, the government will automatically represent the entire society, and will represent all the people. This does not necessarily follow. It must also be asked how the representatives act.

The crucial questions are: Whom do the representatives represent? How is the government run? The primary challenge in democratic governance is ensuring that the representatives represent those who elected them. How does the system prevent other elites, such as the wealthy, from co-opting the representatives? How will the representatives resist associating with and being under the influence of other elites of the powerful and wealthy? Recent events show how difficult this is.

Rubin argues that most discussions of how well representatives operate are in terms of their legitimacy, which he dismisses as an obsolete and misleading term. He would rather discuss how the people feel about their government in terms of how well they comply with the rules and demands of government.[35]

In making this shift from legitimacy to compliance Rubin avoids questions of how the government operates. He suggests that as long as the people feel good about their leaders and comply with government demands, the government is a good government. This leaves open the question of what it is about the government that induces the people to comply with it.

Held[36] lists seven levels of compliance, from coercion to active agreement with the actions of the government. People could comply with the government as much out of fear or inertia as out of any positive feelings about their government. It is thus not sufficient to judge a country's governmental effectiveness or democratic success in terms of whether its people comply with the demands of the government.

The issue that Rubin ignores—how the government makes decisions about policies and programs—is an essential part of the description of any government, and is crucial to the assessment of how democratic the government is. The essential question is whether decision-making takes place by majority rule or some form of consensus or supermajority through which minorities can control legislation. This decision-making aspect is independent of the question of how representative the government is.

A government can be unrepresentative, but majoritarian, as the British government was until the 1800s, or representative but not majoritarian, as the present U.S. government is. A majoritarian government is one in which the policy-making body makes its decisions on the basis of a simple majority of the members.

Most discussions of democracy have tacitly assumed that decision-making is by majority rule, but with the United States as a world power which claims to be democratic, but is not majoritarian, it has become necessary to fudge this aspect of democracy. This obfuscation is evident in the work of several major scholars of democracy.

Dahl cites four strong arguments in favor of majority rule as the decision-making rule:

1. "Majority rule ensures that the greatest number of citizens will live under laws they have chosen for themselves."[37]
2. Majority rule is decisive, does not favor one voter over another, does not favor one alternative over another, and is responsive to the smallest preference in the voting population. He remarks that this has even been mathematically proven.
3. Majority rule is most likely to produce the correct decision.
4. Majority rule maximizes the average benefit of the laws among all citizens.

Dahl says these advantages occur only when majority rule is used to decide between only two alternatives, such as a yes–no vote on a bill. Problems arise when more than two alternatives are offered, as in an election in which there are more than two candidates. Legislative decisions about policies and programs, however, rarely involve more than two alternatives.

As Dahl himself admits, "since the policy alternatives are typically framed to require one to vote either for or against a proposal, the defects of majority rule in the face of more than two alternatives are avoided."[38] Thus the problems deriving from having more than two choices do not apply to using majority rule in the context of legislative decision-making.

In Dahl's view some problems still arise with majority rule, but these may be more theoretical than real. Cases exist in which using majority rule to maximize average benefits for all of the citizens is not desirable because the result deprives some individuals of their basic rights. The current controversy over how to deal with terrorists is an instance of this kind of problem.

In other cases the overwhelming consensus is that certain issues or basic human rights, such as in the Bill of Rights, will not be considered as subject to a vote, in spite of momentary majority passion, such as religious beliefs or practices. These are possible misuses of or exceptions to the use of majority rule, but Dahl does not cite any actual cases in which majority rule was actually so misused.

Overall, the Dahl's objections to majority rule as the decision making rule in the legislative context are not significant. Nevertheless, he concludes that majority rule cannot be considered the single rule for decision-making. In his opinion, "The quest for a single rule to specify how collective decisions must be made in a system governed by the democratic process is destined to fail."[39] After showing that majority rule is the best decision-making rule, Dahl retreats from any conclusion about how collective decisions should be made.

One suspects that Dahl is unwilling to confront the fact that the U.S. government does not use majority rule, but in any case, he has not shown that using majority rule as the single or primary decision-making rule is inadequate. While different governments use majority rule to varying degrees and most people consider them democracies, perhaps we ought to judge how democratic these different governments are based on how much they use majority rule.

Ackerman[40] provides another example of the avoidance of majority rule in his comparison of the British and American governments. He begins by presenting a positive account of the British parliamentary system, a majoritarian government. He admits that the British system is more responsible, more transparent, and more decisive than the American government. But then he seems compelled to defend the American system, though he admits it is often non-responsive, non-transparent, and indecisive.

Ackerman's defense of the American system is not persuasive. He admits that to win the argument he has to redefine the question. His first argument is that a "parliamentary system allows the governing party to project an image of mobilized national commitment that doesn't really exist." The American system, on the other hand, "refuses to grant any single governor an effective monopoly over lawmaking in the manner of a victorious Prime Minister."[41] For Ackerman, this is somehow a positive aspect of the American system. The ability to project an image of mobilized national commitment, though, is part of the ability of the British government to be decisive. The lack of any effective monopoly over lawmaking in the American system is part of what makes it indecisive.

He admits that the Prime Minister may have "the soft support of the private citizenry," but then asks, "Why should the Prime Minister have the power to take decisive action on the basis of soft popular support? Isn't it more democratic to require her to convince independent politicians/statesmen that, despite the softness of support among the private citizenry, her proposal serves the permanent interests of the community?"[42]

Ackerman does not say what he means by "soft" support, or what the "private citizenry" is, as opposed to the citizenry in general. His claim that the Prime Minister does not have to convince independent politicians/statesmen that her proposal serves the permanent interests of the community is false. The Prime Minister must persuade the politicians/statesmen within his own party, and does so in party conferences where policies are worked out.

The difference between the British and the U.S. systems is that the Prime Minister does not also have to persuade politicians/statesmen from outside his party who have no interest in supporting his policies, and in fact want to defeat them. Ackerman's underlying assumption is that it is good that in the U.S. system politicians from outside the majority party need to be convinced that a proposal serves the interests of the community. The need to do so in the United States is part of what makes the system indecisive, non-transparent, and unresponsive.

Thus Ackerman's major argument against the British system is not convincing, and when the underlying assumption is articulated, it turns out to be an argument against the U.S. system. His argument is a covert, convoluted, and not very persuasive attempt to promote some kind of supermajoritarian or consensual decision making rather than using the simple majority.

Ackerman then goes on to rehearse the kind of arguments presented by Madison in the Federalist Papers, and by Dahl: the possible oppressions that majority factions might visit on minorities. Yet he, too, presents no evidence that the British government or any other parliamentary system has been oppressive.

He also suggests that the United States does not have the national elite of Oxford and Cambridge intellectuals the British have, which he believes makes a parliamentary government possible. The question here is which comes first, a national elite or the government that supports and needs that elite. A national elite does exist in the United States, albeit not as well defined as in Britain.

A third example of attempts to dismiss the value of majority rule can be found in Levinson.[43] He discusses the process of legislative decision-making, but only in the context of his discussion of the pros and cons of a bicameral legislature. He distinguishes between majoritarian democracy and consensual democracy, or decision-making on the basis of a simple majority or some form of supermajority. He considers that consensual, supermajority decisions are preferable. Dahl also, in his rejection of majoritarian decision-making, seems to approve a more consensual process.

Levinson refers with approval to the comments of the Iraqi President Jalal Talabani that "Without the Sunni parties there will be no consensus government[,] . . . without consensus government there will be no unity, there will be no peace."[44] Levinson comments: "It is hard to disagree with Talabani, and one might apply his comment to politics well beyond the borders of Iraq."[45] On the contrary, it is easy to disagree with Talabani.

Iraq is not generally seen as a particularly well functioning government, and part of that is precisely because of the requirement that there be a consensus—more than a simple majority—to make decisions. Different ethnic and political positions need to be represented, but requiring a consensus rather than a simple majority only delays and prevents decision making, as is obvious in the years of U.S. involvement with that country.

From a political point of view, it might be wise to avoid using the term "democracy," or to define it in a more limited way, as representation only, to avoid criticizing the presidential form of government. Democracy for most people, though, refers to a government whose goal is to promote liberty and freedom from oppression by the minority of the powerful and wealthy. As such, democracy necessarily includes majority rule.

A democratic state makes policy decisions through its elected representatives by a simple majority rule. Simple majority rule is empirically, as well as theoretically, the best way to ensure that representatives of a government remain responsive and responsible to their constituents. For a government to be democratic, it must exclude consensual decision-making, in which a supermajority is required. Rule by a minority of the decision-making body is not democratic, but neither is rule by consensus, in which a minority can block decision-making, or make a good bill not a better bill, but a bad bill, as in the recent health care debate.

Executive Legislative Integration: Accountability

The need for integration of executive and legislative functions of government is a second characteristic writers on government have ignored or assumed without comment. Integration of the process of governance is required for any large organization. The principles of governance of large organizations apply to the government of a country as much as they do to any other organization. Regardless of the exact nature of the organization, be it the management and administration of a corporation, a non-profit organization, or a government, the basic model applies, and so comparisons can be made between corporate governance and political governance.

In corporations this external world consists primarily of the shareholders of the corporation, but also the governments with which they interact, other corporations, and the general public. With countries, the external world is the country's citizens, but also other countries and other international bodies.

The relevant external population, the shareholders in corporations and the citizens of countries, choose the members of this policymaking body through elections. The shareholders of corporations vote based on the shares each individual owns; their influence is a function of the number they own. The citizens of a country are each allowed only one vote, and have a choice of candidates. Both have a formal election process. In Rubin's terms, they are both interactive republics—his term for a democracy.

This policymaking body, the board of directors of a corporation, the board of governors of a nonprofit organization, or the legislature of a government, gives directions to the chief executive officer as to how to implement the policies they set according to the goals and purposes of the organization. For a corporation the purpose is to produce a particular product or service at a profit to the shareholders. A government's purpose is to benefit the citizens of the country.

It is then the CEO's responsibility to direct the operations of the other units in the network to effectively and efficiently realize the policies. In all corporations, and most governments, the CEO is hired and fired by the policymaking body, giving him a direct incentive to realize the policies decided on by the policymaking body. He knows that if he does not do a good job, he will be fired. He has authority over all the subordinate units in the network, but he generally delegates to other levels to get the job done.

Such an organization is described as a well-functioning or well-integrated organization. For a democratic government, this means the legislature and the executive are well integrated. This feature of any well-run organization is perforce also characteristic of a well-run democratic organization. The U.S. government is not a well-run organization, and in this respect is less than a fully democratic government.

Thus democracy should be defined as having three characteristics: A democratic government is representative, operates by majority rule, and is integrated, where lines of authority and accountability are clear and consistent. (A fourth criterion of political parties could be added, but these may be better seen as inevitable results of the first three.)

These are tendentious, argumentative criteria for the meaning of the term "democracy" since they lead to certain unpleasant conclusions about the American government. The term "democracy," contra Dahl and Rubin, is not just an idealization or a useless term for describing modern government. It is a term that has clear relevance to the evaluation of governments. Democracy in the modern sense is a description of how the government *functions*, not of how the people *feel* about it.

British vs. American Governance

Using the definition of democracy as a government that is representative, makes decisions by majority rule, and has an integrated organization, the British government is and has been a democratic state at least since 1832, when it became more representative. All decisions made in parliament are made through the simple majority will of its members,[46] and the legislature controls the executive through the cabinet ministers.

In the House of Commons, the parties elect their chief executive officers; the leader of the party with the majority becomes the Prime Minister. He is charged with implementing the policies developed in the party conference. Formally, the Prime Minister consults with the King or Queen, who appoints his or her ministers, but this is only a function of historical tradition. The monarch has little real power.

The difference between the Prime Minister and other CEOs is that the Prime Minister is selected from among the members of the legislature; in many ways he dominates the legislature through his control of the executive. This often occurs in corporations as well: The CEO dominates the board of directors, and gets them to agree to the policies he wants. In both cases, though, the ultimate authority lies with the policymaking body: They can fire the Prime Minister/CEO and hire another one if it becomes necessary. Ultimately British citizens can elect a different party, resulting in a different CEO.

The British government is a party government. The voter votes for an individual as a member of a party, not as an individual. He knows that if the party he votes for becomes the majority, its programs will, by and large, be carried out. "The government can be expected if not to implement every detail of the party programme, at least to act continuously in the spirit of it, and so to translate into governmental terms the message conveyed by the electors."[47] Each party elects its leaders through a majority vote of the party members in a party conference, during which time they work out the policies they will promote if they become the majority party.

If the party becomes the majority party in the House of Commons, its leader becomes the Prime Minister, the one who chooses the other ministers for the Queen to appoint. These ministers become the government; they are the leaders of the majority party and they control the executive departments. The minority party also has a leader who leads the opposition to the government. He also chooses members who would be ministers if they were in the majority; when in the minority these members lead the opposition as a shadow cabinet.

The process of legislation is highly formalized and rigidly controlled by the party in power. The majority party writes all significant legislation with the assistance of the executive departments. The majority party controls the schedule of debate, and cuts off debate if it feels it has gone on long enough. The Speaker of the House has a crucial role in the management of debate. He has a formally impartial position in the House of Commons so he can try to ensure that all parties in the debate and all points of view are heard. The opposition only offers amendments to bills introduced, and the amendments must be relevant to the bill.

Each party controls, through its party whips, how its members in the House of Commons will vote. Each member receives a list of the pending votes indicating how to vote and the importance of the vote. Failure to vote according to this list results in sanctions. The majority party thus knows beforehand how the vote will go, and is able, most of the time, to see its policies and priorities enacted into legislation. There is usually no necessity for the majority party to work with or compromise with the minority party.

The minority party is literally out of power, and can only wait until it can achieve a majority status to have any effect on legislation. It has no way to constrain the rule of the majority except with issues that are controversial even within the majority party. Its role is to make sure the majority party governs well, openly, and honestly. Given this stark difference in power between the two or more parties involved in government, elaborate rules and traditions have developed to assure amicable relationships among individual members.

Another salient aspect of British government is the complete control that the leaders of the majority party, the prime minister, and the cabinet officers have over the executive departments and agencies. There is a strong and stable civil service in Britain that maintains a degree of independence from the legislature, but the overall policies and direction of the executive is in the hands of the leaders of the House of Commons. Executive officers, corresponding to our departmental secretaries, are impartial and dedicated to following whatever direction they get from the ministers. What resistance there is from the executive toward the legislature is no more than bureaucratic inertia.

Principled opposition of the executive to legislative direction does not exist in Britain as it does in the United States. In the British system the executive works with the legislative to formulate policy and legislation, and carry it out. There is no reason, as there is in the United States, for conflict between the executive and the legislative arms of the government.

The differences between the British and the American governments are stark. The House of Representatives has been representative of the voting population from the beginning, but with a Senate minority able to block legislation, and the presidential veto requiring a two-thirds vote, the government does not always operate by majority rule. In the United States there is majority rule within the House of Representatives, but not necessarily in the Senate.

Because legislation has to be approved by both houses and by the President, the system does not operate democratically. The Senate can force approval by a supermajority, and so a minority in the Senate can block the expression of its own majority as well as the majority of the House. The President can veto legislation and so require a supermajority of both houses. Thus, on controversial issues in which "only" a majority approves legislation, the majority will can be blocked.

These constraints are held up as virtues of our system because the will of the majority needs to be restrained, but the result is that the democratic process is often thwarted or at least delayed. The checks on the expression of the majority have rendered overall decision making less than democratic. Decision making in the U.S. government has been forced to operate by consensual majority, requiring more than a simple majority. This requirement of consensus makes it an undemocratic state. Requiring a supermajority does not make it more democratic, it makes it a paralyzed, ineffective, gridlocked government.

The power of a majority party to express its will and enact the legislation it has advocated is diminished, leaving the legislature the less powerful branch of government, and making the government less responsive to the needs and desires of the people. The people lack respect for the government because it does not adequately reflect the will of the majority of people. Polls of the popular approval of the President and Congress reflect the people's understanding that the government is not responding to the majority will.

Americans have been taught to fear simple majority rule in order to persuade them to accept the violations of majority rule in our government. Bad things will happen to the country if majority rule is not restrained and limited. The Founders structured our government to protect the people from the "tyranny of the majority" for fear it will somehow oppress the people. Yet, outside the federal government, in local governments and in other political and non-political organizations, majority rule is simply assumed. If we believe in majority rule in every other context, then in what sense do we have to be protected from majority rule in the federal government? In what sense can this be considered tyranny? How is it that the British government and other parliamentary governments have functioned well enough on the basis of a simple majority rule?

Minorities do need to be defended against violations of their rights; this is the reason the original Bill of Rights was enacted so soon after the Constitution was ratified. It is not clear why, in addition, we need to make the decision-making process undemocratic. To do so does not in any way enhance the rights of minorities; all it does is allow some minorities to impede the decision-making process—often to the detriment of other minorities for whom the decisions are being made. The entire history of race relations and the civil rights movement is testimony to the tyranny of one minority, southern whites, over another minority, southern blacks, enabled by the undemocratic aspects of our government.

The U.S. government is not well integrated. It is only in the United States and those countries that have copied the American form of government that the execution of policy is not controlled by the legislature. The policymaking body in the United States has been divided into two separate and independent bodies, the

Senate and the House of Representatives.[48] The result is that the two separate policymaking bodies compete with each other, diluting and weakening their combined authority.

The process of determining policy becomes unnecessarily complicated and difficult. This leaves the CEO of the government, the President, uncertain about what the policy is, and encourages him to set policies himself, independent of the policymaking body. The natural tendency of any CEO is to dominate the policymaking body, and the CEO in the United States is encouraged even more by playing one policymaking body off the other.

The second way the U.S. government is not well integrated is that its CEO, the President, is separately elected by the citizens of the country rather than by the legislative, policymaking body—rendering the President independent of that body. The legislature does not hire the President, and cannot fire him if he is not doing the job the legislature determines he should be doing.

The legislature is thus powerless to command the CEO, and depends entirely on his cooperation with their directions. The legislature is emasculated, unable to fulfill its function in the organization. The inevitable tendency is for the President to dominate the legislature and force their submission to his policies. This has been the case since the country accepted the Constitution.

Those who defend the virtues of the U.S. governing system have the burden of proof that the U.S. system is superior to the model of governance common to all other large democratic organizations. If they cannot, then we should change our government to conform more to the basic model for governing large organizations.

If all that is necessary to motivate change in the U.S. government is to establish that it is not democratic, we could stop here. However, several other aspects of our government obstruct direct movement toward making it more democratic. The first of these is the separation of powers.

II

PERPETUATING AN
UNDEMOCRATIC GOVERNMENT

5

THE SEPARATION OF POWERS

The model of government used in the United States, of separated powers and "checks and balances," has little basis in any general theory of government, or in any other political system. Most students of government[1] know these concepts do not help to describe even the operations of the American government, but the model persists in the popular media. The only argument for the separation of powers model is the appeal to authority: the Founders promoted it.

Myths

Montesquieu[2] originated the idea of a separation of powers as a description of the British government, which he held up as a model of how to prevent an undue concentration of power in any one of the three branches of government. He confused the functions of government (legislation, execution, and adjudication), with the physical parts of the government (Parliament, King, and judiciary).

Montesquieu borrowed from Locke,[3] but Locke's functions of government were not those posited by Montesquieu. Locke proposed three functions of government: legislative, executive, and federative functions. He places the first in Parliament, and the last two in the King. The federative function related to foreign relations. He thus had two parts of government fulfilling three functions. The judicial part was only mentioned in passing.

It was Montesquieu who made the judiciary equal to the legislative and executive functions, and identified the functions of government with the King, the Parliament, and the judiciary. In taking over Montesquieu's tripartite division, the Founders identified the three parts with the President, Congress, and the Judiciary, in particular the Supreme Court. This described the reality of the state as they knew it, but it also presumed that two of these parts at least, the King or President, and Parliament or Congress were necessarily at odds, both trying to take over the functions of the other.

In eighteenth-century Europe this opposition between King and Parliament was clear. In particular the King was assuming the functions of the Parliament in many countries, such as France, Montesquieu's birthplace. This was not the case in Britain, however, where the Parliament was taking over the functions of the King.

For the Founders, the conflict between these two "branches" was a natural and intrinsic feature of any government. They thus built into the new U.S. government the conflicts between the King/President and Parliament/Congress that they just assumed was a necessary characteristic of government.

The opposition between the King and Parliament was not necessary, rather it was a function of only transient historical circumstances. This became clear as the history of British and other European governments unfolded subsequent to the formation of the U.S. government. In Britain, Parliament became the dominant, supreme power. In other European countries, the King, for a short period became the supreme power; then, through evolution or revolution, the legislature became supreme.

No practical political need forced the creation of a kinglike President, independent of the legislature, to oversee and compete with the legislature in controlling the executive functions of government. An executive component of government is necessary, but it does not have to be, and cannot be, independent of the legislative and judicial components. There is no evidence to suggest that such a government, outside of Montesquieu's imagination, was ever viable or functional.

Montesquieu was writing about the English government from the outside, from France, which at the time had a clear absolute monarchy. He admired the English government, but his view of it was shaped by his familiarity and allegiance to the absolute monarchy in which he lived. This bias induced him to see in England the same monarchy he was familiar with in France, put into the mixed government Locke described. Montesquieu was less aware of the growing importance of Parliament in the English system.

When Montesquieu's version of the British government was written, in 1748, the King was still seen as the head of government, but after the Settlement of 1688, the King could rule only through Parliament. After 1688 all revenue measures had to be initiated in the House of Commons. This meant the King and his ministers had to negotiate with the House of Commons to finance projects and policies. Such negotiations were accepted as part of the process of governing, and did not immediately change the perception that the King dominated the process. The influence of Parliament and its ministers increased only gradually after 1688.

No principled opposition between the executive and legislative prevented the close coordination of policymaking between the British King and the Commons. The executive was never separated from the legislative in Britain, as Montesquieu thought, or as it is in the United States. The King's ministers were expected to be members of Parliament, either as members of the House of Lords or of the House of Commons.

As time went on, the value of having the minister for finance, the Chancellor of the Exchequer, as a member of the House of Commons became more and more apparent. As a member of the House of Commons, ministers could organize and lead the Commons—and see to it that the King's priorities, as determined by his ministers, were enacted and funded.

Members of Parliament who supported the King's programs came to be known as the Whigs or Court Whigs. They were not a monolithic group with absolute control over Parliament, nor were they as organized and disciplined as modern parties, but they supported the King's programs. These programs became more Parliament's programs than the King's, as the King delegated more and more authority to his ministers. A tradition developed that a minister would resign if he felt forced to accept policies with which he did not agree.

The Tory party, along with the Country Whigs, who gave only conditional support to the Whigs, were the opposition to the Court Whigs. As the opposition, their job was to criticize the King's proposals, and try as much as they could to defeat them. For over fifty years, from 1688 on, the Tories were the opposition party, largely because they had the additional stigma of supporting the old Stuart Kings, who were replaced in 1688. By association, the Tories were also suspected of supporting the return of the Catholics to power in Britain.

The threat of the return of Catholicism to Britain and the destruction of the Protestant establishment was a major force in British politics from 1600 on, amounting to a kind of hysteria similar to the American fear of Communism in the twentieth century. It did not diminish until the late 1700s, when the fear of France diminished. This fear prevented the Tories from being a part of the ruling coalition. By the time the animus against Catholics and the Tories weakened, both the Tories and the Whigs dissolved as distinct parties, and members of Parliament eventually reorganized into Conservative and Liberal parties.

The Tories strove to develop a principled argument against the ruling party: They adopted Montesquieu's arguments about the need for the separation of powers as a vehicle to criticize the government. These were tactical criticisms, not impartial attempts to formulate political theory. They argued that by mixing executive and legislative positions, the King improperly influenced the process of determining public policy.

The King did have an influence over executive appointments, and so impacted many members of Parliament, but this power diminished over time because of Tory criticisms and the ongoing professionalization of the civil service. No one ever questioned, however, that the King's ministers and their executive functions should be an integral part of the legislature.

The British simply never accepted the presumption that the executive and legislative should be separate and independent. Even the Tories, if they had been in power, would have used these sources of influence to achieve their own ends as much as the Whigs did. Unfortunately, the American colonies accepted the Tory criticisms as general political theory rather than political polemics.

Montesquieu's view that the British system or any other was a government of separated powers was simply wrong. His was just an erroneous theory. In creating three centers of power in the government, though, the Founders created the facts called for by a false theory. Rather than using a theory that fit the facts of government, they created the facts to fit a fallacious theory. We now have three centers of power, the President, Congress, and the Supreme Court competing to fulfill the functions of government—because of bad theory.

Realities

American acceptance of Montesquieu's totally unfounded "principle" of the separation of powers is more an excuse to maintain the basically medieval, monarchical form of government the Founders were familiar with, than a newly discovered founding principle of government. By adopting Montesquieu's ideas, essentially a reactionary judgment on the ongoing evolution of the British system, Americans elevated them to the status of theory. His ideas did, however, fit the realities of the colonists experience with colonial governments, governments that were artificial and not completely sovereign governments.

Colonial governments were modeled on the monarchical governments of the 1600s. All the colonies were established in the 1600s, starting with Virginia in 1607, except for Georgia, which was chartered in 1732. The colonies were all founded, to a greater or lesser extent, on the model of the monarchy that existed then in England: The governor of a colony served as the representative of the owners of the charter, and had absolute power. Legislatures were eventually formed to provide input from the colonists to the governor, but ultimately they had only an advisory role.

Government in the colonies habituated the colonists to this medieval outlook. The colonists themselves created the local parts of these governments,[4] but with the understanding that they were ultimately responsible to the owner of the charters by which the colonies were formed. There was a clear separation and opposition between the local communities and councils, and the governor. The governor was appointed by the owners of the charter, and ultimately by the King, who granted the charter to the owners. It was the governor's and his government's job to restrain the local legislature, to make it conform to the wishes and policies of the owners of the colony.

Legislatures were formed in each colony, but they were subordinate to and could be overruled by the governor. A congruence of interests between the governor and the legislature never existed, although at times, for some governors, there were working agreements. Thus the colonists' immediate experience of government was even more like an absolute monarchy than the government that existed in England at the time, where the King could rule only through Parliament.

The governors' domination of colonial governments had two effects on the American thinking about government: Most colonists did not have to be concerned about affairs outside their local community. The governors could be counted on to take care of issues involving the whole colony, such as international relations. The people could concentrate on local government, which the governors largely left alone.[5] Thus local leaders could operate as if there were no important issues outside their community, with no external threats or concerns beyond conflicts with the local Indians.

This long tradition of focusing on local governments in the colonies, and ignoring larger colonial, national, and international issues encouraged the ideal of direct democracy, such as town meetings, where everyone participated in decisions for the community. This orientation became a hallmark of American thinking about government.

The colonists came to see their colonial legislature, and later their state legislature, as buffers between the local towns and the colonial governor. The legislature was not seen initially as part of colonial government. Government was what the governor did.

There was little sense that the legislature was in any way representative of the entire colony. Members of the legislature were instead expected to represent only the local communities from which they came; representatives were given highly specific instructions on what to ask of the governor, and how to deal with him.[6]

The governor and his officers *were* the colonial government, and the legislature's role was separate: to protect the people and the communities from the colonial and later state governments and to petition the government for favors or relief. Otherwise the legislature acted as the accountant and auditor of the government's actions, and as such had to be separate and independent.

This expressed the view of many, even in England. It was only beginning to be understood in Britain that the legislature could be more than a monitor of government, that it could be an integral part of the government itself. In the America of the late 1700s, this notion was almost completely unknown.

When the colonists achieved independence from Britain, they had little experience running a government that had to deal with issues beyond the local communities. Their initial response to independence was to try to extend their experience with local governments to the state and national level, and to apply the principles of government they had learned from their reading of the British writers of the 1600s. All this occurred in the context of the severe economic stress in the colonies.

A second source of models for the Founders was their collective memory of the Old World. The colonists came to the New World with the knowledge and attitudes of their time, and this was reflected in their practices. Many, if not most, settlers from England who populated the American colonies, arrived in the 1600s.

They came to escape religious persecution in England, but another major reason was to evade the violence and conflict of civil war between the King and Parliament. Religious and political conflicts were not all that separate. Their religion encouraged them to believe that the solution to the conflict in England was in a better monarch, rather than parliamentary dominance. For them, just as God ruled over the spiritual world, the monarch properly ruled over the secular world.[7]

The American colonies were strongly monarchist for most of their history until just prior to the revolution. Even during the revolution Americans may have been against the British monarch, George III, but many were still receptive to the monarchical form of government.

The colonists were aware of the writings and debate about the forms of government that characterized seventeenth-century England,[8] but these were debates within the context of a monarchical government. Most of these works, Locke's in particular, were written before the Glorious Revolution of 1688; the writings supported the form of government prior to that revolution: that of a competing monarch and parliament.

Strife and dissension in England through most of the 1600s led to several covert plans for another civil war. Locke was involved in some of these plans, and was forced to retreat to France in the years before the Revolution of 1688 to avoid arrest. Locke's *Treatise on Government*, completed around 1683, five years before that Glorious Revolution, with much of it completed even earlier, was critical of the English government at the time, and in particular of the actions of the King. When he was writing the *Treatise*, he could not have known how the conflicts he knew about would be resolved.

Locke's prescription for the way government ought to be run essentially amounted to the elevation of the status quo, with the caveat that the parts of the government should work harmoniously. His *Treatise* became popular as an idealization and justification for monarchical or "mixed" government, but it became almost immediately irrelevant to the description of actual English government after 1688.

The colonists had absorbed the ideas of Locke and others: the ideal form of government was a mixed government in which all classes of society, monarch, nobility, and the commoners were equally represented in the government. They were aware of the changes taking place in the English government in the years after 1688, but British government, even in the 1760s and 1770s was not yet one in which the Parliament was clearly supreme. The colonists in any case generally did not approve of the increasing power of Parliament, feeling Parliament was just interfering with the king's business, promoting corruption and discord.

The American government was modeled in part on the English government as it existed in the mid-1700s, but in the context of the monarchical governments that dominated Europe. All the European governments had changed drastically from what they had been in the 1600s, when most English colonies were founded.[9] It was not obvious to the colonists that the changes were positive.

European governments had become much more powerful and wealthy, engaged in heavy taxation and extensive warfare. From the outside, the major changes were this increase in power and the ability to tax and oppress their people. England was seen as no different than other monarchies, most of which had absolute power.

The English had gone through their Glorious Revolution in 1688, in which the King was forced to work through Parliament rather than against it, but it was not yet clear, at least to the colonists, that this was going to leave the King no more than a figurehead. George III still tried to influence the policies of the government, through offers of seats in the House of Lords, or other forms of patronage, and sometimes through outright bribery of members of parliament. He was the last gasp of the old system while the new parliamentary system was growing; but from the colonial view, George III was a reversion to an absolute monarchy.

The House of Lords had not yet become an anachronism: The lords were still vital to governing, although by this time their importance was more in the infiltration of the House of Commons with Lords or of members of Commons under the influence of the Lords. In any case, colonists' loyalty was primarily to the monarch rather than to Parliament. The English government was evolving away from the Elizabethan structure on the basis of which the colonies were formed, into the modern parliamentary system, but it is not clear that the colonists approved. For them, the ideal was a balance between the King and Parliament.

Even though many of these changes in structure were in process in England in the late 1700s, the world appeared to the American colonists as one in which governments were and should be monarchies, led by a strong executive. They were influenced by their own immediate experience with colonial governments, and their reading of the conservative, even reactionary English Tories and Country Whigs. The colonists might have recognized that England was not an absolute monarchy, but they were not sure that it should not be, or that it would not return to one. From their perspective on the periphery of the British Empire, British government was just as oppressive as any other government.

Much of what the colonists read about events in England were comments of those on the reactionary fringe of British politics, such as Lord Bolingbroke: "precisely those with the least respectability and force in England."[10] "Bolingbroke, who is all but forgotten today but was considered essential reading by John Adams and Thomas Jefferson, was the crucial intellectual figure in this period."[11] Bolingbroke was a member of the Tory opposition to the dominance of Walpole, England's first true Prime Minister, in the early 1700s, a time when there were no recognized, organized parties.

Bolingbroke was an open supporter of the Stuarts and Catholicism, and even had to retreat to France for a period because of this support. He was opposed to the changes taking place in the British government following the 1688 Glorious Revolution and wanted to return to the status quo, where there seemed a balance between the monarch, the aristocracy, and the people. He held that the Elizabethan Age of the late 1500s was the ideal. Bolingbroke viewed Locke's writings as the ideal description of how governments should be. He and his followers had a "fierce and total unwillingness to accept the developments of the eighteenth century."[12]

Given these sources for models of government, it is not surprising that the American colonists were receptive to Montesquieu, writing in 1748—he also idealized the mixed government advocated by Locke. Montesquieu went even further than Locke by saying that in the ideal system, the three functions of government, the executive, legislative, and judicial should be separate and independent. Montesquieu justified this separation and opposition between the executive, the governor, and the legislative (the colonial assemblies that the colonists knew intimately). For the colonists and the Founders, this was the way government was and should be.

Americans sided with Bolingbroke and his arguments that the English government's growing power of Parliament was corrupt, and should return to the ideal of the balanced government of 200 years earlier, or at least of that before the 1688 settlement. The American understanding of England was based on Locke's writings, filtered through the writings of Montesquieu, and the reactionary opposition (such as Bolingbroke) to the developing parliamentary system. The advocates of the American Revolution saw their cause as a protest against the supposed corruption of the developing parliamentary system.

The Founders could not have known that the models they were using in forming the U.S. government were about to disappear along with the Tory party that made them. England was in the process of evolving into a truly parliamentary government, and France was on the verge of a bloody revolution that resulted, eventually, in a similar parliamentary government.

6

SUBORDINATION OF THE HOUSE

The Constitution the Founders wrote was ratified in 1788, but remained merely words on paper until the first session of the first Congress in 1789, when aspects of the structure that had been left vague or ambiguous in the Constitution were defined. The government that emerged was a function of the representatives' previous experience, beliefs, and prejudices.

Unlimited Debate

In the first years of the Republic, the House of Representatives was the primary legislative body. The government had been set up on the model of the British government, as the Founders understood it. The Founders adopted the idea that the best government is a mixed government, representing the three classes of society: the monarch, the aristocracy, and the democracy. The President was the equivalent of the monarch, the Senate was the equivalent of the aristocracy, and the House of Representatives was the equivalent of the democracy. Each form had to be represented in a complete government.

Taking their cues from the British government, Americans also accepted the English idea that the lower house, the House of Commons in England, and the House of Representatives in the United States, was the primary legislative body because it had the power to raise and allocate funds. This was how the government worked in the early days. The Senate saw itself as better than the

House, made up the "better sort of people," just as the Lords were the better sort of people in Britain. The Senate saw itself as the American House of Lords. Nevertheless, the Senate generally deferred to the House. The House passed bills, and the Senate reviewed them, suggested amendments, and returned the bill to the House for final passage.[13]

This left the Senate with little to do in these early years; it met only briefly and conducted little business. Senators had been given a six-year job with little to do, and as the government settled into its routines, and fears of democratic excess faded, the Senate was becoming irrelevant to the process. If their only function was to review what the House had done, and the House was doing an adequate job, the Senate was increasingly superfluous.

The superiority of the members of the Senate was not quite so obvious when they had little to do. The Senate, if it were to maintain its original position, faced the propsect of gradually declining into irrelevance. By 1809 the Senate "could very well travel down the same path of obscurity and marginality that its mother chamber, the British House of Lords, would take."[14]

Instead, over the next twenty years, the Senate "reconstituted" itself, becoming the Senate we have become familiar with. It first claimed that it was as representative as the House of Representatives, though this was simply not true. Second, it copied much of the internal structure and procedures of the House, and asserted that it had as much authority to initiate and approve legislation as did the House. It claimed that it was a co-equal branch of the legislature. None of this was part of the original design or intent of the Founders. It was not in the Constitution and was not intended to be how the government worked.

The Senate thus became a rival to the House in carrying out the legislative process. This was still not enough to justify its continued existence, however. The goal was not just to develop a meaningful role for itself, but also to maintain its status as different from and superior to the lower house. The Senate had to justify its existence as more than just another lower House.

The claim to be a distinctively different contributor to the legislative process took place in the early 1800s. The transition rested on its claim that unlike the House of Representatives, Senators were allowed unlimited debate, and thus were able to consider the issues more comprehensively.

The first step was to eliminate the right of any member of the Senate to cut off debate and vote on an amendment or bill. The Senate insisted on having the fewest formal rules possible for managing its deliberations, and in 1806 it eliminated the rule for calling for the question—the standard way debate is ended and votes are taken in a deliberative group.[15] Senators felt it was not necessary to have a formal rule to stop debate. They argued that the Senate was small enough that such formal rules were not necessary; they extolled the virtue of allowing unlimited debate.

This all sounds noble and virtuous, but its effect was a requirement for unanimous agreement for passage of bills, giving the minority the power to force compromise that would satisfy the opposition—or abandonment of the bill. This simple practice became the source of minority obstruction of the democratic process. The Senate may not have done this consciously or maliciously, but the result is the same.

This change set up the role of the Senate as the means by which the minority could block the will of the majority, either on its own or with the support of the President, thus rendering the government less democratic. The Senators who did this knew, or should have known, that this gives the advantage to the minority in debate over any measure, allowing the minority to debate forever, or until the majority gives in and accedes to its demands.

Senators may have justified this, as they do even now, on the grounds of "bipartisanship," or the virtues of unlimited debate and unanimous agreement on important legislation, but the result was to give the minority the power to block the will of the majority. There was no longer any way for a Senator to stop debate and force a vote on a bill.

There are costs to such obstruction: Someone or some group has to speak continuously so debate does not end. There are costs on the other side too: The majority has to maintain a quorum of Senators to prevent adjournment, thereby giving the opposition a rest. Both sides lose time to consider other legislation.

In the early years the Senate did not initiate legislation, but it blocked the will of the majority, as expressed in bills passed by the House. In the early 1800s, this meant that the South could prevent measures that threatened the South and its practice of slavery. Even in 1806 the South was aware that it could soon be in the minority, with the expansion of the country to the west; they saw this as a threat to the institution of slavery.

Obstruction is necessary only when the minority in the Senate is threatened by the majority in the Senate, acting in support of the majority in the House. If the majority in the Senate is opposed to the majority in the House, minority obstruction is not necessary to block the actions of the House. A simple majority of the Senate can block the House.

The lack of any rule for ending debate in the Senate continued into the twentieth century; a partial limit on debate was established in 1917, with a vote for cloture. Even now, though, the minority in the Senate can force the majority to make compromises to please the minority, and so can influence legislation even without an actual filibuster. In fact, it is almost easier to block the majority, since now it is only necessary to announce your intention to do so.

The Lower House

Early Americans did not hold the members of Congress, especially those in the House of Representatives, in very high esteem. Some indication of how the people felt about their representatives is revealed by how much the representatives felt they could pay themselves. Members of the first Congress set the pay for themselves at $6/day plus travel expenses during the session, not enough to support an individual.[16] The Senate wanted a higher pay, but the House rejected this effort. This low pay contributed to the large turnover in Congress, and demonstrated the low expectations members had for themselves as part of government. Membership in Congress was not expected to be a career; it was expected to be only a temporary service to the government.

In contrast, the President was paid $20,000/year, an amount at least ten times that of a Congressman, in recognition of his supposedly greater responsibilities. It was expected that Congressmen would have only a minor role in running the government. The American attitude toward government service was similar to the British: Service is an obligation and responsibility, not a source of wealth. The British did not pay their representatives at all, but the British government at the time was not representative of the population, and the executive and legislative functions were not separated. Their tradition of service without pay, as an obligation and responsibility of citizenship, was possible in Britain because many members of parliament were independently wealthy, and those who were not could often obtain jobs in the executive departments.

Since American representatives were more truly representative of the general population, they were not expected to be independently wealthy. Since they could not accept executive positions in addition to their legislative work, they needed some reimbursement. The compromise was to pay them for their service, but not enough to meet their needs. This was consistent with the federalist attitude that the representatives should be chosen from "the better sort" of people, those who were independently wealthy. Surprisingly, the Jeffersonian Democratic Republicans, the more "democratic" party, did not promote better pay for the representatives.

In this context of low expectations, Congress began to make the Constitution a reality. The defining issue in establishing a government involved how the legislative and executive branches were going to relate to each other. As Remini notes, "The relation between the executive and the legislative branches had not been made clear in the Constitution. But Madison had no fear: 'In our government,' he said, 'it was less necessary to guard against the abuse in the Executive Department because it is not the stronger branch of the system, but the weaker.'" As Remini comments, "Little did he know what the future would bring."[17]

The first step in setting up a government was to establish the actual executive apparatus beyond the President. The executive departments, treasury, war, and state, were created in the first Congress by statute, after extensive discussion about how these departments should be formed, and to whom the executive officers were to be responsible, i.e., who could hire and fire the officers. Madison summarized the different possibilities: 1) leave the power to hire and fire with Congress; 2) use the impeachment power if it became necessary to remove an executive officer; 3) give the Senate the power to remove officers; or 4) give the power of removal to the President.[18] Madison favored the last of these alternatives, out of deference to the President, in particular to President Washington.

This was "a clear Constitutional problem. Who has the power to remove executive officers? . . . The Constitution deliberately left the matter to Congress to decide. And Congress ultimately decided to duck the question—a practice habitually adopted in the future . . ."[19] Congress went along with Madison and created the tradition that the President has the power to select and dismiss, hire, and fire the heads of these departments.

Much of the debate related to whether or not it was appropriate for the House to address the matter at all; many Congressmen felt this would bring into question their own implicit assumption that the President had the inherent power to remove members of the executive. Thus Congress declined the opportunity to take charge of the government.

Madison and others, as representatives, just did not trust themselves, the representatives of the people, to be competent and responsible participants in governance. In the House there were doubts that the masses of people and their representatives were really competent to run the government. This was an expression of the old Aristotelian notion that a democracy of the people was a degenerate form of government. In structuring the federal government the way they did, giving away the power to hire and fire executive officers to the President, Madison and the first Congress confirmed this prejudice that Congress was subordinate to the executive.

The assumption that the President had an inherent power over the rest of the executive, and needs this power to restrain the legislature, was a continuation of the view developed in the colonies that the executive is the real government, with the legislature having only an advisory role. In revisions of the state constitutions following their initial formulations, the states returned to this assumption. The prevailing view had the legislature as separate from the government; it acted only as a vehicle for communication between the government and the people.

Several other factors contributed to the acceptance of a low status for Congress. The Founders' close relationship with the President, and the general reverence they had for Washington undoubtedly influenced Congress. Many people at the time, including, to some extent, Washington himself, saw the President as equivalent to the King in other countries.

Madison's original proposal for the Constitution presented to the Convention, his Virginia Plan, was to have an executive elected by the legislature, but this was defeated in the Convention.[20] Many at the Convention wanted a stronger, monarchical executive, and Madison was forced to acquiesce. Members of the Convention were probably influenced by their negative experience of the dominance of the legislature in state governments before these governments reestablished a strong executive.

Much of this negative experience was gained during great economic stress, when the problems of credit and debt overrode and distorted the normal functioning of government. The Founders' experiences were derived as much from these credit problems as from the "tyranny" of the legislative majority. Nevertheless, from these negative experiences Madison was apparently convinced that there was much greater danger from an out-of-control legislature than from a tyrannical executive. The consensus at the time seems to have been that the President would defer to Congress.

The three original executive departments were headed by three secretaries: of State, Treasury, and War. The House of Representatives did not organize itself to take charge of these secretaries. The leaders of the House majority did not appoint members of the House to whom these secretaries reported, and to whom they were responsible. In no sense did the House consider itself in charge of the executive branch; instead it gave the President the authority to hire and fire the heads of the executive. Members of the House did not believe it possible or appropriate for the secretaries of the executive departments to be directly responsible to the House.

The House did pass legislation regarding the roles and responsibilities of the executive departments, so it did interact with them. The House did so by forming standing committees to deal with legislation relative to each department. The first of these was the House Ways and Means Committee, responsible for raising and budgeting revenues for the government. Without recognized, official parties at the time, membership of the committee was formed on the basis of interest in the issues. Each committee thus became a miniature legislature, in which the issues were debated by those most involved.

Other standing committees proliferated as Congress' work became more involved, with each one focused on developing legislation to be passed by the House and the Senate. These committees were not focused on controlling how the executive implemented legislation. Control of the legislation once a bill is passed was and still is assumed to be the responsibility of the executive. Given that much of the time legislation was initiated by the executive, as for example Hamilton's credit and banking proposals, Congress was left to act as no more than a glorified debating society. Even after the recognition of parties in the late 1820s, in large part the executive initiated the legislation and then controlled how it was implemented after getting it passed through Congress. Again, from the very beginning, the established structure left Congress playing a subordinate role in governing.

The history of standing committees provides insight into the role of Congress in the operation of government.[21] Standing committees were first developed in England in the late 1500s and early 1600s, when Parliament was first developing its independence, and saw itself in opposition to the King and his court. As Parliament became more integrated into the operation of the government, and came to dominate the rest of the government after 1688, standing committees became less important, and survived only as relics.

Nevertheless, standing committees were adopted in the colonies in deliberate imitation of the British practice in the 1600s. They survived in the colonies because they were useful for governments in which the legislature felt itself in opposition to the governor, as was true in many, but not all, the colonies. That standing committees were developed in the federal government, and continue to be used even now, is further evidence that Congress sees itself, and has always seen itself in opposition to, rather than in cooperation with, the executive.

In Britain, policies are worked out in party conferences with assistance from the executive departments before legislation is ever presented to the House of Commons. The role of that House is solely to approve or disapprove of the legislation as amended in the legislative process. It does not by itself *develop* the legislation, and so does not need an elaborate committee system. What committee work is done in the House of Commons is strictly controlled by the majority party and is limited to minor changes.

It is not clear that the parties in the United States have ever carried out a similar policymaking process separate from the committee work in Congress. Much of the work developing legislation is done in the committees in Congress, which have members of both parties, and thus the members of the minority party can distort or even derail majority party programs.

Congressional committees are good at dealing with input from the opposition to make sure the legislation is well structured, but committees are not a good place for the majority party to work out the policy itself. This process must be carried out by the majority in its own conferences or caucuses. Without such a separate party process, much initial policymaking is left to the executive departments under the control of the President, not the majority party.

Each house of Congress has tried to deal with the separation of executive from legislative functions and the opposition between them by trying to duplicate the executive branch in its committees.[22] The House Ways and Means Committee tries to do what the treasury does, the foreign affairs committees try to do what the State Department does, and so on. With the assumption of antagonism between the executive and legislative, each committee does not trust the department it is responsible for, and tries to develop expertise and knowledge to compete with the executive.

More recently, even the staff of each Congressman has expanded to such an extent that every Congressman duplicates the departments of the executive in the Congressman's areas of interest. All of this is in the name of congressional oversight over the executive departments, as if they were inherently antagonistic to the legislature. Still, Congress does not pretend to control the executive departments.

According to the separation of powers theory, legislation is supposed be written in Congress, without interference from the executive. In fact, the executive writes most bills, but even when the executive writes a complete bill, Congress typically modifies it, and even writes an alternative. Since these changes are made in the relevant standing committees, with more than just minor changes, the majority loses control over the bills the legislature considers. A bill, whether proposed by the executive or a member of Congress, goes to a committee with both majority and minority members that has complete control over what gets reported to the full House or Senate.

Each standing committee operates as a miniature legislature, where both the majority and minority parties have almost equal influence on the final product presented to the full House. The party leaders in the House can only control, through the Rules Committee, whether and how the resulting bill will be considered by the full House. In the process, the programs and policies of the majority party may be weakened and distorted to an extent that they are often no longer representative of the positions of the majority party.

Because both the House and the Senate can independently pass their own bills, an additional division of responsibility is added when the two Houses have to reconcile different bills. Control of legislation is thus fragmented among several interested parties, the executive, the party leaders in the House, the party leaders in the Senate, and the responsible committees, many of which have overlapping jurisdictions and work at cross purposes. The minority party has an excessive ability to influence the legislation through its representation in the committees. This diffusion of authority and responsibility for legislation results in lawmaking that ultimately no one party or individual is responsible for. A voter for a party, voting on the basis of the positions of the party, can have no confidence that the party will deliver on its promises.

Government in Operation

As indicated above, the initial formation of the executive caused some controversy. The establishment of the judicial system was relatively non-controversial. Only later, when the federal courts were used to assert federal dominance over state courts and state laws, did the court system become controversial, but by then it was too late. Having established the executive structures and the judiciary, the next step was to put the government in operation.

The first order of business for the new government was to deliver on its promises during the ratification debates. Congress passed the Bill of Rights because it had promised to do so in the ratification debates. Revenue sources were established, but they were all indirect, in the form of tariffs on imports and a few excise taxes that the people did not feel directly. The federal government found that it could rely almost entirely on taxes on imported goods to fund its operation. This exclusive use of indirect taxation, thus shielding the general populace from any direct awareness of the fiscal needs of the federal government, continued well into the twentieth century, perhaps contributing to the anti-tax attitudes today.

The first session of the first Congress, lasting for six months from March to September 1789, accomplished five things: It established the first executive departments; it established the judicial system; it passed the Bill of Rights; it established a revenue stream for the federal government; and it started the debate over the permanent residence of the federal government. Nothing was done about the military in this first session; in fact, nothing was done for years, until the deterioration of relations with France following the Jay Treaty with England in 1795. At that point, the Department of the Navy was created, and a standing army was established. Then in 1800 the standing army was again disbanded, forcing the national government to rely on the state militias for national defense.

Thus the government delivered on the claims the federalists made during the ratification debate: It did not try to interfere with local and state militias, and the standing army was neglected, leaving no way for the federal government to "oppress" the people. In later sessions of the first Congress, Hamilton's work to create a common monetary system by assuming the state debt and creating the national bank resolved the credit crisis that made it difficult to collect taxes, carry on commerce, and operate the government. Ultimately, taxes were even lower for the people than they had been before the adoption of the Constitution.

The immediate fears of the anti-federalists, that a national government, through a standing army and the power of taxation, would oppress the states and the average citizen, were thus quickly assuaged. This attitude, that the federal government should have as little impact on the individual as possible, leaving the individual states as the primary focus of political attention for the individual, became a major theme in the subsequent history of the United States.

7

THE EXECUTIVE: MASTER OR SERVANT?

The Role of the Executive

The years 1789 to 1828 were the generation of the Founders: those who were involved in the framing of the Constitution or had firsthand knowledge of the intentions of the Founders and were actively involved in running the government. The first six presidents were all members of that group: Washington, Madison, and Monroe were members of the Constitutional Convention; Jefferson and Adams were in France as ambassadors but were closely connected to those at the convention, especially Madison and Hamilton; John Q. Adams, the transitional figure, was the son of John Adams, a diplomat, and Monroe's secretary of state. These six presidents thus shared the perspective of the Founders.

The presidency was created to be the head of government as well as the head of state (to use the British distinction, where the head of state is now the monarch, but the head of government is the prime minister). The Founders viewed the President as an executive who was allowed broad leeway in foreign affairs, but depended on Congress for revenue. The assumption was that Congress, especially the House of Representatives, would be the dominant body.

In actual operation it became more and more obvious that the President dominated both foreign and domestic affairs. When

Congress made executive officers responsible to the President rather than to Congress, Congress established itself as the subordinate body in relation to the President.

The consequence of making Congress subordinate to the President is that the President and the executive becomes the primary policymaking force of the government. Presidents in the Founding generation tried hard to maintain the appearance of the supposed separation of powers, presenting themselves as no more than executors of Congress' policies, but this was never the reality.

Even George Washington had his agenda for Congress, and he worked hard to see it realized. Washington and others of the Founding generation felt they had to be deceptive and dishonest to maintain the pretense that they were only executors, when in fact they set policy in consultation with their department heads, their cabinets.

The legislation to implement the policy was presented to Congress, which debated it, changed details of it, and then approved or disapproved. In these terms the President was similar to the modern prime minister in the British government. The difference is the prime minister in Britain is part of the House that approves the legislation, and is selected by the members of the house, or its majority.

The U.S. President, on the other hand, is elected by the people at large, and so is independent of Congress. The President can operate independently of Congress if he chooses—and has done so many times. The constraints of needing the confidence of his party and support from members of his party, as in Britain, do not apply nearly as strongly in the United States.

The President and his department heads dominated the second session of the first Congress, as might have been expected. Congress, even Madison as a member of the House, began to protest against this domination. Almost immediately after giving the President the power to control the executive and set the agenda for Congress, Madison began to complain about the things Washington and his cabinet were doing.

Hamilton, Washington's secretary of the treasury, reported to Congress on his proposals for assuming state debt, creating a national bank to fund the federal debt, and repair the country's financial system. Hamilton proceeded to act as a British minister of finance would, enlisting support among the members of Congress for his proposals, and actively working with congressmen to further Washington's objectives. He was not and could not be a member of Congress, though, and this limited the extent of his influence.

Madison led the resistance in the House to Washington's plans. He objected to Hamilton's proposal to have the federal government assume the state debts, which would involve exchanging federal bonds for state bonds held by the current holders of state bonds. Hamilton believed this would put the credit of the U.S. government on a stable basis.

Madison and his followers felt that some attempt should be made to reimburse those who originally took on the debt, rather than those who currently owned the debt. The government could have at least assumed the state debt at less than its full value, but "Just how the government would go about distinguishing between original and secondary holders [of debt] and trying to adjust a fair balance between them struck most representatives as unworkable."[23] Most northerners felt that speculation in state bonds, taking on the risk of loss, was both legitimate and admirable.

Congress voted against Hamilton's plan to fund the country's debts, in part because his opponents used Hamilton's open and honest attempts to influence members of Congress as an objection to his programs. It was not until the famous Compromise of 1790 that the issue was resolved, but not by Congress. Jefferson, the secretary of state, and Hamilton, the secretary of the treasury, two executive officers, devised a bargain by which the debt funding would be passed in exchange for placing the nation's capitol on the Potomac. The bargain was sold to Madison and the rest of Congress, who this time went along. Even as early as 1790 Congress was not in charge of developing policy.

Madison, along with Jefferson, also objected to the creation of a national bank, arguing that this went beyond the powers delegated to the federal government. Their argument was that the federal government was strictly limited, and that state governments had primary authority over the people. Madison and Jefferson believed the federal government could do only what it was expressly allowed to do by the individual states as delineated in the Constitution. This did not include establishment of a national bank. Fortunately, Madison's opposition was not enough to prevent the establishment of a national bank.

With the executive departments, the judiciary, and a sound credit system, the federal government was in operation. In the first years of the republic, the presidency was what the Founders expected it to be, at least on the surface: Washington and Adams were outwardly deferential to Congress, but they recognized that they were the analogs to the kings in European governments: They held receptions, greeted dignitaries, gave guidance to Congress about what it needed to be concerned with, and if necessary rejected measures Congress had taken.

Congress under Madison's leadership resisted the temptation to address the President as royalty, but this was only a superficial concession to popular sentiment. It did not take long for people to realize that the President was a separate power center analogous to a King who dominated the legislature through his control of the executive. Washington received advice from his secretaries Hamilton, Jefferson, and Knox, and transmitted it to Congress. This pattern persisted with future presidents. Adams and Madison were not very good at providing this guidance, but others, like Jefferson and Jackson, were quite effective.

Madison was as close to Washington as to Jefferson and Hamilton in their history, but as a leader of the legislature and not part of the executive, he soon found his influence diminishing. Madison left Congress when Washington's term ended, perhaps recognizing that with Washington gone he would not have the special bond of friendship with the President. Madison had perhaps expected that Congress would be the dominant branch, but by the time he left, he seems to have recognized that the President dominated.

The election of 1800 is said to have been a turning point in the development of the U.S. government.[24] It has been called a revolution in that there were threats and fears of civil war if Jefferson were not named President. According to Ackerman, Jefferson was the first plebiscitary President, the first to claim to represent all the people. Other historians[25] view Jefferson's presidency as the first step in the democratization of government. Jefferson, according to Wilentz, was acting in opposition to the anti-democratic Federalists, who supposedly wanted a monarchy.

It is true that the Federalists were anti-democratic in wanting to preserve the restrictions the Constitution placed on the expression of the popular will. It is not clear, though, that Jefferson and his Republican party were any different. They instead accepted and learned to use the restrictions. The evidence Wilentz uses to support his argument that the Jeffersonians were more democratic consists mainly of a detailed, state-by-state review of the changes in the requirements and qualifications of who could vote. In the early 1800s the extensive enlargement of the franchise in most states enabled eventually practically every adult white male in the country to vote, with few restrictions on property or residence.

These changes, however, were not primarily the result of Republican policy,[26] and in any case, they did not change in any way the basic structure of the government for which the people were voting. With respect to these structures, there had been no change, so voters were still voting for an undemocratic system. Jefferson, as much as the two previous presidents, accepted that system, worked within it, and did not try to change it. Jefferson only continued and extended the dominance of the executive over the legislative.

This was not entirely his fault: Jefferson "found that Republican members [of Congress] were unable or unwilling to exercise leadership. They looked to him for guidance. . . . In effect they abdicated responsibility for directing national policy."[27] To use a further extended quote from Remini,

> Like other Presidents, Jefferson also regularly proposed a legislative agenda in his annual messages to Congress,

various parts of which were referred to select committees, and he himself actually prepared a number of bills that he sent to supporters for introduction to either the House or the Senate. During a period when the separation of branches was held sacrosanct and the idea of a President actually writing the legislation he wanted passed was anathema, this practice not only undermined the centrality of the legislature in the American system but also greatly increased the power and authority of the chief executive. It was the beginning of executive encroachment on the powers of Congress.

Here, then, is one of the most important themes woven into the history of Congress. The Founders had created a government with three separate branches in which the legislature was the centerpiece and given delegated powers to run the country. But in time, Presidents attempted to gain control of national policy by exercising Congressional powers, such as the power of the purse through "backdoor spending" and impoundment, and the right to declare war. Periodically, a contest would develop between the two branches over which one should run the country. In the course of two hundred years, the pendulum would swing back and forth.[28]

This pendulum has swung back and forth with the leadership strength of the incumbent president. Strong presidents lead the legislature, while weak presidents leave the legislature floundering with little incentive to get things done. A minority in the Senate is always able to block legislation and cause gridlock.

Budgeting and Appropriations

The separation of powers myth was most acutely expressed in the process of raising and allocating funds for the government. Development of the budget for the different departments was a jealously guarded power of Congress. Power over the budget was, after the example of the House of Commons in Britain, what supposedly gave the House of Representatives its power over the executive. It was the reason Madison felt Congress was the stronger branch of government.

In the first years of the republic, however, Hamilton, as the secretary of the treasury, was very much involved in the budgeting process; he was as much a part of the legislature as of the executive. In creating the Treasury Department, Congress recognized that the role of the Treasury was as much a legislative role as an executive role. Hamilton readily and openly accepted this role, acting as much as a legislator as an executive, interacting directly with legislators and lobbying for his programs. The prohibition on being a member of the legislature limited his influence, however, and created resentment of his activities among those who opposed his ideas. Members of Congress were afraid the executive was taking away their power to control spending.

Congress became uncomfortable with Hamilton's influence; they were afraid that if they allowed him to continue, Congress would become even more subservient to the executive. Congress recognized the subordinate status it had given itself in giving the President control of the Treasury Department, and was afraid the President would simply dictate policy to Congress through the Treasury.

Hamilton was restricted because he was open and honest about the interaction between the legislative and executive functions. Congress, believing in the separation of powers, limited Hamilton's involvement in the budgeting process. Thereafter, the individual departments of the executive submitted their own budgets independently, and it was left to Congress to coordinate them. The opposition and potential antagonism between the parts of the government was there from the beginning.

Between 1789 and 1921 Congress had no formal process for coordinating and integrating the budgets of the individual departments. This was in part because the U.S. government had a surplus until the early 1900s, except for the Civil War period, and thus experienced no strong need to coordinate budgets. The departments received what they requested. The only political issues were how to allocate the tariffs to raise the money needed, and how to please the business and agricultural interests on which congressmen depended.

It was not until the 1900s, with the Spanish-American War and the entry of the United States onto the world stage, that costs for the government increased, and budgeting became an issue. In 1903 the government experienced its first deficit, and Congress began to realize that budgeting was a more difficult process, and required more coordination than Congress had provided. Several congressional committees formed to recommend how to deal with the budgeting process. Congress' solution was to create an agency that would produce this coordination, one that would be responsible to Congress, not to the President.

President Taft was very much interested in this issue, and in 1910 he and Congress created the Commission on Economy and Efficiency to develop an overall budget. President Taft, however, felt that developing a budget was properly an executive task, and so he should have control of it. Although the commission was created to be responsible to Congress, Taft took control of it. He populated it with people who would do what he wanted, and tried to impose his own budget on Congress. Congress responded by simply ignoring the commission.

Taft's efforts were seen as a power play between him and Congress.[29] He wanted to establish his own control over budgeting rather than establish a process to help Congress control the budget. In addition he wanted more central, presidential control of administration in general, and of the civil service. This was, in his view, only an extension of the movement toward professionalization of the government—a movement whose logical endpoint was the complete exclusion of a Congress corrupted by money and politics from the process of governing.

Congress reacted strongly against Taft's efforts, determined to retain its distinctive power over the budget and appropriations. Although Taft's commission developed a budget for the government, Congress ignored it, as they believed that budgeting was Congress' job. The antagonism between Congress and the President evident 120 years earlier with Hamilton, reasserted itself. It was not until

1921 under Harding that the Budgeting and Accounting Act was passed, creating the Bureau of the Budget. The Bureau of the Budget was an executive agency under the power of the President. The power of the legislature to control the budget was reduced.[30]

This did not last long: Congress reserved the right to change the budget the Bureau of the Budget presented to them, thus nullifying the Bureau's ability to impose discipline on Congress. Through "backdoor spending" Congress circumvented the restrictions the President was trying to impose on Congress. The President, increasingly frustrated with what he saw as the irresponsibility of Congress, tried to find ways to force Congress to accept the executive budget.

Several presidents, from Truman on, controlled the budget by impounding funds. Nixon was especially egregious and belligerent about impoundment. Congress responded strongly to Nixon's actions as a usurpation of legislative authority. Through several court cases the ability of the President to unilaterally impound funds was restricted. Then in 1974 Congress passed the Budget and Impoundment Act, setting forth the terms by which impoundment was allowed and not allowed.

This resolved impoundment, but the act also reduced the responsibility of the President for the budget by making it depend on congressional budget resolutions. The Congressional Budget Office (CBO) was created, an agency whose directors are directly appointed by and report directly to Congress, not the President. Two parallel agencies were carrying out the same tasks, one for Congress, and one for the President.

This time, rather than continuing to fight Congress over who was in control, the President was content with his own agency, even though it largely duplicated what the CBO was doing. The government has evolved from insisting that different functions be rigidly allocated to different branches, to simply duplicating the different functions in each branch of the government, as noted with respect to congressional committees and staffs.

After 1974 Congress could claim it was again in charge of the budget, but it had only returned to the status quo ante. Congress is unable to impose enough self-discipline to stick to its budget. The President continues to try to control spending. Under Reagan the executive tried to restrict spending by refusing to allocate enough personnel to a department or agency to do its job, or trying to reallocate money according to presidential priorities rather than congressional intent. Congress made several attempts, such as the Gramm-Rudman Act, to discipline itself, but without success.

At present the process of budgeting, authorizing, and appropriating money is hopelessly dysfunctional, resulting in appropriations being regularly put off until the end of each year. The government often continues in operation only through multiple continuing resolutions. Congress does not have an efficient, effective process of determining policy and providing funds for its execution. The existing committee structure of Congress is part of the problem, but the deeper issue is the continuing antagonism created by the supposed separation of the executive from the legislative.

On the basis of separation of powers, the U.S. Congress accepts that it does not and should not control the actions of the executive. The control of the executive branch is the responsibility of the President according to the separation of powers doctrine. At the same time, Congress is in control of the executive budget through its revenue-raising role.

Its responsibility to raise and spend funds should give Congress the power to control the executive, including the President, as has been the case in Britain for the House of Commons. The separation of powers myth, however, makes the President the master of the executive, and so makes Congress' control of the budget and appropriations ambiguous and uncertain. The result is a continual jockeying for power between the President and Congress—created only by the artificial separation of powers.

In a federal agency such as the Bureau of the Budget, the issue is not whether the Bureau of the Budget or its successor, the Office of Management and Budget, is properly executive or legislative in the mythical world of the separation of powers. The larger challenge is the fact that under the separation of powers, control of executive agencies and departments is eternally ambiguous; it invites conflict and disrupts the smooth functioning of the government.

The issue of who is in charge results only from the misguided notion that there should be a separation of powers between the President and Congress. In a well-functioning government (described in chapter 4) the executive carries out the will of the legislature, and by extension the people the legislature represents. Relations between the executive and the legislative should be cooperative, with both formulating policy, then the executive carrying out the legislature's directions. Issues of who is in charge should always favor the legislature. The executive's purpose is to serve the legislature, not be its enemy or competitor.

Executive-Legislative Conflicts

The continuing struggle between Congress and the President over who is in charge extends beyond the budgeting process. Continuing and debilitating controversy interferes with efficient, effective governance in at least four other areas:

- The power to remove executive officers;
- The legislative powers of the President, including signing statements and executive orders;
- Claims of executive prerogatives and presidential immunity;
- War powers.

The power to remove executive officers was established in 1790 when the House refused to grant the power to the President only because that would imply the President did not already have the power, and that Congress could then take it away. Although Congress thus implicitly assumes the President has this power, when the President does go against the will of Congress, its abuse tends to be quite significant. The first such incident was when Jackson dismissed his secretary of the treasury because he would not comply with Jackson's directions to remove federal money from the national bank. Jackson went explicitly against the will of Congress.

The second instance was with Andrew Johnson after the Civil War: Congress tried to restrict his removal power to prevent him from removing the secretary of war. Congress directed the secretary of war to impose federal rule on the southern states; Johnson acted against the will of Congress in resisting this direction and trying to fire the secretary of war.

The third example of the President acting against the will of Congress was Nixon's order to his attorney general to remove the special prosecutor, Archibald Cox, to prevent him from pursuing the Watergate scandal. Both his attorney general and the assistant attorney general refused, and they too were removed.

In all three instances, the President was explicitly acting against the will of Congress. Although the President has the power to remove, it is not clear that his power includes acting against the will of Congress. Only the myth that the powers of the President and of Congress are separate enables the President to act against Congress.

In the normal process of government operation, the legislature passes a bill, and the executive implements it. In implementing the bill, specification of what the bill means for particular situations is almost always necessary. Regulations and procedures have to be changed or created. For example, a simple bill to change the pay levels of civil servants requires specification of who is covered, when the changes will take place, how benefits and taxes are calculated, and so on. Most of the time problems do not arise from this process.

Ideally coordination between the legislature and the executive is seamless, with no conflict between the law and the regulations, and most of the time the President simply tells the relevant executive officers to do what the legislature has said to do in the legislation. This is the way the Founders imagined it would happen. In our government, however, the President is able to impose himself between the legislature and the rest of the executive, setting up a conflict between the President and Congress.

The President has authority independent of Congress, which he has used to act against the legislature, and so disrupt the normal process of governing. The first clear instance of this took place when Andrew Jackson issued an executive order to his secretary of the treasury to remove funds from the national bank. This was an order in defiance of the will of Congress—but he got away with it. Another example of presidential defiance of Congress can be seen when Theodore Roosevelt declared 13 new national parks just before he signed a bill Congress had passed specifically forbidding him to do so.

Such executive orders have become a popular way for presidents to shape legislation in ways to their liking rather than as intended by Congress. Again, most of the time problems do not arise with this added step, but when Congress and the President have different views about what should happen, it *is* a problem for the whole government.

A subtler example of such conflict was Nixon's opposition to civil rights legislation. He directed that the Justice Department hire personnel in the civil rights division who would not enforce the legislation. Similarly, Reagan issued secret executive orders for arms sales to Iran and arms assistance to the Contras in El Salvador in direct defiance of the Boland Amendment forbidding such assistance. Such conflicts exist in our system only because the doctrine of the separation of powers endows the President with his own independent power.

In the normal process of developing and formulating legislation, the legislature needs relevant information from executive agencies and departments about their operations and procedures. Normally, access to this information is automatic and in the interests of both the executive and the legislature. Because of the separation of powers doctrine, however, the President can decide whether or not to give some information to the legislature.

The first such instance arose when George Washington refused to give the House information about how the Jay Treaty with England was negotiated. Washington appealed to executive privilege or presidential prerogative. The question of the extent to which the President can withhold information from Congress has been present throughout our history, but has arisen most notably in more recent years with Nixon, Reagan, Clinton, and Bush.

The idea that the President has the power to decide whether to give information to the legislature is a product of the time when a monarch in England had a separate power base from parliament, and could assert his power to refuse to cooperate with parliament.

It does not exist in Britain today, and did not even exist in the Britain of the 1790s: the monarch can act only through parliament.

In the modern British government, we do not find examples of information being withheld from parliament because the executive and legislative are completely integrated. The fact that the President has such power is a product only of the separation of powers doctrine that preserves the old monarchical point of view.

The separation of powers between the executive and the legislative is perhaps most critical in matters of foreign affairs. The Founders gave a great deal of power to the President in the Constitution, but tried to limit his ability to use this power by reserving to Congress the power to declare war. This attempt at separation of *war declaring* from *war making* has generally failed.

From Jefferson's dispatch of the navy to the Mediterranean to fight the Barbary pirates, to Bush's war in Iraq, presidents have found it easy to make war without a congressional declaration, and then get a declaration if necessary after the fact. Here the supposed separation of powers has failed—because it never existed in the first place.

These conflicts and tensions between the executive and legislative branches of government, from budgeting to war powers, arise and persist only because the separation of powers is assumed to be an appropriate and desirable aspect of any government. In reality, it is a made-up aspect of the U.S. government only, and serves only to waste time and impede the efficient operation of government.

Government cannot be neatly divided into legislative, executive, and judicial branches. Government is a dynamic, interdependent interaction of these functions, and the functions cannot be easily placed in separate physical or conceptual locations. The real question is, "Who has the final authority in the overall process?" It is counterproductive to allow this question to be an ongoing point of contention, with no resolution.

Conflicts between Congress and the President cry out for resolution, and under the separation of powers doctrine, that resolution has become the domain of the Supreme Court through development of the doctrine of judicial supremacy.

8

JUDICIAL SUPREMACY

By elevating the judiciary to equal status with the legislature and executive, and creating the Supreme Court, the Founders created another power center for government—one that had never existed. In Britain and most other countries, the judiciary is subordinate to the authority of parliament, and is generally content to stay that way. The court's role is only to apply the law to particular cases. It leaves the formulation and interpretation of law beyond the particular cases to parliament. Questions of how to interpret the law are based on precedent, and any changes in interpretation are left to parliament. Parliament is the final authority on what the law is.

It is different in the United States. The Founders were intent on making the judiciary independent of the executive because of their adherence to the doctrine of the separation of powers; they also believed that the governors of the colonies had used the judiciary to oppress the colonists. Thus the judiciary was set up as a part of government independent of both the executive and the legislative. It is not clear that the Founders knew the implications of creating a Supreme Court independent of the rest of the government.

The final authority for interpreting the law is ambiguous in the Constitution, divided between the President and Congress. Congress has the authority to make the law; the President, as executor of the law, has the authority to decide how the law is implemented. Where there is disagreement about what the law is, Congress is free to pass new legislation to clarify the law, but the

President is also free to use his influence to persuade Congress to interpret it his way. It is understandable that the courts are used as mediators between the President and Congress and between the federal government and the states.

Congress in a sense continued in the role the colonial legislatures had: as the vehicle by which the people petitioned the governor and his executive staff, not as a part of the government itself. Colonial assemblies wrote laws, but they were subject to the approval of the governor and to his interpretation. This perception of the role of the legislature continued into the early operation of the federal government, and Congress did not expect to interpret the laws it wrote. If Congress was not going to interpret its laws for the rest of the government, and the President and the executive departments *did* make such interpretations, only the courts were left to give a final interpretation.

Creating the Supreme Court for this purpose, rather than having Congress be the final resort for judicial appeals, invited individuals and states to bypass Congress as the arbiter of what the laws were, even when Congress made the laws. Thus, even though Congress enacted the laws, it was not considered the final authority on the intent and interpretation of the laws.

The implicit judgment seems to have been that Congress was not competent to interpret the laws it had enacted. Fittingly, Keith Whittington,[31] in his discussion of the development of judicial review, chooses to discuss judicial review primarily in terms of the judiciary's relation to the President. Congress was simply not a factor.

In the early years of the republic especially, the states competed with the federal government for dominance. Only a supposedly neutral third party could adjudicate rival interpretations of the laws Congress passed, not Congress itself. Thus when the Alien and Sedition Acts were passed in 1799, the resulting dispute led some of the states to call for the judiciary to declare the acts unconstitutional. Those who supported the acts did not appeal to the supremacy of the national government and Congress to defend the acts.

Judicial Supremacy

As Whittington puts it, the state legislatures that supported the Alien and Sedition Acts

> could have asserted Congressional supremacy in construing the terms of the U.S. Constitution and denied the authority of a state legislature to challenge the federal legislature on matters of national concern. Especially in this early period before the firm establishment of even the power of judicial review, pointing to Congressional passage of the acts as conclusive to resolving such constitutional disputes would seem to have been a natural move. [Instead the states] overwhelmingly and somewhat surprisingly resorted to the assertion of judicial supremacy.[32]

Fortunately the dispute over the Alien and Sedition Acts faded as the acts expired or were repealed in later sessions of Congress. The rivalry between the states and the national government continued, however, and it was clear that the states were not going to accept the superior authority of the national government without argument.

Thus the courts were forced into arbitrating between the states and the national government, even though the federal courts were part of the national government. The states gave the national judiciary the status separate and independent of the rest of the national government, just as the separation of powers said it should be.

It is Chief Justice John Marshall (Chief Justice of the Supreme Court from 1801–1835) who is given credit for first asserting that the Supreme Court had the authority to review and make judgments of the constitutionality of federal and state laws. This was an unprecedented role for the judiciary in a government. To give the judiciary the power to decide whether a law was a valid allowable law, had never been done before. Marshall asserted the right of the courts not only to apply the law to specific cases, but also to interpret the law in relation to the Constitution.

He could have instead said that the issue before the court was not clear on the basis of the Constitution alone, and requested the House (the dominant house of Congress at the time) to enact laws clarifying the issue. The burden and responsibility of interpreting the law and the Constitution would then have belonged to the House, not the courts.

Instead Marshall chose to relieve the House of both the burden and the responsibility of deciding what the Constitution meant in cases before the court. The Supreme Court under Marshall took responsibility and authority from the House, and diminished its authority in relation to other parts of government.

The House gave up its authority to control the executive offices when it gave the President the power to select executive officers. It gave up authority to control legislation when it allowed the Senate to delay and obstruct legislation through the filibuster. Finally, the House gave up its ability to interpret its laws when it allowed the Supreme Court to judge the constitutionality of the House's own laws. The House did not think it had much authority in relation to the other parts of government.

Marshall's assertion of the authority of the courts was a tactical and political act. Marshall was one of the Founders. He was actively involved in the debates over the ratification of the Constitution, and he felt he knew what the Founders meant when they wrote the Constitution. Marshall did not have to defer to others for the correct interpretation.

Further, he did not agree with Jefferson and the Republican party about the future of the country. Marshall was a Federalist who believed in strong federal government, whereas Jefferson and his party believed in the centrality of the states. Marshall did not want the House to interpret the Constitution because he was afraid they would interpret it in favor of the states, and thereby threaten the continued existence of the United States.

Fortunately for the early republic, Marshall's orientation was to enhance the authority of the national government in relation to the state governments. Thus he held that the federal government was superior to the states in contracts and commerce and his decisions generally favored the authority of the federal government. To quote Smith:

Judicial Supremacy

A list of Marshall's great decisions reads like the ABCs of American Constitutional law. Judicial review—the authority of the Supreme Court to declare acts of Congress and the executive unconstitutional—traces to his landmark opinion in Marbury v. Madison. The implied powers of the national government evolved from the decision in McCulloch v. Maryland. In the leading cases of Martin v. Hunter's Lessee and Cohens v. Virginia, the Marshall Court established its jurisdiction over state courts when a federal issue was at stake. The sanctity of contractual arrangements, a concept that underlies the growth of modern business, found expression in Fletcher v. Peck and the famous Dartmouth College case. Perhaps even more significant, in Gibbons v. Ogden, Marshall struck down state efforts to restrain competition and thereby helped to fashion the seamless web of commerce that characterizes the American economy.[33]

Marshall's actions and biases on the Supreme Court were not easily accepted. As an advocate of limited government and states' rights, Jefferson in particular opposed what Marshall was doing. He initiated a 30-year struggle with Chief Justice Marshall over the meaning of the Constitution. For Jean Smith,[34] in her biography of Marshall, this was a dispute over states' rights versus national power, whereas for Ackerman[35] it was a dispute over executive versus judicial interpretations of the Constitution.

In either case, the legislature was left out as irrelevant. Jefferson believed the power of the federal government was strictly limited to those powers explicitly listed in the Constitution, leaving much of the governance of the country to the individual states. Marshall had a much broader and more national view of the powers of the federal government. He understood that the courts needed to help promote commerce and development by breaking down barriers set up by the states.

Jefferson was generally against any court decisions that would enhance the power and reach of the federal government—excepting his own personal and presidential power. These biases found a most congenial home among those who believed in states' rights and the preservation of slavery. Jefferson's efforts had made Congress largely compliant with his positions; only the courts opposed him. Jefferson tried to shift the bias of the courts toward his own way of thinking and to use the courts to persecute his enemies, in particular Aaron Burr and his associates; he accused Burr of treason but the courts threw out the charge.

Jefferson's efforts to control the courts reinforced the view that the courts in the American system were a third, largely independent center of power, acting as mediator between the dominant executive and the subordinate legislature, and between the states and the national government. Having the courts provide the final interpretation of the validity of laws did not make the system more democratic—but it may have been what has made the system work for so long.

Marshall's actions, as one who wanted a strong federal government, were reasonable at the time. The role Marshall gave to the courts—of acting to uphold the power of the federal government over the states—was necessary in the early years when the power of the federal government was not well-established. It was necessary for a third party to support the supremacy of the federal government over the states. He planted the seeds for the opposite outcome, however, where the courts supported the states over the federal government.

Marshall's assertion of judicial review was shortsighted in the sense that he did not consider that such review may not always be in favor of the federal government. He could not guarantee that the Supreme Court would continue to defend and promote a strong federal government—and it did not. After Marshall was gone, and Jackson was able to appoint justices who supported states' rights, the downside of using the federal courts to mediate between the federal and state governments became apparent. The composition of the Supreme Court changed, and it began to support the states, and later business, in opposition to the national government.

The first expression of this came in the Dred Scott decision of 1857, in which the Supreme Court tried to do what the minority

South could not do in Congress: impose the southern view on the majority. The Court's decision tried to force the country as a whole to see slaves as property, with the same rights for the owner of slaves as for the owner of any other property. Justice Roger Taney handed down the opinion that slaves were property, and like any other property could be transported to any state in the country and remain the owner's property. Since many other states had declared slavery illegal, it is not surprising that this decision could not be benignly accepted as a settled rule of law for the entire country. Instead it became a precipitating factor in the eventual conflict.

Lincoln spelled out the flaws in this decision in his Cooper Union speech that catapulted him into the presidential race. But the decision stood, just because the Supreme Court handed it down. Congress did not feel it had the authority to contradict the courts, allowing the courts to be the final authority. In the absence of effective legislative governance, government was de facto by the courts. The court's decision and the passivity of Congress were factors that precipitated the Civil War.

Nothing was done legislatively until positions became so hardened that it required war to force the southern states to give up their official approval of slavery.

After the Civil War, in 1864, Congress, then consisting only of representatives from the North, passed the 13th Amendment outlawing slavery. Before Congress met again, Lincoln's successor, Andrew Johnson, said the southern states could rejoin the union, with the only condition being that they accept the 13th Amendment. And so, by 1865, the 13th Amendment was ratified.

When Congress finally met, it decided not to admit the southern states to Congress until they also accepted the 14th (1868) and 15th (1870) Amendments, outlawing discrimination against blacks, preventing former Confederate leaders from holding office, and requiring that blacks be allowed to vote. The South reluctantly accepted these restrictions. The southern states joined the union with Republican, pro-black governments and representatives. For a brief period race relations improved.

The improvement did not last, however, in large part because of the Court's interpretation of the 14th Amendment. The argument of the Court in the Slaughterhouse cases (1873), and then in *United States v. Cruikshank* (1876) was that the powers of the federal government were limited, and did not include the authority to force the states to conform to the Constitution and its Amendments with regard to state matters. The states' treatment of African-Americans was held to be a local state matter.[36]

The Court gave a narrow interpretation to the 14th Amendment, one that allowed states to ignore it. In the Slaughterhouse cases, which addressed the right of the state to close down an unsanitary slaughterhouse, the Court decided that the 14th Amendment applies only to federal rights, not to rights provided by the states. This happened because the counsel for the plaintiffs, future Supreme Court Justice Stephen Field, made the sweeping argument that the 14th Amendment applied not only to people, but also to corporations, and did not allow "discrimination" against the slaughterhouse.

He argued that the 14th Amendment banned the states from discriminating against corporations such as the slaughterhouse, even though the discrimination at issue was part of what governments had been doing for years in regulating corporations, in this case, health regulations. The Supreme Court decision written by Justice Samuel Miller upheld the right of the states to regulate corporations, but felt it had to respond also to the plaintiffs' arguments, even though they grossly distorted the intent of the amendment.

He accepted its premise that the 14th Amendment applied to corporations as well as persons, but then wrote that "The clause [No state shall make or abridge the privileges and immunities of the United States] was not 'intended' to protect 'the citizen of a State against the legislative power of his own state.'"[37]

Thus the court ruled that the state did have a right to close down the slaughterhouse, but it had the effect of nullifying the intent of the 14th Amendment with regard to state actions against blacks as well. Individual states, the court concluded, could discriminate against both corporations and individual citizens. Only the federal government was not allowed to discriminate against the people. Each state could continue to discriminate against some of its people, and they did.

This ruling was followed three years later by Cruikshank (1876), in which the killers of blacks in Colfax County were to be tried. The Slaughterhouse reasoning was used to argue that since the murderers in the Colfax massacre had not violated any specifically federal rights, they could not be tried in federal court. The result of both these decisions was that violence against blacks by private individuals could not be touched by federal courts, and could be addressed by state courts only if they wanted to.

Thus, although officially slavery had been eliminated, it continued, through the intimidation and segregation of blacks, enabled by the failure of the federal government to enforce the 14th and 15th Amendments to the Constitution. The courts reinterpreted the intent of Congress, and thereby subverted Congress's authority. Congress did nothing.

The South was free to reestablish slavery in all but name. Attempts by Congress to make the South comply with the intent of the 14th and 15th Amendments were uniformly ineffective. Just after the war, while the anti-slavery Republicans still dominated Congress, the federal government passed far-reaching laws and amendments designed to change the culture of the South, and to bring it more into the mainstream of American values.

In 1870–71 three bills to enforce the 14th and 15th Amendments were passed, but they were never enforced; 20 years later a southern dominated Democratic Congress repealed them. In 1875 an attempt was made to pass a bill that would force the southern states to allow blacks to vote, but it was defeated. A Civil Rights Act was passed in 1875, but it was ineffective when the federal courts rendered it irrelevant in the Cruikshank case.

Thus the Republican program faltered and eventually fizzled in the face of President Johnson's resistance and the courts' reinterpretation of the intent of Congress. The southern states were allowed to revert to their previous attitudes and treatment of blacks. As the Republican majority decreased in the 1874 election and after the unreconstructed southern states were admitted back into the union, the southerners defeated the measures the Republicans had passed, and prevented any further legislation.

The finale came in 1877 when the South agreed to let Hayes be the next President on the condition that all remaining federal troops be pulled out of the South.[38] After that, regardless of what the federal government said, it was up to the states to enforce the laws, and the southern states did not. A final attempt in 1890 to force compliance with the 14th Amendment was dropped in bargaining to get the Sherman Silver Purchase Act passed. This last attempt ended efforts by the federal government to force changes in the South until the 1960s.

The 14th Amendment did not disappear, however. The courts found a new use for the amendment: it became a way of preventing governments from regulating business. Though the federal courts nullified the intent of the 14th Amendment as it applied to blacks, they used it to prevent government interference with business, in what Jack Beatty[39] calls an inversion of the Constitution.

He argues that this result was primarily the work of Justice Stephen Field. In many decisions over his long career, especially in his role as the judge for the Ninth Circuit Court covering California, Field upheld the right of the corporation, such as the Southern Pacific Railroad, to be free of discriminatory taxation or regulation by the state or local communities. In decisions of the full Supreme Court, Field was limited to dissenting from the majority opinions, such as in the Slaughterhouse cases and in *Munn v. Illinois* (1876), which upheld the right of the states to regulate business.

In his Ninth Circuit work, however, he was the lone authority (each Justice at that time was the sole head of a Circuit Court), so he could establish a set of precedents for considering corporations as individuals. In such cases as In Re Ah Fong (1874), and *San Mateo v. Southern Pacific Railroad* (1882), Field held in favor of business against the state. In the latter case Field argued that the Southern Pacific Railroad should be considered a person, and as such under the 14th Amendment, could not be discriminated against by San Mateo County.

Through a recording error not discovered until 1963,[40] it became settled law that a corporation was to be considered as a person, thereby protected by the 14th Amendment from discrimination by any state. Outside of this error, there is no precedent for the Supreme Court ever to consider a corporation as equivalent to a person, to be protected by the 14th Amendment. It is simply not true that the 14th Amendment was ever meant to apply to corporations. But Stephen Field convinced the court that it did apply, and Congress was silent.

This legislative silence, aided by business payoffs to members of Congress, allowed the courts to rule in favor of business, rejecting any effort by Congress to attend to the effects of capitalism on the welfare of its victims. The federal government, the courts judged, had no authority over business, in the same way it judged that the federal government had no authority over a state's discrimination against African-Americans.

The 14th Amendment was then used to prevent even the states from discriminating against business. The result was that corporations were free from any control at all, and were justified in calling on the government to defend them against discrimination, such as in labor disputes.

Whittington, confirming this view of the courts in the late 1800s and early 1900s, states:

> Empowered by national elected officials and dismayed by the radical proposals for economic and social reform that were winning support in legislatures, the federal judiciary seized the opportunity to make expansive claims for its own authority to interpret and apply the Constitution in the late nineteenth and early twentieth centuries.[41]

In his view the conservative business establishment represented by the President and Senate supported this authority.

The Supreme Court, along with the President and the Senate, suppressed the expression of the will of the people to make social and economic changes by rejecting as unconstitutional legislation against the interests of business.

> By the first decade of the twentieth century, the Court was voiding nearly one Congressional statute and over three state statutes per year on constitutional grounds... [After the election of 1912] the Court was able successfully to exercise judicial review at an even greater rate over the next two decades. Anti-judicial sentiment was unable to coalesce into a political majority [until the onset of the Great Depression].[42]

The sentiments behind the actions of the Court and its supporters were clear. "Calvin Coolidge argued, 'Majorities are notoriously irresponsible,' and judicial review was essential to prevent political majorities from voting away even 'the most precious rights.'"[43] Reaction to the Supreme Court's actions described it as a judicial oligarchy. Even Theodore Roosevelt called for reform: "If the courts have the final say-so on all legislative acts, and if no appeal can lie from them to the people, then they are the irresponsible masters of the people."[44]

As the railroads, steel, oil, and other large businesses became more powerful, the national government was essentially absent except as a source of largesse for these businesses. The railroads played the states against each other by paying off the state government regulators; oil followed, giving kickbacks to the railroads for favorable treatment. Carnegie's steel mills freely oppressed labor with little fear of government intervention; when intervention came it was in support of the capitalists. No national authority could mitigate or mediate the effects of capitalism.

The argument was that the federal government had no authority to dictate how businesses treated their workers, or how they dealt with sanitation conditions or child labor or labor unions and labor strife. This was the responsibility of the states—and they could be bought off. The federal courts rejected Congress' efforts to assert its authority over business and Congress did not complain. Congress fell under the influence of the money that powerful businessmen put into the hands of congressmen.[45]

The late 1800s and early 1900s were a time of westward expansion and the growth of big business, from railroads to coal and steel and oil. These were national developments with national implications. Governance, however, was still largely carried out by the states, with the federal government no more than a resource for the states and their constituents: farmers, ranchers, and miners, but primarily business.

The federal government gave away land, mining rights, and money in various forms, such as subsidies for the railroads, with little expected in return. Regulation of the use of these resources was left to the courts, with the states and corporations secure in the expectation that the federal courts would rule against federal or even state efforts to regulate individuals and corporations.

The executive and legislative branches were weak and ineffective with respect to civil rights in the South and the regulation of business, because the courts ruled. The courts became just another way the structure of our government operated to suppress the will of the majority. Even if a law was passed in Congress and signed by the President, such as a law regulating working conditions in factories, if the courts judged it to be invalid or unconstitutional, it had no effect. The courts thus obstructed the expression of the majority will.

9

ANTI-PARTY POLITICS

Political parties are an essential part of governing. They are the means by which people can express their positions on the issues of the day. The party that best reflects the positions of the majority of the population can elect a majority of the representatives to Congress. The majority party takes control and works to enact those measures that promote the positions of the party and of the people it represents. Or at least that is how it should work, and how it does work in parliamentary governments such as Britain's.

Every country in the world that has a representative assembly as part of its government has political parties. Parties provide vital information for the voter in determining which candidate to vote for. The parties with which the candidates identify are integral to who they are and what they stand for. The party that elects the majority of representatives to the House and the Senate takes control of the chamber and its procedures. It controls the legislative issues to be considered each session, and the progress of the legislation.

Over the last thirty to forty years a body of political science literature has grown that maintains that political parties are *not* vital to determining the outcomes of the legislative process.[46] These conclusions are based on two arguments. First, that party affiliation is not a strong factor in predicting the outcome of legislative debates. Such tests of predictive power are based on narrow statistical models of the variance accounted for by a selection of factors. Such models assume normally distributed, linear relationships among the variables. They are essentially atheoretical, i.e., lacking theory about the underlying process. They are, in addition, extremely sensitive to the dataset used, limiting their generalizability.

The second argument is that parties are not important for American governments because they are weak. This is a more substantive argument, and in many ways it is, or has been in certain periods, true. However, this argument reflects a deeper aspect of the profession of political science that avoids evaluative, comparative judgments about the American government. In comparison with parties in Britain and other parliamentary governments, American parties are weak. Parliamentary parties have substantial control over the selection of candidates, financing of their campaigns, and their roles in the legislature: American parties have much weaker control in all of these areas, especially campaign finance.

Having weak parties interferes with the ability of the government to represent the will of the majority, even when the majority party is in power in Congress. According to the general principle that a democratic government is one that operates by majority rule to enact the will of the majority, a weak majority party that is unable to enact its programs makes the government less democratic. To the extent that American parties do not perform their role in the deliberative process well, to the extent that they are weak and dysfunctional, the government is less democratic, functional, and competent.

The acceptance of America's weak party system as an intrinsic part of the government is, arguably, less a reflection of the objective, non-judgmental standards of science, than of the long history of anti-party attitudes in the United States. Parties were not a recognized part of politics in revolutionary America. They existed, but they were not considered part of the apparatus by which a government operated.

Madison in Federalist Paper no. 10 derided them as factions, and hoped their influence would be diluted by the size and geographic extent of a national government. The attitude was that parties distort and prevent the search for the common good—and need to be ignored as much as possible. In particular, it was believed that the choice of an individual for executive office should be based on a criteria of professional competence, not party affiliation.

In the early years of the republic, people were chosen for executive offices on the basis of competence. The British admired the professional standards the United States seemed to be using.[47] Parties were necessary, however, for choosing candidates for elective office: representatives, presidents, and senators. Representatives are chosen by the people of their districts through direct elections. Senators were originally chosen by the state legislatures, and so indirectly by the people through the election of members of the state legislatures. Presidents are chosen by electors chosen by each state, but the electors themselves quickly came to be chosen through elections, in which each elector candidate pledged to vote for a particular candidate of a particular party.

Whatever the particular details of election, parties were essential to the process. The first such parties were the Federalists and the Republicans. The Federalists corresponded to the British Whigs, comprising those who supported President Washington, while the Republicans were the loyal opposition, corresponding to the Tories in England.

The Federalists survived only about the first twelve years of the Republic. They were decimated when Jefferson took over the presidency, and never recovered. The Jeffersonian Democratic Republican party was no more than an instrument of Jefferson's control over Congress. It survived through the administrations of Madison and Monroe, but withered with John Q. Adams to the point that Jackson felt that he had to revive the spirit of Republicanism in 1829.

For awhile it seemed, especially under Monroe, that the country had achieved the ideal of a one-party state, in which there were no factional disputes. Eventually, however, the Republican party split into those who supported the national government and national development, and those who felt the states should be the primary focus.

Those Republicans who favored the states became the Democratic Republicans, and eventually just the Democrats, while those who favored national development became the National Republicans, eventually the Whigs, and then the Republicans again. In the years before 1828, these parties were concerned almost exclusively with local and state elections. Congressional caucuses of the senators and representatives of each party chose the presidential candidates. Thus a small group of national leaders chose the candidates for the national executive officer, with the same concern for competence as for any other executive office.

This process of choosing the President ended in 1828 when Andrew Jackson was chosen by the state Democratic party leaders, and then by the people in the states. The system of choosing the President had changed.

Electing the President

The election of 1828 was the first presidential election in which recognized parties, organized state-by-state, chose the presidential candidates. National conventions of the state parties, rather than the national congressional leaders, chose the candidates. Power was transferred from the national party caucuses in Congress to the state party leaders. Since it was the states that held the power in the convention, the convention selected as a candidate for national office the person who could appeal to the largest number of states—this became the new criterion.

National party leaders lost control of the nominating process for presidential candidates; they also lost control, if they ever had it, of the candidates for congressional office. Representatives came to Washington primarily as representatives of their district and state, only secondarily as representatives of their party. At the national level, parties were only loose confederations of various state parties. Political parties, though recognized as part of the political process, remained weak at the national level.

Changing the *process* by which presidential candidates are chosen also changed the *criteria*. The intent of the Founders was that the President would be chosen on the basis of his managerial and executive skills, since his job was executor of the programs and policies of the legislators. The implied subordination of the President to Congress was never actually true, but the selection of candidates for President by congressional caucuses was an attempt to maintain the appearance that the President was responsible to Congress. This tenuous connection was eliminated by national party conventions.

The dynamics of a national convention of state parties suggests that the person chosen is most acceptable to the most states—not necessarily the one who would be the best executor of national affairs. State delegations were concerned primarily with promoting the interests of their individual state; national issues and national leadership were of secondary concern. With a weak national government subordinate to the states, it was not expected that the leadership at the national level was important. This was true for most of the presidents chosen after Jackson until the twentieth century.

Ideally, the most popular figure in the party is also the best leader, or the person that would, at least, reflect the priorities of the party, and be amenable to the leadership of others in the party. This is not necessarily the case, however. According to James Ceaser, "The Founders' intent was to prevent the selection of a president from being determined by the 'popular arts' of campaigning, such as rhetoric. [The Founders] were deeply fearful of leaders deploying popular oratory as the means of winning distinction."[48] But this is just what the process of presidential elections became.

If the process by which we elect our presidents were one that always, or even just usually resulted in the election of a wise and good individual that we want, one in whom we can justifiably place our trust to lead the United States well, then we would not need to worry. This is not the case. As Anne Appelbaum suggests,

> the American nation has devised a Presidential election system that actively selects for egotistical megalomaniacs: You simply cannot enter the White House if you aren't one. . . [Candidates] are self-centered, driven, ambitious,

calculating, manipulative politicians—because they have to be. That's what it takes to be President of the United States, and we might as well get used to it.[49]

A self-centered, driven, ambitious, calculating, manipulative person may also have wisdom, humility, and empathy, but this is not guaranteed. Thus we are forced to choose a president who is eager to use power for his own ends. We can only hope the person's goals have some relation to the country's needs.

Since presidential candidates have to appeal to the entire country, it is in their interests to say as little substantively as they can in their speeches. In early party campaigns, the candidates actually spoke little. They left it up to their party organizations in each state to campaign for them. Rallies and parades, songs and slogans enlisted the party faithful to vote for the candidates. They depended on the oratory and emotional reactions that the Founders had condemned. The pressure was to dumb down the speeches, providing as little substance as possible. Such appeals are the definition of demagoguery.

Demagogic appeals have been characteristic of our presidential elections since Andrew Jackson, when elections were first organized and run by state parties. As recent studies of decision-making have shown,[50] people are not completely rational in choosing whom to vote for; they use short cuts and heuristics such as party affiliation as guides. This is perfectly appropriate when choosing someone to represent the people from a district or state in a legislative body: it is something entirely different when choosing someone to be leader of the entire country.

In this country we are forced to choose our legislative representatives and our leader, our chief executive officer, by the same elective process, as if the President were no more than another representative. Yet the President becomes the leader of the country and of his party. After election, the President can and often does operate contrary to and in defiance of Congress and even his own party. The President controls the party, rather than the party controlling him. The person is, in terms of the definition of democracy, a chief executive officer who is neither integrated with nor responsible to the legislature.

Selecting leaders in Congress, and more generally in parliamentary systems, is quite different from electing U.S. presidents. The voters of each district or state elect representatives and senators on the basis of their party, their popularity, and because they are leaders in their community. Selection of the *leadership* within Congress involves a separate process after the election of representatives. Each party selects its leaders from among the members of the party in the House or Senate on the basis of firsthand knowledge of their qualities and their policy positions. Thus the selection of leaders in Congress, as in other parliamentary systems, has two steps: selection as a representative, then selection of the leader of those representatives.

Since in the United States the President is only one person, separation of the process of selecting executive leaders into two steps is not possible. When the selection is made at the party convention or in the national election, as it is, in terms of popularity, there is no chance for the party or the people to make a second assessment of the candidate's leadership qualities. It might be said the state party leaders acting at the national convention correspond to the members of Congress in the process of choosing the national leader, but state party leaders are choosing *candidates*, not necessarily leaders. Their primary consideration is popularity and electability, not leadership qualities, and their concerns are not with national leadership, but local state issues.

Jackson was elected on the basis of his popularity, primarily because of his reputation as the hero of the Battle of New Orleans. It was clear to the national party leaders in 1824 that he would not be the best person to promote the party agenda, but his popularity overrode these objections.[51] Their judgment was confirmed in 1829: Jackson set the priorities for his presidency, not the party, and he used demagoguery and propaganda to promote his view of what needed to be done. He set the pattern for future presidencies.

The Spoils System

The second aspect of the shift of power from national party leaders to the states involves the change in the process of selecting individuals for executive offices. Jackson instituted a system whereby federal employees were fired and new ones hired on the basis of whether they were friends of the President or loyal to him and his party, not in terms of their competence for the job.

Thus began the spoils system that lasted through the Civil War and after, and was the focus of reform in the late 1800s and early 1900s. Jackson cared about the employee's loyalty to the President, and to the local and state party leaders he controlled. Local congressmen and party leaders could in turn influence and exert some control over the national executive.

Beginning with Jackson, party organizations became the means by which the personnel of the federal government were chosen. For both parties, governing came to mean doing favors for constituents by providing jobs for them and allocating funds or land to them in return for their support in elections. After Jackson, the parties consistently elected weak presidents who would acquiesce to party demands for patronage, with the possible exception of Lincoln. From 1836 to 1900, except for Lincoln, there was a succession of weak, ineffective presidents resulting in more floundering in Congress in the absence of leadership from the President—except for the more important activities of rewarding supporters.

Another expression of Jackson's effort to control and reward the party faithful and punish the other party, was his control of internal improvement bills. Jackson's famous veto of the Maysville road-building bill is an example. An ambitious project for building a national road from Buffalo, New York, through Washington, D.C., to New Orleans had been defeated in Congress as too ambitious and too much an extension of federal authority. The Maysville bill was much less ambitious, in that it involved a road entirely within one state. Both houses passed it, but Jackson argued that the federal government should not be involved in projects within a single state. States should be required to pay for their own improvements.

Both Wilentz[52] and Howe[53] point out that Jackson was not entirely against federal support of internal improvements. From Wilentz' view, Jackson vetoed the Maysville bill to placate southerners who were vehemently against any federal involvement in internal improvements. For the South, support of internal improvements was just another part of Clay's American System for national development and expansion—a threat to the autonomy of the individual states. For the South especially, the government should not do things that would make the states dependent on the federal government.

According to Howe, Jackson's support for certain internal improvements and rejection of others was more cynically just another device by which he rewarded his friends and punished his enemies, so increasing his control over the government. Such selective patronage of different states and districts by the majority party continued even after the Civil War.

Parties in the United States were and are primarily local institutions, concerned with promoting the interests of the local district or state. Only once every four years do these local parties get together to choose a candidate for the only national elective positions, the President and Vice President. National party organizations exist now, but they are focused on elections, not on party policies. The national convention constructs a platform, but this is for the purpose of supporting the electoral process and satisfying various special interests, rather than setting policy for Congress if it gains the majority. Candidates do not campaign on the basis of the platform, and are not called to account if they disagree. The President, not Congress after all, sets policy, and neither Congress nor the party ultimately has any control over the President.

Candidates' treatment of the party platform shows the irrelevance of party positions in the United States. In their election speeches, presidential candidates define their own positions, which may or may not be congruent with the party platform. When presidents are elected, they are free to develop their own policies. Similarly, congressmen may or may not agree with the party platform.

Thus political parties did develop in the United States, but they never became the national vehicles by which the will of the majority is expressed, as they did in Britain and Europe. In Europe a political party is responsible for developing a political program that, if it becomes the majority party in the government, it implements. Voters for candidates from the party can be fairly confident that the party candidates and the party they come from will realize the programs they advocate.

This was never the case in the United States. Political parties in the nineteenth century were first and foremost vehicles for political patronage, the means by which the resources of the nation were funneled to the individual states. The federal government was no more than a cow to be milked. It had no real authority to be anything else. The federal government until well into the 1900s did not require any obligation or sacrifice from the states or individuals: military service was not mandatory, and taxation was entirely indirect, with no visible impact on citizens.

After 1877, after the country had chosen to ignore the plight of blacks in the South, and the federal courts had shifted the effects of the 14th and 15th Amendments from blacks and the South to the protection of business, the attention of the parties shifted to what they could do for their constituents. Though the doctrine of the separation of powers dictated that members of Congress could not themselves hold executive offices, both parties quickly found that the promise of federal employment to their constituents was an effective means for achieving party discipline. The hope for a federal job gave individual party workers incentives to work hard and get out the vote for their party.

Starving the Beast

Since the rise of parties in the early 1800s, critics of American government have focused on removing the influence of parties from the process of choosing candidates. These reformers were high-minded intellectuals who believed decisions about candidates are best made in a thoughtful, rational way, without appeals to emotions and passions.

Their reform efforts were directed first at the use of campaign slogans, songs, parades, and social gatherings in campaigns. The reformers were against the political machines that ruled the cities through favors and patronage. Political decisions, they felt, should be made for the common good, not on the basis of emotional appeals or party identification.

Progressives extolled the virtues of the independent voter and the independent member of Congress, but did not seem to understand or care that making independence a virtue defeats the purpose of representation. An independent congressman who represents only him or herself, or even only his or her constituents, is powerless in a large body such as the House or Senate.

Only by joining a larger organized group, a party, will a member of Congress have any influence or authority. To have influence requires reciprocal support of party programs, and this reciprocity must be enforced.

To the Progressives, a mostly Republican subgroup in Congress, the problem was the dominance of parties and partisanship. Parties, in their view, existed only to promote special economic interests. To improve itself, society had "to reduce the role of parties in national affairs."[54] This was expressed best in Herbert Croly's 1909 book, *The Promise of American Life*.

The solution for these reformers to what they saw as excessive party influence was a strong President leading an impartial bureaucracy. Parties needed to be controlled so they represent only the public interest, not the corrupt influence of big business. Progressive Republicans advocated the regulation of party finances to prevent the Republican party from becoming just the tool of big business.

Reformers directed their efforts toward reducing the influence of money in politics and parties by "reforming" campaign finance laws. The goal was to starve the parties to reduce their power in the political process.[55] Although noble and well intentioned, such appeals to rational decision-making were unrealistic and misguided, and did not succeed in reducing the power of parties.

A review of the history of campaign finance legislation shows that campaign finance laws were actually passed for primarily partisan reasons. Changes in campaign finance laws were not impartial, high-minded attempts to further the public interest. Each new campaign finance law was passed only because it gave an advantage to one party over the other. Each party used reformers from the other party to advance its own party objectives.

The Democrats co-opted the Progressive Republicans to pass the first campaign finance law that restrained the Republican's ability to raise funds. The Tillman Act of 1907 was promoted and passed by a rabid southern Democrat to weaken the Republican party, which was coming to rely more and more on contributions from big business. The Republicans were better at raising such funds, whereas the Democrats relied more on local, in kind resources.

In 1910 and 1925 Democrats, again with the help of reform Republicans, passed the Federal Corrupt Practices Acts to force disclosure of contributions, and set limits on the size of contributions. The Republicans watered down the provisions so their effects were minimized; even so, they further affected political campaigning and hurt the Republicans most.

These acts limited corporate contributions and thereby changed the way parties raised funds. For the reformers it was an effort to encourage the parties to seek out and accept only small contributions from individuals, and so avoid the taint of being bought by big business, but its effect was quite different.

Enforcement of these acts was lax, so Republicans did not suffer as much as the Democrats hoped, but it did change the orientation of fund raising to emphasize more small donations—and encouraged more deception about the large donations. Funds from large donors were funneled through state organizations not covered by the acts. The laws did not substantially change the influence of money in campaigns, as the reformers wanted.

The Republicans got their revenge in the 1930s and 1940s during the New Deal and World War II. Labor unions were gaining power in politics, and the Republicans wanted to limit their influence. The Hatch Acts were passed in 1939 and 1940 to limit federal employees' and labor unions' ability to participate in political activity. These groups were seen as sources of support for the Democrats.

Later the Smith-Connally Act was passed in 1943 to limit union activities during the war, and then the Taft-Hartley Act was passed in 1947 to make the Smith-Connally limitations permanent. Both bills limited unions' ability to use union dues for political purposes.

Though the Republicans were ready to organize and find ways of circumventing the campaign laws prohibiting large donations, the Democrats were more resistant to getting themselves organized. As a result, in the 1960s and 1970s the Democrats struggled to generate enough funds for campaigns.

The solution for the Democrats was to pass the Federal Elections Commission Acts of 1971 and 1974, in which a program for public financing of campaigns was started, and the Federal Elections Commission was established.

Finally in 2002 the Bipartisan Campaign Reform Act was passed, which banned parties from using "soft" money, "funds raised in amounts greater than federal contribution limits, and from sources banned under the Tillman Act (corporations) and the Taft-Hartley Act (unions)."[56]

Thus, basically three approaches were used to reduce the influence of money and power in campaigns: limiting campaign contributions, increasing disclosure requirements for donors, and public financing.[57] None has reduced the influence of money but they have served to maintain the weakness and ineffectiveness of the parties.[58]

Restrictions on campaign contributions have not reduced the amount of money going into campaigns: they have only redirected and fragmented the process of raising money. Efforts to regulate campaign finances became a game of creating regulations that reduce the amount of funds available for campaigns, and then finding ways around the regulations. As soon as a law is passed, armies of lawyers find ways around the law, leaving only a more fragmented and chaotic financing system. The parties became dependent on independent fund-raising organizations. Similarly, requirements for public disclosure of the donors to campaigns are easily evaded and circumvented.

The primary result of all the legislation limiting fundraising for political campaigns was that it prevented the development of parties with a clear national identity, with national rather than local goals and responsibilities.[59] There are now national party organizations, but they function primarily as fundraising organizations, only one of many such organizations. The President, rather than the national political parties, continues to be the focus of national attention.

National Republican and Democratic party organizations exist, but the accumulation of campaign finance regulations has fragmented the political process. Parties are only one of many organizations involved in carrying on a political campaign. Political Action Committees, candidate fundraising organizations, supposedly independent political interest groups, separate congressional and senatorial campaign committees, all contribute to campaigning. The parties, as indicators of a candidate's positions are weakened.

Weakening the parties was the intent of campaign finance laws, with the pervasive influence of the Progressive movement and its focus on fighting corruption, but it is not clear that corruption has been reduced. The result is that political parties are not the only funding source for candidates—and thus have limited power to discipline their members. Both Democratic and Republican members of Congress take independent positions in defiance of their leaders, with few consequences. This relationship between a member of Congress and his party may be changing, especially in the Republican party, when it functions as an opposition party. Both parties realize that without party discipline it is difficult to get things done in Congress in an efficient and timely manner.

However, "Since the Tillman Act of 1907, each succeeding wave of reform has weakened the capacity of national committees to organize presidential [and other] elections, even as the federal government became increasingly important in the lives of Americans."[60] Other roles of the parties, such as recruiting potential candidates for office and developing policy positions, have become less important.

The limits on contributions have not kept the Republican party from being identified as the party of big business and the Democratic party as the party of labor, but they have forced business and labor to be more devious in how they use their money. Contributors have learned that they can contribute to individual candidates without regard to parties; in doing so, they diminish party influence in Congress. If a candidate does not depend on his party for support, if he depends instead on the support of individual contributors, then his contributors can have more influence on his vote than his own party. Party labels become uncertain predictors of how a candidate will vote.

Political parties became such an insignificant force in the operation of government that some political scientists have constructed models of government and the legislative process that do not include parties.[61] Lack of clear party leadership was most evident in the 1950s and 1960s when the alliance of conservative Republicans and the white South ruled.

Trying to mandate that all political contributions be small, individual contributions, runs into two problems: the problem of collective action as discussed by Mancur Olson.[62] Potential contributors who make only small gifts to an organization have little incentive to contribute. It is not in their interest to give, since their contributions are not likely to have much effect on the organization.

It is more in their interest to be a free rider, letting other people support the organization. Allowing only small individual contributions, then, without requiring them, will not raise enough money for the parties to survive. Large donations from individuals or groups are necessary to enable the organizations to solicit and provide incentives for small donors.

Making the government responsible for managing campaign finances raises an inherent conflict of interest. The majority party controls the government, and it is in its interest to maintain that control. The minority party seeks to become the majority and replace the current government. In such circumstances there will always be the suspicion that the government agency managing public campaign financing is favoring the party in power. No matter how carefully the agency created to manage public financing is created to be independent of the rest of government, the possibility of corruption will be present.

In addition, there is no historical evidence to indicate that parties have ever needed government assistance to survive. Parties have attracted enough contributions from private individuals and groups to do quite well. If they cannot, they wither and die, to be replaced by other parties. Trying to interfere with the free market for party support through public financing only distorts the political process by artificially prolonging no longer popular parties.

Good government reformers saw parties as the problem in the United States; unfortunately, they did not consider more broadly that the structure of the government itself may be the problem. The American party system is described as a weak system in comparison to other democracies, and much of this weakness is a function of the problems of getting legislation through Congress, and in controlling the executive.

The Progressive Republicans of the early 1900s misdiagnosed the problems of getting bills through Congress, and in the end contributed to the problems they were trying to resolve. Their mistake was in believing that the parties as they existed at the time were the cause rather than an effect of the problem.

Parties are an intrinsic part of the process of dealing with national issues, not an obstacle to it. They need to establish national identities separate from state parties, be ready to campaign solely on national issues, and be able to carry out the appropriate functions of a national party, including long-range planning, attracting staff, recruiting candidates, and developing support.

10

PROFESSIONALIZATION

As the size and complexity of the national government increased, pressure developed for a professionalization of the bureaucracy of government. The sheer number of offices in the government made the transition from a government dominated by the courts and state parties, to a modern national bureaucratic state inevitable. It was a transition going on in many other countries. In the United States, however, there was a distinctly anti-party cast. The federal bureaucracy had to be professionalized to get party influence out of government.

Two major areas where this professionalization took place were in the growing civil service and the military. Both areas were major sources of political patronage that congressmen could use to reward faithful party workers. Professionalization threatened to diminish the power congressmen and party leaders used to motivate party members. Thus these changes did not occur without a fight. It was a long, slow process of change, but it was not slow and painful just because of the resistance of the states and state political parties. The built-in conflicts between the President and Congress, and between the House and the Senate made the development of a professional civil service and military even slower and less complete than it should have been.

Civil Service Reform

The ability of congressmen to offer jobs to the residents of their districts or states was a major form of patronage; it was how congressmen influenced their local districts, and thus were re-elected. As the population increased and the country gained more territory, the number of federal jobs increased, from 53,000 in 1871 to 256,000 by 1901.[63] The burden on individual congressmen became overwhelming. Pressure increased to professionalize at least some of these positions, and so reduce the strain on congressmen and the President. Congress, however, wanted to retain control over the most powerful positions and so resisted doing anything at all.

The Radical Republicans, those who had been most vehement about eliminating slavery and discrimination against blacks, were also learning about good government from developments in Europe. They were members of the first professional societies in the United States, such as the American Bar Association, and the American Social Science Association.

In 1871, under pressure from these reformers, Congress delegated to President Grant the authority to prescribe rules and regulations for admission of persons to the civil service. Grant did not use this authority, and only paid lip service to those who were advocating civil service reform to keep them in the party. Grant created a Civil Service Commission, which proposed rules and standards for the civil service, but then just ignored them. This was a great disappointment to the reformers, and led them to reject trying to work within the parties to produce reform.

The reformers' effort in 1871 and 1872 "was the last major effort of the 'best men' to tie their political fortunes to the instrumentality of a party."[64] From then on, they argued there was "a crisis of institutional authority that could persuasively be laid at the doorstep of party hegemony."[65] They rejected parties, party machines, and the professional politicians who in their view thrived on the ignorance of the voters, were void of principles, and systematically excluded those who were competent.

These attitudes about political parties recall the arguments of the early Federalists about the evils of parties and factions, that the government should be run by the elite, aristocratic element of the population, who would be above the crudity of politics and factional conflict. This is a continuation of the anti-party position: it rejects the value of parties in a legislature as tools for organizing and managing debate, and inevitably supports the President and his executive power, independent of party, over Congress and its politics.

The reformers could have taken a different position, one that showed an understanding of the value of parties both inside and outside Congress. They could have then directed their reform efforts at developing national party leaders who understood that it is in the party's interest to have more rules and standards by which congressmen choose federal employees. The goal of promoting competence and professionalism in the executive would be the same, but it would be done from within the parties, and within Congress, not from the outside.

This was what happened in Britain and other countries in their civil service reforms. Britain in 1870 "linked the parliamentary party organization, the recently enfranchised commercial classes, and the Oxbridge intellectuals in a new mode of governmental operations."[66] This linkage did not happen in the United States because the reformers found it much easier and intellectually less taxing—given the separation of powers—to promote a bureaucracy controlled exclusively by the President.

The first real attempts at civil service reform were directed at the Customhouse in New York—and were part of an intraparty conflict over control within the Republican party. The so-called Republican Stalwarts, the older party leaders who had supported the Grant administration, had their strength in the party machines in the big cities of Boston, New York, and Chicago.

The up-and-coming party leaders, the Half-Breeds, focused more on the expansion of industry and the West; these upstarts had to defeat or take control of these party machines to take their place in the hierarchy. One of the ways to do so was to attack the

New York Customhouse, a major vehicle for the party machine to dispense patronage to its members.

The Half-Breeds got President Hayes to "issue an executive order to end political activity on the part of federal officeholders and to forbid political assessments on them."[67] Although there was resistance from New York Senator Conkling, Hayes ultimately changed the Customhouse, and even extended civil service rules to all principal customs houses and post offices in the country. In the end, though, his order was largely ignored. Without congressional support providing the machinery to implement the rules, Hayes could do little to enforce them.

It was not until the assassination of President Garfield by a disgruntled federal office holder with the encouragement of the Stalwarts, that Congress felt forced to pass legislation to reform civil service. This was the Pendleton Act, which passed in 1883 and created the Civil Service Commission (CSC). It became the vehicle by which the reformers hoped to reform federal employment, but was marginalized for years after its creation.

The CSC did not have enough funds or personnel, and few enforcement powers. Only gradually were employees placed under the control of the CSC; however, it did succeed in ending party assessments of employees for the support of the parties. The parties learned to obtain funding from other sources. The Republicans learned to appeal directly to businesses, and the Democrats, to southern and western farmers, and eventually to labor unions.

Federal employees effectively were not subject to civil service rules and requirements until the election of Theodore Roosevelt, himself a dedicated civil service reformer. Roosevelt placed more employees under civil service rule, and tried to sever the political ties employees had with the parties and Congress. He wanted to make civil service an exclusively executive entity. He "looked toward the creation of a stable career service directly attached to and exclusively managed by executive officers."[68] These efforts eventually became a contest between the President and Congress over who was in charge of the bureaucracy. The implicit conflict between the executive and the legislative, which had been more or less dormant since Jackson, now became explicit again.

In the process of asserting the President's budgetary authority, Taft's "Commission on Economy and Efficiency developed a program that would institutionalize executive control over civil administration in ways that far surpassed the scope and implications of the Roosevelt initiatives."[69] In the meantime, Congress was explicitly rejecting the idea that the executive could have exclusive control over civil service personnel. It passed the Lloyd-LaFollette Act, which "effectively nullified the Roosevelt-Taft initiatives on behalf of exclusive executive control over civil service personnel."[70] This was Congress' attempt to reassert control over the selection of federal employees.

Much had changed, however, since the high point of the patronage system. Federal employees had unionized and gained some control of the conditions of their employment. The Lloyd-LaFollette Act concerned the rights of employees to petition Congress or provide information to Congress, not the power of Congress to appoint the employees.

The attempted reassertion of congressional influence over federal employees continued in President Wilson's administration. He was relatively more amenable to these efforts. Congress continued to create agencies, such as the Bureau of Efficiency to oversee the Civil Service Commission, that were responsible only to Congress, as a way of monitoring and controlling the executive agencies. Wilson, like Roosevelt and Taft, asserted that such agencies were unconstitutional, that according to the separation of powers, he was entitled to impose himself between Congress and executive agencies.

Professionalizing the civil service was never completed. The highest offices in the executive branch continue to be subject to patronage, but now the President, not Congress, controls that patronage. The net effect of the process of professionalization has been to shift the power of patronage from Congress to the President, weakening Congress, and making the President even stronger. It has not made the country more democratic.

Military Reform

The development and reform of the military was another area in which the goal was to remove politics and party influence. In one sense it was much more an in-house affair: Debate over reform was carried out almost entirely within the military bureaucracy. In another sense it involved a much deeper split in the national psyche. From the beginning of the formation of this country, there was a common fear that the national government would become omnipotent and oppressive to its citizens through the development of the military, especially a standing army. Americans felt the British government and other European governments, in creating military establishments, were becoming oppressive to their own people.

Brewer[71] points out that from the inside, British citizens in England did not feel oppressed, but those on the outside, such as the Americans, thought they were, and wanted to avoid this fate at all costs. One of the ways to do so was to keep military power away from the central government and dependent on local, state initiatives. Each separate state was allowed to have its own militia independent of the national government; the national government was intended to be dependent on these state militias for military actions.

The federal government was dependent to a large extent on the state militias in the early military campaigns, from the War of 1812, the Indian wars, and the Mexican War. It changed with the Civil War, in which, ultimately, a million men served in the U.S. army. These soldiers quickly demobilized at the end of the war, though, and the U.S. army returned to a small force of about 30,000 men, occupied primarily with fighting Indians in the western territories. The tradition of depending on the state militias continued to be strong.

After the Civil War, the other primary factor in supporting the independent state militias was the desire of the South to prevent any effective effort by the federal government to enforce its laws. With the agreement in 1877 to allow Hayes to be President in return for the federal army staying out of the South, it became convenient for the South to argue that the state militia was the proper means for enforcing federal law in each state. For the Democratic party, which came to represent the South, it was vital to maintain the state militias—and state control of the militias.

In every state, militias were a source of patronage jobs for local state parties. The army staff, centered in Washington, came to be independent of the line officers in the field; they were more concerned with tending to the needs and wants of congressmen and the state militias than with the needs of the U.S. army. The staff was headquartered in Washington with direct access to congressmen, while the line officers were scattered in the territories, far from their congressmen.[72]

Three sources of conflict arose for the military: between state militias and the federal, U.S. army; between the southern desire for a weak central government and the northern recognition of the need for a strong central government; and between the central army staff and the decentralized line. In response to these conflicts, as with the civil service, a group of people advocated military reform. They took their ideas from a study of European governments and military establishments and advocated that the U.S. army copy the organization and structure of those militarily more advanced governments.

These conflicts persisted because after the Civil War the country had no real need for a strong, well-organized military establishment until at least the Spanish-American War in 1898, and maybe not even until World War I. In that period, the United States was under no threat from other powers, and could easily believe that an army was not even needed, except possibly for protection from Indians, and domestic crises. The 1877 Railroad Strike was one such crisis, and made people aware of the need for a functional military, but the result was only that the state militias became more organized, and means were found to allow the federal government to use the state militias to put down further labor violence.[73]

Progress in the development of the military consisted primarily of increasing the organization and professionalism of the state militias. The regular U.S. army gave state militias more money and responsibility in return for more regulation of training and standards and procedures, but they remained independent of the regular army. Meanwhile, the regular U.S. army continued to be disorganized, as was made glaringly evident in the preparation for and execution of the Spanish-American War. The logistics of equipping and transporting large numbers of troops was a disaster.

The logistical disaster of the Spanish-American War was not enough of a shock, however, to induce Congress to reform the existing system; problems remained during World War I and after. Congress provided little support for the President and the military, and resisted the efforts of the military to organize itself into a modern, effective force. Congressional resistance, combined with the lack of a perceived external threat, prevented real modernization until World War II. Following World War II, the national government, and in particular the President, had just what the Founders feared: a strong, professional military under the control of the President, enabling him to engage in foreign adventures, and oppress even Americans. Wilson in World War I intimidated and spied on German-Americans, and Roosevelt in World War II interned Japanese-Americans.

III

CONGRESSIONAL GRIDLOCK

11

COMPROMISING OVER SLAVERY

Separation of powers, judicial supremacy, and the anti-party bias of groups wanting to reform government have combined with the basically undemocratic character of the form of our government, to produce weak Congresses, in particular a weak House, relative to the presidency, the Senate, and the judiciary. Congress is unable to do the job it was intended to do: express the will of the people. This is most apparent in how Congress dealt with slavery.

In many ways slavery is the central issue in the history of the United States: Slavery was a point of contention when the Constitution was written; it dominated discussion over every other aspect of U.S. development and expansion until the Civil War; and it was the elephant in the room for another century until the civil rights movement in the 1960s. The history of slavery is a history of repeated compromises with the South, followed by willful neglect of what was going on there.

As part of giving up control of the executive to the President in the first session of Congress, legislators came to look to the President for direction in making policy. Since every President up to the election of Lincoln was either from the South or sympathetic to the southern point of view, it is not surprising that Congress did not take any meaningful action to deal with slavery. Congress just tried to ignore it.

Slavery was a perennial concern for the people in the country, however, and Congress was faced with a steady stream of petitions from citizens to abolish it, starting with the effort of the Quakers in 1790. Such petitions were consistently dismissed, and from 1836 to 1844 the House annually passed a resolution, the so-called gag order, stating that any petitions concerning slavery or the abolition of slavery would be tabled immediately and not discussed at all in the House. This prevented any further discussion of slavery in the House for eight years. After all, the House had been arguing about this issue for almost fifty years, and nothing had been accomplished; maybe it was time to avoid it completely.

The Senate, on the other hand, represented the states; senators simply wanted to prevent federal interference in state affairs, especially with respect to slavery. With the President and the Senate telling the House to ignore slavery, the House actually did no more than rant and rave about the issue, with no constructive resolution. They could rant and rave and yell and scream at each other, even beat each other up, because they knew nothing would actually change. The President did not push for change, and the Senate would block any real House efforts. In presidential elections, none of the parties wanted to discuss slavery for fear it would alienate the South and jeopardize the election of its candidate.

It was in the South's interest to promote a federal government that was weak and limited, with the individual states wielding the most power. This became the device behind which the slaveholders could hide and prevent the federal government from interfering with their practices. The threat of secession was an influential part of this presumed power of the individual states. States' rights were what motivated Jackson in his campaign to reduce the power of the federal government.

In the early years of the republic, controversy over slavery was avoided through an informal rule that each newly admitted free state had to be paired with a slave state, so parity between the North and the South was maintained. The South thus maintained a balance at least in the Senate between slave states and free states. This balance allowed the South, acting as a group, to defeat any challenges to its way of life.

The Missouri Compromise

The first threat to this balance of power in Congress came in 1819 when Missouri applied for admission as a state. The United States was expanding to the west, and as the population increased, new states were formed. Until 1819 there had been a relative parity between new slave states and new free states. This was challenged when Missouri applied to become a state.

The southern states wanted slavery to be permitted in Missouri, but the rest of the country, which by that time had the majority of the population, did not want to allow slavery to continue to expand. The result was the famous Missouri Compromise, by which slavery was allowed in Missouri, but not north of it, and Missouri was paired with the new state of Maine, carved out of Massachusetts.

The Missouri Compromise is the first instance of congressional gridlock—and the failure of expression of the majority's will. In 1819, "Representative James Tallmadge of New York offered an amendment to the enabling act, prohibiting the further introduction of slaves into Missouri and mandating the emancipation of all slaves subsequently born in the state on reaching the age of twenty-five."[1] This amendment passed the House 79 to 67, in spite of the protestations of the southerners.

If this had finished the matter, the history of the United States might have been quite different. Southerners had not yet hardened themselves into unyielding supporters of the institution of slavery; some even admitted that slavery was a moral evil that would have to disappear eventually. If the House vote had prevailed, not only would the subsequent history have differed: the Civil War might never have happened.

But this was not to be: Southerners in the Senate stopped the will of the majority, as expressed in the House, by forcing the House to compromise with the minority southern position. Southerners forced adoption of a compromise that allowed them to cling to the hope that their way of life could be preserved in spite of the majority's condemnation of it.

After controversy and effort lasting into the next year, the South claimed some satisfaction—and hope that they would continue to have their way in defiance of the clear will of the majority. The South had learned that although it could not force its will on the majority, it could block the majority from expressing its will. The ability of a minority in the Senate to block the will of the majority in the House was to become a perennial problem for our government.

After the Missouri Compromise, the issue of slavery was put aside, and the use of the filibuster and other obstructive tactics diminished. The Jeffersonian Republican party split into those in favor of the use of federal power to assist in the development of the country, and those who, like Jefferson, were threatened by increases in national power. For a brief period, the forces of expansion and national development were ascendant. The so-called National Republicans were in favor of a national bank and federal assistance in developing the frontier.

Jackson's election was a renewal of the reactionary, anti-national attitudes first expressed within the federal system by Jefferson. The Democratic Republicans, led by Jackson and Van Buren, were apprehensive about such assertions of national authority, and fought against them.

Slavery fueled these fears. Sentiment in the rest of the world was shifting strongly toward abolishing slavery, putting pressure on the United States and the South to follow suit. As the United States became more integrated into the international market economy, these sentiments were especially threatening to those who wanted to preserve slavery in the South, even though cotton was very much a part of the international economy.

Those who defended slavery were threatened by the imposition of the authority of the national government—even when it was helping the states develop internally. Over the next thirty years, from 1820 to 1850, slavery was not directly addressed, but it festered below the surface as the government dealt with other issues.

Nullification

One of these other issues was the nullification theory devised by John Calhoun. John Calhoun, the Senator from South Carolina and Vice President under both J. Q. Adams and Jackson had been a strong National Republican, in favor of expansion and internal improvement. Toward the end of the 1820s, however, in reaction to the growing pro-slavery, state's rights' positions of those in his home state of South Carolina, he changed his orientation.

In 1828 Calhoun wrote an anonymous essay in which he argued that each state had the right to nullify the laws of the federal government if the state felt the laws were unconstitutional. Ostensibly his arguments were directed at the tariff legislation passed by Congress. He argued that South Carolina could nullify the tariffs within its borders. In his scheme, the rest of the states would then have to collectively decide whether they agreed or disagreed with South Carolina: only if the other states disagreed would South Carolina have to decide whether it was going to stay in the union or secede. Only at that point, for Calhoun, would secession be raised. Ultimately Calhoun's arguments were a rejection of the sovereignty of the federal government.

Rejection of national sovereignty was a complete reversal of Calhoun's previously nationalistic positions. His reversal was motivated by fears that the South, and South Carolina in particular, might be forced to accept the end of slavery. His writings were at first anonymous, but by the time Jackson was elected President he was known to be the author.

South Carolina, and Vice President Calhoun, felt that tariffs passed in Congress as part of Henry Clay's program for promoting American manufacturing and commerce benefited the North, and were unfair to South Carolina and the South in general; they threatened to raise prices in the South without any benefit to the South, and were seen as part of an effort to threaten the southern way of life, in particular the institution of slavery.

Many Republicans thought Jackson, a southerner, would agree with Calhoun's position on nullification (by 1830 Calhoun was known to have written the essay), but to the dismay of the South, Jackson rejected the arguments, and maintained that the union must be preserved. As Howe[2] remarked, Jackson did not like having his authority questioned. This precipitated a direct confrontation between the federal government and South Carolina (and between Jackson and Calhoun) that threatened to escalate. Debate continued until 1832 after passage of another tariff bill. South Carolina declared the new bill null and void in its state, forcing a confrontation with the federal government.

Jackson issued a proclamation denying that a state could nullify a law passed by the federal government. He asked Congress to pass a "Force Bill" that would give him the power to use force to collect the taxes. This act was passed, but a violent confrontation was avoided when Henry Clay engineered a compromise in which the tariffs were reduced, allowing South Carolina to save face and claim a victory with the reduced tariffs. Once again Congress was put in the position of negotiating a compromise between the white South and the rest of the country.

Indian Removal

Indian problems in the South were only indirectly related to slavery, but how the problems were resolved encouraged southern resistance to the federal government. Jackson had no sympathy for the Indians. During the War of 1812 he massacred thousands of Creek Indians, then forced the remainder to give up much of their land. By the time Jackson became President, the state of Georgia had completed the confiscation of Creek land, with the acquiescence of then President John Quincy Adams.

Georgians wanted to do the same to the Cherokee tribe, though the Cherokees had tried hard to assimilate into the U.S. culture. Wilentz[3] suggests that had Adams not acquiesced in allowing Georgia to eliminate the Creeks, the southern states might not have pursued their opposition to the federal government with regard to the Indians. However that might be, with Jackson Georgians had a sympathetic ear.

The Cherokee nation had declared itself a republic, and therefore claimed the right to deal directly with the federal government, a provision explicitly written into the Constitution (Article I, Section 8). But Jackson refused. Instead he pushed through Congress an Indian Removal Act in 1830, which continued the Adams policy of allowing the states to take their own measures to deal with the Indians, under the guise of helping the Indians to do what was best for them: to leave.

Wilentz writes that Jackson sincerely believed moving the Indians to western lands was best for them, but the law was vaguely worded, inviting whites to use it to exploit Indians. As Wilentz put it, "Bereft of long-term planning and a full-scale federal commitment, the realities of Indian removal belied Jackson's rhetoric."[4] Jackson felt that allowing the Cherokees to create a separate state within the state of Georgia was unconstitutional, a position enthusiastically supported by the white settlers.

Even when the Supreme Court explicitly pointed to the Constitution and decreed that the state of Georgia had no power to expel the Cherokees, that it was a federal issue, Jackson chose to ignore the Court, and allowed the state to proceed with the expulsion, resulting in the infamous Trail of Tears.

In contrast to his position on the nullification issue, Jackson supported the states against the federal government on the Indian issue. As long as federal power was not threatened, he supported the power of the states. If he had wanted to support a real change in the social system and wanted to uphold the Constitution, he would have asserted the authority of the federal government to deal with Indian issues. Congress' support for his actions indicates that Jackson did reflect the will of the majority. Of much greater consequence was that Jackson's treatment of the Indians encouraged the South to resist the federal government and harden its position on slavery.

The Compromise of 1850

After Jackson's presidency, political debate returned to the issue of slavery. The issue intensified because Congress could not confront it directly and resolve it. Between 1836 and 1844 any debate on the issue was deliberately prohibited. In 1846, only two years after the gag resolution had finally been defeated, the slavery issue came up again with admission of new states, where it could not be avoided. This time the dispute was over the admission of New Mexico and California following the acquisition of Mexican territory in the Mexican War under Polk.

Slaveholders wanted these states admitted as slave states, and also wanted to strengthen the fugitive slave laws so slaveholders could retrieve their "property" from the free states. Again, the anti-slave majority in the House passed a law making New Mexico and California free states, but the Senate blocked the will of the majority, forcing another compromise. The Compromise of 1850, four years after the issue had been raised, admitted New Mexico and California as free states, but with a stronger fugitive slave law and no abolition of slavery in the District of Columbia.

Remini[5] interprets this last compromise as giving the country ten more years in which to find a Lincoln who could successfully deal with slavery. All of this delay and avoidance, however, served only to harden both sides in their positions: by the time Lincoln took office, the issue could be resolved only by attempted secession and war. The failure of the federal government to deal decisively with the moral and economic issues of slavery prior to the Civil War is the cause of the war. This failure is one consequence of a government structure in which the will of the majority can be thwarted.

Failure to deal with slavery more decisively was not the fault of the people through their representatives in the House. The House wanted to end slavery. It was, rather, the fault of the overall structure of a government in which the Senate could thwart the will of the people, and the President could discourage and even veto the majority's expression. The government did not resolve slavery earlier because the majority view of the people, as expressed through the House of Representatives, could not prevail.

Civil War

The Civil War's immediate impact on Congress was that the departure of the southern states and their representatives made Republicans the clear majority in Congress. The Republicans passed significant legislation that promoted national development and national issues; these measures had been bottled up in committees prior to the war because of the resistance of the South. Much of this legislation favored the wealthy northerners, but several bills were significant for the future of the country: the Homestead Act, the Morrill Land Grant Act, the U.S. Internal Revenue Act, and the Pacific Railroad Act. Without the resistance of the South, it was finally possible for Congress to deal with national issues.

With a united government directed at prosecuting the war, Congress also felt it should have more say in running the war. The leaders in Congress decided they should be the ones who determined how the war was conducted. Their attempts to interfere became an annoyance to the President. Under the circumstances, the efforts of Congress to assert itself during the war were ludicrous, even comical.

Congress did not try to control the War Department, as the ministers in Britain did. Instead Congress formed a Joint Committee on the Conduct of the War, and then proceeded to investigate the War Department. The members of the committee had no war experience, and distrusted the War Department. They did find fraud, abuse, and poor management, but they also initiated resentment and annoyance because the reality was they were not in charge.

Congress wanted to be in charge, but in wartime there is pressure to have one man manage the war, not a committee of kibitzers: In the government at the time, that meant the President. It was the wrong time to attempt a change in the way the government operates. Congress' efforts were going against a tradition of over seventy years that gave the President authority over the department heads. It was ridiculous for Congress to try to direct the operations of the executive departments in wartime when the heads of those departments were responsible to the President; unsurprisingly, it did not succeed.

Slavery persisted in this country for seventy years after the creation of the United States because the federal government was weak. A minority in the Senate or a veto by the President blocked the clear majority of the population—who wanted to join the rest of the world and end slavery. Individual states wanted the federal government to be weak, and took advantage of the structure of the federal government to preserve this weakness. The consequence of the weakness of the House of Representatives was that we had to go to war to try to resolve the issue, rather than deal with it peacefully through a meaningful political process. In spite of all the violence, the continuing lack of effective political processes meant the issue, even after the Civil War, was not fully resolved.

12

SLAVERY IN ALL BUT NAME

Reconstruction

One of the more absurd aspects of the American presidential system is the provision for a Vice President. This would not be true if the Vice President, upon succession to office, could be counted on to carry on the policies and programs of his predecessor. Most of the time this happened, but it is not guaranteed. The most catastrophic example of this failure to carry on with the policies of his President and party was Andrew Johnson, who succeeded Lincoln after he was assassinated.

After the war, Congress expected to be involved in reconstructing the South.[6] They were ready to take charge of the government and put an end not only to slavery but also to the culture that promoted it. The challenge was how to reintegrate the South into the country in a way that would preserve and promote the values and ideals about which the war was fought. After Lincoln's assassination, Congress expected the new President, Andrew Johnson, to cooperate with these efforts. Congress soon found, however, that the new President had his own ideas of what should be done, and became an obstacle to Congress.

Congress adjourned on April 15, 1865, and did not normally reconvene until December. Johnson could have called a special session to deal with reconstruction; instead he used the intervening months to implement his own version of it. He unilaterally proclaimed that the southern states could rejoin the union if they would repeal the secession ordinances, disavow the Rebel debt, and ratify the 13th Amendment outlawing slavery.[7]

These requirements were less than southerners had expected, and they rushed to conform. They held new conventions and wrote new constitutions accepting these requirements, but they also wrote the Black Codes meant to ensure that the status of blacks did not actually change. Many members of the former Confederacy were elected to Congress.

When it reconvened in December, Congress did not feel the southern states could be simply readmitted to the union without more meaningful changes in how those states operated. Some recognition was necessary that blacks had the status of citizens with rights. Although Johnson had accepted that the southern states were again part of the union, Congress refused to admit them to Congress. A kind of standoff persisted between Congress and the President for over a year.[8]

Congress without the southern representatives passed two bills, one extending the reach of the Freedman's Bureau, and the other defining the civil rights of blacks. To their surprise, Johnson vetoed both bills, making it clear that he favored the South, and was not going to cooperate with Congress. Both vetoes were overridden and then the 14th Amendment was passed, making it part of the Constitution that blacks could not be discriminated against because of their race.

Frustrated in this way, Johnson asserted his control over the executive officers, removing those who were sympathetic to Congress, and replacing them with persons who agreed with him. The result was that although the laws were passed, they were not carried out. These actions demonstrate most starkly the consequences of having the form of government we have—one that allows the executive to negate the will of Congress. Though Congress overrode Johnson's vetoes, Johnson felt justified in continuing to defy Congress and refusing to implement Congress' laws.

This defiance emboldened southern states to resist the new laws, and riots and killings in Memphis and New Orleans increased the alarm. Johnson "referred to the U.S. Congress as illegitimate, inspiring rumors that he might disperse it by force—and apparently he was pondering the idea."[9] When Johnson tried to rally support by making a tour of the northern states, however, he succeeded only in making himself more unpopular.

The elections of 1866 returned a large Republican majority to Congress, which still was not admitting the representatives from the southern states. The new Congress passed the Military Reconstruction Act, and three subsequent acts whereby the "existing governments were superseded by military authority. . . . [and] the army would oversee registration of a new electorate, which would include the African-American population and exclude those proscribed from office by the proposed Fourteenth Amendment."[10] Johnson continued to resist the efforts of the Republicans to change the South.

Although black suffrage was not popular even in the north, suffrage was necessary to enable election of those governments in the South that were sympathetic to black civil rights, and to the Republican party that supported those rights. The Republicans offered the South a deal: if this new electorate of blacks was allowed to participate in forming a new state government, and if the newly formed government was acceptable to Congress and ratified the 14th Amendment, the southern states would be readmitted to the union. New governments in the South were thus formed, and in 1868 the states were readmitted to the union and to Congress.

All the new state governments were Republican, and thus supported the Republicans in Congress. They made it possible to elect Grant in 1868 as the next President. At first the new governments seemed to have some success in promoting the condition of blacks in the South. The 15th Amendment was passed in 1870, giving blacks the right to vote; some parts of the white population were beginning to give grudging respect to some blacks. But it did not last.

In 1868, at the end of his term, an effort was made to impeach Johnson because of his resistance to Reconstruction; the specific charge was that he had violated the Tenure of Office Act by which

Congress had tried to limit the President's power to fire executive officers. A clear majority of the Senate wanted to impeach him, and so assert the authority of Congress over the President, but since impeachment required a two-thirds vote, the ability of Congress to restrain the President through impeachment failed. A minority in the Senate kept the majority will from being carried out.

This famous impeachment attempt failed by one vote in the Senate, partly because of poor arguments from the prosecution, but perhaps mostly because the issues were considered political rather than judicial. The President could be impeached only for high crimes and misdemeanors, whatever those terms mean, but not when the two branches simply disagreed over political measures and the President had a minority of supporters on his side.

The failure of the impeachment effort resulted in reinforcing the understanding first promoted by Jackson, that the President is an independent actor who can act on his own interpretation of his responsibilities—in opposition to the will of Congress or the meaning of the Constitution.

The effort to reintegrate the South into the rest of the country failed. Perhaps Congress was trying to do too much in its attempt to change the South, but at least it had a plan for how to do it and the will to carry it out. Johnson's actions were not directed at promoting another plan for integrating the South into the Union, and blacks into the South, as much as they were an attempt to thwart Congress and, again, deny that there was a problem. The four years of Johnson's term, in which substantial progress could have secured a real change in southern culture, were wasted through the opposition of the President.

Two economic events destroyed the progress that began tentatively after 1868. The first was railroad speculation. It was pervasive all over the country, but the Republicans, in their effort to integrate the South into the larger economy, encouraged the new southern states to promote railroads. A great deal of speculation and corruption resulted.

When the Credit Mobilier scandal erupted, in which many railroads simply collapsed, the southern states suffered also. The southern whites encouraged their northern sympathizers to blame the collapse and suffering on corruption in the black governments, giving the North an excuse to discount and ignore white southern repression of blacks.

When violence against blacks increased, Grant sent federal troops to stop it. This made Grant very popular, and enabled him to be re-elected with the support of southern blacks, who were briefly able to vote.

The second event was the depression in 1873 that followed the railroad bankruptcies. The depression made it difficult for southern governments to continue integrating blacks into the economy, and encouraged whites to reassert their supremacy. The price of cotton went down for years, and violence against blacks rose again. President Grant was reluctant this time to send more troops South, so intimidation of blacks only increased.

The result was that by 1877 white supremacists had regained control of the governments in the South, essentially by force and intimidation. They prevented blacks from voting in the elections, and the Democrats—i.e., white supremacists—swept into power. The final straw came in 1877 when the federal government agreed to withdraw its troops and leave the enforcement of civil rights to the states. The federal government had given up its efforts to promote civil rights in the South.

Other than the end of legal slavery, nothing really changed; the South was allowed to continue its repression of blacks for almost another 100 years. The Supreme Court cooperated by distorting the meaning of the amendments Congress passed, construing them to apply only to the federal government, allowing the states to ignore them. By 1877 the military had been withdrawn from the southern states, and they were allowed to revert to their racist practices.

No period in our history demonstrates more the dysfunctional consequences of our government's structure. Once again the President thwarted the will of the majority and allowed the minority to continue activities that were clearly at odds with the values of American society. Congress, in turn, was unwilling or unable to defy the President.

This period further cemented the dominance of the President and the subordination of Congress that started with Jackson's assertion of presidential power in defiance of Congress in 1832. Jackson's precedent justified Lincoln's later assumption of dictatorial powers during the Civil War, and then the defiance of Andrew Johnson after the war.

The other major structural event of this period was the unexpected impact of having the President succeeded on his death by the Vice President. With both Tyler in 1841 and Johnson in 1865, the program for which the President and his party were elected was completely lost and the direction of the country changed—all without any input from the people. In both cases the Vice President was at odds with his party's plans and prevented the party from realizing its goals.

Segregation

With the failure of Reconstruction, subjugation and re-enslavement of blacks in the South continued. Though officially slavery had been eliminated, the practice continued, enabled by the failure of the Supreme Court and the executive to enforce the 14th and 15th Amendments to the Constitution. In the Slaughterhouse cases (1873) and *United States v. Cruikshank* (1876) the courts argued that the powers of the federal government were limited, and did not include the authority to force the states to conform to the Constitution with regard to state matters; the states' treatment of African-Americans was held to be a local, state matter. Congress supinely accepted these arguments without protest or any effort to correct the Court's interpretation of the 14th Amendment. The South was free to re-establish slavery in all but name.

As the Republican majority decreased in the 1874 election, the southerners defeated the measures the Republicans had passed, and prevented any further civil rights legislation. In 1870–71 three bills to enforce the 14th and 15th Amendments were passed, but they were never enforced, and twenty years later a southern-dominated Democratic Congress repealed them. In 1875 an attempt was made to pass a bill that would force the southern states to allow blacks to vote, but it was defeated. A Civil Rights Act was passed in 1875, but it was ineffective when the courts rendered it irrelevant.

The end came in 1877 when the South agreed to let Hayes be the next President on the condition that all remaining federal troops be pulled out of the South. After that, no matter what the federal government said, it was left up to the states to enforce the laws, and the southern states did not. A later attempt in 1890 to require a federal investigation of an election if 100 voters petitioned for it was dropped in bargaining to get the Sherman Silver Purchase Act passed. This ended any attempts by the federal government to force changes in the South until the 1960s.

Theodore Roosevelt's 1906 dismissal—without any judicial proceeding—of an entire battalion of black soldiers in Brownsville, Texas for their supposed guilt in a firefight, is an example of the continuing power of the South to have its way with respect to the treatment of blacks. Though Roosevelt was in some ways sympathetic to blacks, this action was an egregious misuse of his authority as commander in chief in peacetime, and a blatant appeal to the South.

None of the soldiers had admitted to causing the firefight; their guilt was assumed. No investigation was made of other reasons for the firefight, though it was obvious that the white citizens of Brownsville did not want black soldiers stationed in their city, and could easily have set up the soldiers. Rather than push for such an investigation, Roosevelt fired the soldiers.

It was not until after World War II when Truman integrated the armed forces, that civil rights for blacks became an issue again; even then it took another twenty-five years to bring about real change. Every President from Truman on had supported civil rights reform, doing what they could to promote change. Eisenhower in the 1950s tried to have a civil rights bill passed, but he only achieved a watered down, ineffective bill. Congress could not act because of the dominance of conservative southern whites. It was not until Lyndon Johnson took over after the assassination of Kennedy in the 1960s that an effective Voting Rights Act was passed—and then only after years of demonstrations and violence.

It took Congress 100 years to fulfill the intent of the 14th and 15th Amendments passed after the Civil War. As soon as the South was readmitted to Congress in 1868, they realized they could prevent any real action to implement these amendments, and they did. These blocking efforts did not end until the 1960s; even then it took years of effort and a major popular movement to accomplish what should have been a clear and obvious change. The southern senators obstructed progress on civil rights from the 1870s to the 1960s.

The civil rights movement in the 1950s and 1960s is one of the clearest examples of the gridlock and minority obstruction that has characterterized congressional activity over the last sixty years. In spite of a clear majority that supported civil rights issues in those years, the governmental structure allowed the southern states, with a minority of the population, to thwart the will of the majority to eliminate discrimination. The inability of the federal government to act decisively could not be more evident. Unfortunately, it is not the only example of the inability of the national government to promote national interests.

13

COMMERCE AND CREDIT

The history of our country's treatment of blacks demonstrates the failure of a government in which the majority of the population does not govern. In the area of economic development, the same constraints on the majority affected the course of our economic history. One of the major responsibilities of a national government is to secure and promote national development. For the United States this involved the territorial expansion and settlement of the country, and the encouragement of trade and commerce both within the country and internationally.

In the early years of the republic, the federal government did act as a national government, promoting the development of the country. The federal government assumed state debts, and thereby established the credit and credibility of the United States in the international market. An essential aspect of Hamilton's plan was to establish a national bank through which commerce and trade could be organized. It is difficult to imagine how the country's credibility could have been established in 1789 without a national bank.

The vast majority of people in the United States wanted national development and expansion. A significant minority, however, did not, or at least did not want the national government to help with national development. This minority position was represented by some of the luminaries of our history, such as Jefferson and Madison. Madison, for example, argued that the federal government did not have the authority to establish a national bank.

From a modern point of view, it is difficult to understand the logic of Madison's argument. Did Madison and Jefferson think individual state banks could do the job of a national bank? That state banks would be accepted by other countries as easily as a national bank? Was their perspective so limited they did not see the need for banks at all, much less a national bank?

If their opposition had been based solely on the limits of the Constitution, they could have called for an amendment that would specifically allow the federal government to establish a national bank, but they did not. If their objection was that a national bank would be taken over by the rich and powerful, they could have proposed an alternative that made it clearer that the government would have primary control. They did not do this either.

Their opposition to a national bank went beyond the constitutional argument: They objected to giving the federal government, through a national bank, increased authority over economic activity, and by implication over the states. They objected to allowing the federal government to establish and supervise a national bank, even if the alternative—state banks—would result in jeopardizing the status and credibility of the federal government internationally. From their point of view, the integrity of the states was more important than the integrity of the national government.

Virginia gentlemen such as Madison and Jefferson may have sincerely believed that banks were not necessary for the conduct of commerce. In the Virginia colony of the 1700s, the British merchants who bought Virginia produce, particularly tobacco, and provided British manufactured items, acted as bankers for the Virginia landed gentry.[11] Going into debt in such a situation meant owing money to a merchant for goods bought, not owing money to a bank for a loan, even though the debt owed the merchant was the equivalent of a loan to the buyer. Even such Virginia gentlemen must have known that behind the British merchant was a British bank.

Fortunately, in the early years of the republic, Madison and Jefferson were in the minority: a national bank was established, and the development of the country proceeded. The First Bank of the United States was instrumental in allowing the country to prosper and expand its boundaries. The Louisiana Purchase, for example, was financed through the First Bank of the United States.

The Era of Good Feelings

In spite of the success of the First Bank of the United States, its charter was allowed to expire in 1811, just before the War of 1812. The South and West did not want a national bank, feeling it would enable the national government to have too much control over the states, and the North did not need it.

This resulted in serious difficulties for the federal government in funding the war. Without a national bank they had to appeal to state banks and private financiers. The largest state banks were in the North, and northern banks were generally unwilling to finance the war because the northern states opposed the war. By the end of the war in 1816, the need for a national bank was recognized, and the Second Bank of the United States was chartered.

Following the War of 1812 issues of foreign affairs faded, as Britain came to dominate the world, and the world left the United States alone, perhaps with some paternalistic shelter of British power.[12] Americans turned inward to their own expansion and development. Monroe took over from Madison in 1817, and the years after the war until about 1819 came to be described as the Era of Good Feelings.

The economy boomed after the war ended, the result of bad crops in Europe and strong demand for cotton and other goods from the United States. Cotton became the major export, bringing in money from Britain, and enabling the southern plantation owners to become rich. Between 1811 and 1816 state banks had proliferated after the First Bank of the United States closed in 1811, fueling a speculative boom in land.[13] Prosperity also led to the development of textile factories in the northeast, and thus promoted industrialization.

The Federalists had disappeared as a functioning party, leaving the government a one-party system. Monroe spent much of his time seeking to accommodate the remaining Federalists and incorporate them into the Republican party. Eventually changes in the economy and society brought about by national expansion split the reigning one-party Republican rule into the National Republicans, who supported national development and the bank, and the Democratic Republicans, who were anti-bank, pro-hard money, and anti-development. The National Republicans continued to support change, while the Democratic Republicans became the party of resistance to change, fueled by southern fears that their culture of slavery may be endangered.

The focus during this period was on development and expansion, and what the national government could do to help bring this about. For a brief time, the House of Representatives with Henry Clay as its Speaker became a force in determining what the government did. Clay promoted his "American System," which included protective tariffs, cheap western land, support for internal improvements, and a national bank. This was a continuation of the Federalist-Hamiltonian program for the growth of manufacturing and commerce described as the market revolution.[14]

Henry Clay was perhaps the last person to believe that the center of government was the House of Representatives, that if one could control the House, one could control the government. He tried hard to control government from the House, and with Madison, he almost carried it off. Finally, though, even he had to admit that the President and the Senate, not the House, ran the government. He spent the rest of his life trying unsuccessfully to become President.

The Era of Good Feelings ended in the Panic of 1819, with the end of the Napoleonic wars in Europe, the recovery of European agriculture, and a shortage of gold and silver from Mexico and Peru.[15] Prices and land values fell; many were out of work and unable to pay their debts.

The Second Bank of the United States, created in 1816, did not handle this crisis well and even exacerbated the problem. It had been a liberal lender in good times, but it tightened its lending when the depression struck, making the downturn worse. It reacted to the panic as any other bank would have done at the time, but as a national bank, it had a greater effect on the country as a whole.

Many new state banks went bankrupt, leaving debtors with no way to pay their bills, and creditors unable to collect. Debtors became angry at the banks, and much of their resentment was directed at the national Bank of the United States.

Resentment of the national bank never resulted in any actual attempt to get rid of it until Jackson took office in 1829 and the pro-expansion, pro-bank National Republicans became the majority. They were in favor of the national government promoting internal improvements and the expansion of federal power; for them the national bank was an essential part of this power. The minority had no way to change the status quo, because there was no new legislation related to the bank. The national bank had been rechartered in 1816, following the War of 1812, and it was not subject to renewal for twenty years.

The party split between National Republicans and "Democratic" Republicans was complete when John Quincy Adams was elected President in 1824, in what Jackson, who was running as an anti-bank Democratic Republican, called a "corrupt bargain." Jackson had a plurality of the votes, but not a majority, and the election had to be decided by the House.

Adams won when Henry Clay, the fourth-place finisher, pro-development and no friend of Jackson, gave his votes to Adams. Jackson and his Democratic Republican party were quite upset with this result; from then on they campaigned hard against this "corrupt bargain" and generally obstructed the policies of the National Republicans.

Unfortunately, Adams was a largely ineffective President. He was stiff-necked, prudish, and overly moralistic, unwilling to use his political power to advance his goals, such as creation of a national university.[16] He was a victim of the obstructionist tactics of the Democrats. It became easy to stall his proposals—and defeat Adams in the next election.

Jackson's Restoration

Before Jackson was elected President in 1828, presidents overtly acted the part of chief magistrate, executing the laws given to them by Congress. They did not give speeches, did not campaign for office, did not even admit they wanted the office. Behind the scenes, however, presidents were the dominant force in government. The progress of the country was the result of their leadership or lack of leadership. The dangers of the lack of presidential leadership were made evident in the Madison and John Q. Adams administrations.

Andrew Jackson's election in 1828 was a turning point in American history. Jackson was against the changes taking place in the United States and thought of himself as a restorer of Jeffersonian ideals. The forces of national development were threatening the status quo he had grown up with and his fantasy of an agrarian paradise inhabited by white people, with other races either expelled or enslaved.

Jackson's actions with respect to the Indians encouraged the abolitionist movement that led to the Civil War,[17] but more insidiously they encouraged the states to ignore and disrespect the national government. He encouraged southern states to think they could ignore the federal government, act in opposition to it, and if necessary, simply secede. He began the spoils system by which government employees were chosen for their loyalty rather than their competence. His only action in favor of the federal government was his refusal to allow South Carolina to nullify federal laws, and this was more a reaction to the challenge to his own authority than it was support of the federal system.

Jackson's most important action, though, was his war on the National Bank of the United States. Jackson was strongly against a national bank, but the rest of the government had accepted it as settled by precedent and the Supreme Court. When the bank charter came up for early renewal, though the legislature easily passed it, Jackson vetoed it. Before its old charter had expired, he shifted federal money to state banks. Jackson transferred federal funds to certain state banks, which came to be called his pet banks because they were chosen largely on the basis of their loyalty to Jackson, in the same way other federal largesse was dispensed.

Jackson deliberately challenged the assumption that a national bank was a proper expression of federal powers. He demagogically used memories of the depression of 1819 to stir up resentment against the bank and to justify his actions. As Howe[18] points out, the economic arguments against the bank were weak, and Jackson had to resort to popular resentment against the rich and powerful.

Congress was stunned by what Jackson had done. Even members of his own cabinet were against the transfer of money from the Bank, and Jackson had to fire his Secretary of the Treasury and replace him with one who would do his bidding. There was talk of impeachment, but ultimately, Congress could do nothing to rein in the usurpation of authority. The requirement that a veto be overturned with a two-thirds majority made it possible for Jackson and his minority of followers to prevent the expression of the will of the majority, who wanted the renewal of the national bank.

Jackson's actions started a long process of conflict, the so-called Bank War. The Bank of the United States had existed and served the nation well for forty years (except for the short interim from 1811 to 1816, when the charter was not renewed).

Biddle, the director of the bank during Jackson's tenure, created a short panic in 1834 to show Jackson the effects of his actions; but Biddle's actions backfired and were quickly reversed. A more serious depression started in 1837, one that particularly impacted the western states Jackson was representing; it occurred due to speculation by state banks, free from the regulation and the restraint of the national bank.[19]

Jackson's actions were undertaken as deliberate reinterpretations of the Constitution and challenges to the will of the people. Jackson felt he, and he alone, was a better representative of the will of the people and interpreter of the Constitution than the legislature. In the Bank War he acted explicitly against the will of the people as expressed in Congress, and the Constitution. It also became obvious that though Congress protested and complained, there was actually nothing it could do to change what the President had done.

Thus it was not until Andrew Jackson became President that the ability of the President to act in opposition to Congress, under the claim of representing all the people, became an explicit factor in governing.[20] Jackson is the first example of the president as autocrat. The tension between the executive and legislative branches that has shaped the history of the country was present from the beginning, but Jackson made it explicit. He asserted the power of the presidency and its independence from the legislature and even the Constitution, perhaps even more than his own party had anticipated.

At the same time he was enhancing the power of the President, Jackson was decreasing the power of the federal government over those who held wealth and power—the same people against whom he was supposedly ranting. By eliminating the national bank, Jackson forced the national government to give up any power to control and regulate the forces of wealth and power he professed to fear.

As with Madison and Jefferson, Jackson's fear was of the power of government, not really of those who were wealthy and powerful. His claim was that the national government had to be kept weak so it could not serve the wealthy and powerful. The perverse result was that the wealthy and powerful found they could control the government *because* it was weak and could not act as a counterweight to the wealthy.

After Jackson left office in 1836, his chosen successor, Martin van Buren, carried on his opposition to a national bank, in spite of the existence in Congress of a majority that wanted a national bank. Through a Senate minority that supported him, van Buren blocked efforts of the majority to create a new national bank. At the end of his term he established his alternative to a bank, the "sub treasury," but it was repealed immediately after his term ended. The next President John Tyler also opposed a national bank, contrary to the position of his own party, and continued to block passage of a new bank.

Tyler was the earliest example of the consequences of having a Vice President who was opposed to the policies of his President and party. John Tyler was elected Vice President with President William Henry Harrison. Unfortunately, Harrison died within months of his inauguration, and Vice President Tyler took over. The Vice President had not been chosen for his leadership, or even how well he reflected the party priorities. He was selected instead for how well he balanced the ticket, with little regard for his positions, or the possibility that he might become President. He was a former Democrat on a Whig ticket, put there to attract voters in Democratic areas. His positions were almost entirely at odds with the party's, making his tenure as President a disaster for the party that elected him.

Tyler accepted the repeal of the sub treasury that Van Buren had spent so much effort on, but was opposed by the Whigs. But then Tyler vetoed bills establishing a new third bank of the United States, going against his own party. For this he was alienated, and in view of his behavior, the opposition party did not accept him either. Tyler became isolated and ineffective, able only to obstruct further progress. Four years were wasted.

Thus after eight more years of struggle, the majority still could not express its will with respect to a national bank. Eventually the state banks adjusted to the fact that the national government was not going to develop a national banking system. The New York banks became the dominant force, and pressure for a national bank diminished. The opportunity for the national government to be involved in development of the banking system, and through the banks, to influence national economic development, had passed.

Once again, the inability of the majority to express its will led to a weakened national government, whose influence on economic and financial progress was diminished. A minority of the population, in the person of Andrew Jackson and his followers, carried out a revolt and imposed their views on the majority. Given our system of government, in which the President is an independent power able to override the majority in Congress, the majority was prevented from expressing its will.

It was not until 1913 when the Federal Reserve was created that the national government re-established a central bank and regained the ability to direct the banking system. Between 1832 and 1913, the country was left to drift on its own without any pressure from the national government to be concerned about the common good. The New York banks' dominance led—years hence—to the rise of a few powerful individuals such as J. P. Morgan, who almost single-handedly rescued the country in the early 1900s.

Freedom for the Powerful

After the Civil War, the national government settled into a long period of Republican party dominance. It was a period in which the rich and powerful dominated the government; they were given the freedom to pursue their goals with little government restraint. From 1860, at the beginning of the Civil War to 1932 when Roosevelt and the Democrats took over, the Republicans were the dominant party. Freedom was for the powerful.

Republicans controlled the Senate for all but 10 of the 72 years. The Democrats controlled the Senate for only five 2-year periods, once in 1879–80, once in 1893–94, and for six years from 1913 to 1918 under Woodrow Wilson. Otherwise, for 62 years, the Republicans ruled the Senate, and thus blocked any legislation coming from the House that the Senate Republicans did not like—even when it was from their own party.

They did not need dilatory tactics such as the filibuster, and its use declined during this period. The Democratic minority in the Senate, on the other hand, was forced to filibuster to block legislation they did not like. During most of this period until 1913, senators were not directly elected. They were selected by the state legislatures, making them representative of the people in the states only indirectly. Senators were more representative of the leaders of the state legislators, and the business interests of each state.

Republican control of the House was not quite as complete. In the 20 years from 1874 to 1894, the Democrats had the majority in the House for 16 years. Over the same period the Republicans controlled the Senate for 16 years, and in only one 2-year period, 1893–94, did the Democrats control both chambers and the presidency, the first two years of Cleveland's second term. The only other complete Democratic control was during the first six years of Wilson's administration.

During and just after the Civil War, the Republicans were the anti-slavery, pro-black party, and retained the loyalty of blacks for many years after they were no longer anti-slavery and pro-black. When it became clear that the South was going to return to its pre-war status of white dominance and suppression of blacks, the Republican party turned to the North and northern concerns, to business and the cities with their largely immigrant populations. They maintained their power by providing patronage and favors to city workers and by doing favors for business leaders. The Republican party came to be identified with the northern cities and big business.

The Democrats were the continuation of the Jeffersonian and Jacksonian orientation toward states' rights and weak federal government. Their power also depended on the patronage they could provide to their workers, but their workers were more rural, small businesses, small farmers, and state and county officials. Their majorities, when they had them, were achieved by appealing to the smaller, more rural parts of the North and the immigrant populations in the cities through organizations such as Tammany Hall.

This was a period of strong party politics, but only at the local or state level. At the national level in Congress, the parties did not establish a national program, and control of their members was limited. Neither party was especially concerned with formulating, proposing, or advocating national policies. The Democratic party was explicitly against allowing the national government to do any more than absolutely necessary, believing that power should remain at the state level as much as possible. It was willing to take offices and money from the national government, but was not concerned with giving power to the national government through the support of initiatives.

The Republicans were equally unconcerned with national policies and projects, but they were more willing to use the national government to benefit their supporters, primarily big businesses. Big business and industry used the Republican party to promote their projects and prevent national government interference with business when unwanted.

Neither party was especially interested in promoting a strong national government concerned with national issues. Both wanted a weak national government. The Democrats wanted it weak absolutely, whereas the Republicans wanted it weak and malleable. Thus this period was exemplified by weak national parties that produced Congresses that resisted the professionalization of the civil service and the military, and rejected national regulation of business, working conditions, and the status of labor.

Congress did change in some ways during this period. After the Civil War the turnover in Congress decreased, and the position of congressman became more valuable and remunerative (through political influence in the allocation of funds) to those who held office, especially in the Senate. The Senate solidified its role as the means for minority obstruction of the majority. It, rather than the President, became the means by which the states and business resisted efforts by the people to change conditions within the states.

The South, given that a relatively small proportion of the population could vote, sent the same individuals to Congress over and over. Time in office became a mark of experience and authority in Congress, and a tradition of allowing seniority in office to serve as a criterion for leadership ensued. Southerners thus became the chairmen or ranking minority member of many of the committees by which the Senate and House did much of their business; in such positions southerners prevented any effort to enforce anti-discrimination laws in the South. This lasted really until the civil rights movement of the 1960s—for almost 100 years. The northern states resisted efforts to regulate the railroads and other large business interests based in the northern states.

Some attempts to increase the power of the majority party in the House were made in the 1890s when Speaker Thomas Reed (1889–99) eliminated the dilatory practices that had grown up over the years to prevent things from getting done. For instance, the minority party would make motions to adjourn or to delay consideration of a measure, just to avoid voting on it. To determine a quorum for doing business, the rule was that members had to answer "present." Often the minority would simply refuse to answer, even though they were physically present, thereby denying the majority a quorum—and the ability to do business.

It was not until Reed became the Speaker that this nonsense was eliminated. He earned the title of "Czar" for his efforts to take control of the process of legislation. As far as he was concerned, "The best system is to have one party govern and the other party watch...."[21] His intent was to make the system work, and his rules lasted twenty years.

When Reed left the speakership in 1899 his successors did not have the same motivation to see that the business of the House got done. Speaker Cannon from 1903 to 1909 used his the power of the Speaker developed under Reed to prevent any legislation that involved a change in the status quo. During Cannon's rule, little of President Theodore Roosevelt's progressive measures got through the House in spite of support there. Roosevelt was successful only when Cannon was not the Speaker. Insurgents in the House finally forced a change in the rules that stripped the Speaker of his power. After Cannon, the House reverted to a system of seniority, in which the committee chairmen had more power and could block legislation.

Discipline and majority control of the legislative process has improved in the House, but no matter how organized and effective the House by itself is, it cannot control the entire legislative process. Procedures in the Senate had not changed and it was still possible for the Senate to use delaying motions and amendments, as well as the filibuster, to prevent the expression of the majority will as expressed in the House. Legislation from the House had to be subordinated to the will of the Senate, giving the Senate the final say about the content of all legislation. So the House's own internal efforts to control its legislative process did not improve the overall process.

The Senate in this period was smug and comfortable, doing what the traditions of the early 1800s enabled it to do: obstruct the "excesses" of the House.

> By 1900 the House of Representatives had become an institution where a determined majority in either party could pass whatever legislation it supported . . . The minority could protest and make its case to the public. What the minority could not do [in the House] was to preclude action that the majority espoused. That was the task and the special role of the Senate . . . By 1900 it appeared that the upper house was as important as or perhaps even ascendant over the presidency.[22]

And yet the Senate was seen as a corrupt institution, where men bought their admission into the Senate by bribing the state legislators who chose the senators. The Senate gained a reputation as a place where money determined the outcome of elections and legislation.

Those who see the Constitution as the perfect expression of how government ought to be ignore the flaws and inefficiencies of the form of the government, and say that this is simply the way government operates. To those who believe a government should be democratic and express the will of the people through majority rule, the role of the Senate was (and is) an undemocratic aspect of government. The effects were first to deny the people a straightforward expression of their will, which led to the distrust of political parties, and second to encourage the irresponsibility of the House.

For example, with reference to Theodore Roosevelt's railroad regulation bill, what came to be known as the Hepburn bill, "there was strong support in the House, but members also had a free vote, since they knew the measure would be decided in the Senate."[23] House members were allowed to vote irresponsibly because their vote was irrelevant given that the Senate would determine its final disposition. Such irresponsible voting was typical of voting in the House—and is true even today.

The politics involved in railroad regulation and the creation of the Interstate Commerce Commission provide a good example of how the structure of the government affected the process of making law. In 1887, Congress passed the Interstate Commerce Act, creating the Interstate Commerce Commission, which was intended to regulate railroad traffic in the United States.

It was the first serious attempt by the national government to regulate the national economy by an agency separate from the courts. Pressure for some solution of the railroad problem had been building ever since the Credit Mobilier scandal and the massive bankruptcy of many railroads in the 1870s, but there had been no agreement about the solution.

Shippers and farmers, represented by the Democratic party, wanted cheap rates and an end to discrimination between long and short routes. They wanted to promote competition between the railroads. They did not believe national regulation of the railroads would be effective, given their experience in the states. They believed that only the courts could be relied on to curb the excesses of the railroads, though the courts were generally on the side of the corporations. They feared that a regulatory commission would only be a tool of the railroads.

The railroads wanted to end the competition between roads that led to rate wars and the threat of bankruptcy for the smaller roads. They wanted to make agreements by which they could pool their rates and cooperate rather than compete with each other. The railroads were willing to allow the federal government to regulate them in return for being permitted to cooperate in setting rates. Labor, not a major player in this discussion, just wanted better working conditions. No one was happy with the existing situation.

When Congress was finally aroused enough to deal with this problem, the Democrats had the majority in the House, and the Republicans in the Senate. The House under the Democrats wrote and passed a bill that reflected the wishes of the shippers and farmers for more competition and the use of courts rather than a commission for resolution of disputes. It prohibited the pooling of rates to enforce competition between railroads, but at the same time it prohibited discrimination between long and short haul routes, which would prevent the competition supposedly desired.[24]

The Democrats' solution to the pressure for railroad regulation was to direct the courts to adjudicate between these conflicting interests, forcing the courts to start regulating commerce. The courts at the time were against federal and even state involvement in the regulation of corporations. Judicial regulation of commerce would have been a major change in the role of the courts in government.

The Senate, with a Republican majority, was more sympathetic to the railroads, and wrote a different bill that was more economically sophisticated, but no less parochial. Their concern was more directly to support what big business wanted from the government, and so they produced a quite different bill. Their bill allowed pooling and created the Interstate Commerce Commission to regulate the rates.

Passage of the Senate bill set up an impasse between the two houses. It was possible to get the legislation through both houses only because the government was temporarily under a Democratic administration (Cleveland), and the northern Democrats wanted the legislation.[25] The southern Democrats were less concerned about railroad regulation, but they wanted to retain their control of the government.

Party leaders took both opposing bills to a conference between the Senate and House. The Democrats agreed to a compromise that did not allow pooling of rates, and prohibited discrimination between long and short routes, as they wanted, but the bill created a commission to regulate rates.

The resulting compromise was against the positions of the majority of the members of the Democratic party, who would just as soon have no legislation if they could not have what they passed in the House. Nevertheless, party leaders forced it on the House and thus the Interstate Commerce Commission (ICC) was born.

Unfortunately, contradictions within the Interstate Commerce Act made it unworkable, and along with the antipathy of the courts to any non-judicial regulation of business at all, this meant that the ICC was not an effective federal agency for many years. The structure for its operation was set up, but it was only a shell, without personnel or power to affect the railroads.

The result of the newly-created ICC was just like the compromises over slavery: there was little or no regulation of the railroads for the next twenty years—even when the railroads themselves wanted it. At least in the area of economic regulation, governing continued to be under the control of the courts, not Congress or even the executive.

This history of railroad regulation is more generally about the question of whether the federal government should be regulating commerce at all, and if so, how. Further, the question itself only arises because the government structure is such that the authority of the people's representatives is weak and uncertain in relation to the states and to the federal judiciary. It is a government unable to express the will of the people.

The Democratic party, continuing to represent states' rights and an anti-federal government position that goes back to Jackson, Jefferson, and ultimately the anti-federalists, was against federal involvement in commerce in general, whereas the Republicans were also against federal involvement, except when it benefited business.

It was not until Theodore Roosevelt became President in the early 1900s that the ICC began to play its part in the regulation of economic activity. Roosevelt believed the federal government had an active role in governing, and this included regulating commerce. He supported the ICC, giving it more personnel and enforcement powers. At the same time, the courts had begun to back off from their resistance to regulation by agencies other than the judicial system, and allowed the commission room to act. Thus it was the President, not Congress nor especially the House of Representatives, who began to assert authority over the courts. The House of Representatives had no authority over anyone.

Without national goals and programs, Congress had little to do other than raising revenue through tariffs, allocating funds to the various departments, and doing favors for constituents. Most of the real political work was done at the state and local level. It is perhaps in this sense that nineteenth-century America was a country where there was almost no national government presence. As Edling[26] points out, the U.S. government was set up to be a "government lite," one that is as much as possible invisible to the people it serves, interfering as little as possible with an individual's behavior.

Skowronek has also remarked on the absence of a national government in early America. "The exceptional character of the early American state is neatly summarized in the paradox that it failed to evoke any sense of the state . . . [Tocqueville] observed that government in America functioned as an 'invisible machine.' A unified legal order was maintained, but the distinction between state and society was blurred."[27]

It was not until 1917 that the Senate was forced to formalize its obstructive behavior by adding the cloture rule for governing Senate procedures. This required a two-thirds, and then a three-fifths vote to stop debate on a bill. Previously Senate procedures had not provided any definite way to end debate in the Senate. Unfortunately the new rule did not measurably improve senatorial procedures, and may even have made them worse by making it easier to block a bill.

The Great Depression and the New Deal brought a sea change to Congress. The Republicans had been dominant, but now the Democrats became the dominant party. In the 78 years from 1932 to 2010, the Democrats had control of the Senate for 58 years, and of the House for 62 years. The difference from the previous period is that the presidency has been shared more equally between the two parties: 42 years of Democratic presidents and 36 years of Republican presidents, as opposed to 16 years of Democratic presidents and 56 years of Republican presidents from 1860 to 1932.

This change in party dominance was in part due to the shock of the Depression, and the discrediting of the Republican approach to the national government. It was no longer possible to argue that the national government existed only to provide support to business—or state and local governments—without any reciprocal responsibilities. For a short period, the demands of labor and business also became concerns of the national government.

The parties were also changing: The Democratic emphasis on states' rights was decreasing, and the Democrats were becoming more the party of labor and the poor. The Republican party split into the party of business conservatives and the party of social conservatives, as the South switched its allegiance from the Democrats to the Republicans. This split has progressed so now the Republican party seems to be almost entirely the party of social conservatives.

The procedures and methods by which legislation is passed have not changed significantly. A great deal of social legislation has been passed, especially in the early part of this period, when the Democrats had the majority in the Senate: Social Security, labor legislation, housing assistance, Medicare, and most recently health care reform. But the legislative process has not gotten any easier or more efficient. There is still the same dependence on the President for leadership; the same ability of the minority to stall, delay, and distort legislation; and the same recurrent experience of congressional paralysis.

A weak Congress has the inevitable effect of encouraging the President to take charge—to become an Imperial President.

IV

IMPERIAL PRESIDENTS

14

BUILDING A NATION

Ensuring Independence

The most persuasive reason given for the establishment of a central government was the necessity to deal with international relations. Perhaps the most pivotal role of the national government is interacting with the rest of the world, both diplomatically and, if necessary, militarily. In the first years of the United States, this meant dealing with Britain and France, who were once again at war with each other, and ready to carve up the newly independent colonies at any sign of weakness. As was standard for most European governments, however, the Founders felt foreign affairs were best left to the President, as head of the executive branch.

The Founders had a vague recognition that it would not be a good idea to let the President start wars; thus the provision in the Constitution that only Congress could declare war. The general conduct of foreign affairs was left to the President, however, and the line between defending the country diplomatically from foreign influence by exerting the influence of the United States on other countries diplomatically and militarily, and going to war was never defined—and has vexed the country since.

According to the Constitution, the President is the commander in chief of the army and navy and the state militias when called to service. He has the power to make treaties and appoint ambassadors and ministers and consuls. This description of the President's powers gives the edge in foreign relations to the President, and this has always been recognized. The President has to share these powers only with the Senate.

Rather than acting to prevent a concentration of power, the separation of powers mythology serves to enable rather than prevent concentration of power in the executive. The President's power in foreign affairs is limited only by the power of Congress to raise and support an army and navy, and to declare war. Unfortunately, once an army is raised, it can be used however the President feels is necessary. It is difficult for Congress to resist supporting an army once conflict has started, even when there is no formal declaration of war.

Thus the President can control Congress by his actions. The President can have it both ways: while presenting the appearance of deferring to Congress, he covertly dominates domestic policy. The President then takes advantage of the supposed separation of powers to deny Congress, and especially the House of Representatives, any role in the conduct of foreign affairs.

The President's control of foreign affairs was evident from the beginning: The American Revolution took place in a time of quiescence between ongoing wars between England and France. A peace treaty between England and France had been signed in 1763 and lasted until 1792 with the rise of Napoleon, who sought to conquer and liberate all of Europe. Following the French Revolution and the rise of Napoleon, war between Britain and France, primarily a naval war, resumed. Under these circumstances, President Washington made a Declaration of Neutrality, saying that the United States did not want to get involved in the affairs of other countries—in particular France and England.

Neither France nor England recognized or respected the Declaration of Neutrality, however, and both countries continued to harass American ships: They captured American ships, confiscated the cargo, and forced the crews to serve the conquering country. The Americans were increasingly irritated with both France and England for these actions, but particularly toward England, which also had troops in the West who encouraged the Indians to harass the Americans.

In 1794 Washington sent John Jay to make a treaty with England, over the objections of his own Secretary of State Jefferson, and without consultation with Congress. Congress, or at least the opposition that was forming in Congress against the President's policies, was quite upset when Jay returned with a treaty that was seen as disadvantageous to the United States. The opposition in the House tried to prevent the implementation of the treaty, but the influence of the President and his supporters was sufficient to push it through.[1]

The House of Representatives was forced to realize that under the Constitution, the representatives of the people had no real role in the conduct of foreign affairs. This is in contrast to the British system, in which Parliament, through the prime minister and his minister of foreign affairs, has a direct role in determining the direction of foreign affairs.

The powerlessness of Congress was cemented with the first claim of executive privilege and presidential prerogative. Washington simply refused to provide documents to the House regarding the details of Jay's mission, thereby squelching an investigation into the development of the treaty. It was not the majority in Congress nor in the House that prevented a hostile investigation into the behavior of the executive; the President himself solidified the subordination of Congress—even the majority in Congress—to the executive.

Madison, as a member of the House of Representatives, tried to assert the power of the House by proposing resolutions "affirming the right of the lower chamber to consider a treaty that required enabling legislation."[2] Appropriations necessary for the Jay Treaty passed by one vote, and Madison's resolutions became irrelevant. In the subsequent history of treaty making, the rights of the House have not been an issue.

The House has acquiesced to the President, and has stayed out of any debate over foreign policy. Members are free to make statements about foreign policy issues, but the House has come to accept its role as limited. In modern times, the President has even tried to avoid the Senate as well by forming foreign policy through executive agreements rather than treaties.

In spite of the objections, the Jay Treaty was ultimately beneficial for U.S. relations with Britain, but it resulted in a deterioration of relations with France; some felt the United States should declare war on France. John Adams, then President, on his own authority, again without consulting with Congress, sent a delegation to France to work out an agreement. This too was ultimately successful, but only because the delegation revealed that France had asked for a bribe for its cooperation. This was the infamous XYZ affair.[3]

Animosity toward France increased and there were cries for war. Republicans such as Jefferson and Madison, who favored the French and its revolution and distrusted the English, accused the Federalists (the majority in Congress) of wanting to ally with England and establish a monarchy. Given that there were no explicitly recognized parties as yet, these criticisms were seen as directed at the government in general and in particular at the President. The Alien and Sedition Acts were passed to try to prevent such criticism.

A huge uproar ensued over these acts, especially the Sedition Act, which was used to arrest critics of the government. Resistance to these acts took the form of the Kentucky and Virginia Resolutions, which asserted the right of individual states to nullify federal actions thought to be unconstitutional.

After 1800, threats to the independence of the United States diminished, but then grew again, briefly, with the last major conflict between England and Napoleonic France. The result was the War of 1812. Madison, by that time, was Jefferson's designated successor, but he did not have the same skills of manipulation and leadership. "Madison offered no leadership and instilled no party discipline . . . With the President willing to take direction from Congress, but the legislature accustomed to leadership from the chief executive, the country floundered."[4]

In 1809, Madison was faced with the challenge of how to deal with the increase in English and French interference with American commercial shipping precipitated by their conflict with each other.

He had no experience with other countries, never having traveled outside of the United States, and his experience in Congress had shown he was more of a compromiser than a leader. His desire to compromise and get along with others resulted in poor choices of advisors and executive officers.

Madison allowed himself to be deceived by Napoleon into believing that if the United States would reopen trade with France, the French would stop harassing American ships. Madison reopened trade, but Napoleon did not stop the harassment—and had never intended to. Britain increased its harassment and encouraged the Indians in the northwest to resist American settlement. Many in Congress, predominantly those from the South and West, were up in arms, especially about the Indians, and wanted to go to war with England immediately. Others, from the northeast, were reluctant to declare war, knowing conflict would disrupt foreign trade, on which federal revenue depended—and which benefited most directly those in the East.

Perhaps as an indirect way to discourage the war fever, the outgoing 1811 Congress defeated efforts to renew the charter of the Bank of the United States, crippling the national government's ability to finance a war. In spite of the war hysteria and without leadership from the President, Congress allowed the charter for the national bank to expire. Neither the House nor the Senate passed a bill renewing the charter, even though the President was in favor of it. "The 11th Congress further demonstrated its incompetence by allowing the charter of the Bank of the United States to expire, despite the need for a central bank to address such problems as reduced revenues and the likelihood of increased expenditures to cope with foreign hostility."[5]

After the actions of the 11th Congress, "the electorate showed its displeasure by replacing more than 70 members with a younger generation of nationalists,"[6] who were much more hawkish. Henry Clay became the Speaker of the House, and "had every intention of determining policy and the legislation to come before the House."[7] He placed people as chairmen of the committees that would support his pro-war stance on relations with Britain, and worked closely with the executive to make preparations for war. Clay dominated the executive, including probably the President. He forced through a large increase in the number of federal troops, and argued strongly for a declaration of war.

Clay's influence on the conduct of the war ended with the declaration. The war became a responsibility of the executive; Congress was no longer responsible. It may have been this very lack of ultimate responsibility—its irresponsibility—that enabled Congress to push so forcefully for war.

Clay was apparently not concerned about how to finance the war; he did not push to revive the national bank. It was not until after the War of 1812 that a Second Bank of the United States was established. Finances were thus a major problem throughout the conflict,[8] but after war was declared, this became a problem for the executive, not Congress.

The war had to be financed through loans rather than appropriations, and in the absence of the national bank, loans had to be sought from the states or private banks. Collateral for such loans was based on ongoing revenue, and since revenue depended so much on foreign trade—reduced in the event of a war—funding for the war effort was necessarily difficult.

Madison tried to appeal to major eastern banks for funding, but they did not favor the war, and refused to support it. Albert Gallatin, the Secretary of the Treasury, had to make special appeals to financiers for loans. Even so, Madison was forced to rely heavily on the state militias and their willingness to fight because he had no money to raise a national army or navy.

In the push for war, there had been little if any effort to enlist the sympathies of the northern states, which were generally and even adamantly opposed to the war. A hysterical Congress run by southerners and westerners, and a President easily manipulated by Congress, forced war on the country. The result was a distinct lack of enthusiasm—and gross incompetence in conducting the war.[9]

The United States lost Detroit and much of the northwest. Entire armies were captured in Canada, and any possible advantage that might have been gained in upstate New York was lost to hesitation and delay. The nation's capital was destroyed, and the only significant victory, at New Orleans, was won only after the war had ended. Only the end of the war between England and France—and the generosity of England, which allowed the United States to return to the status quo ante—saved the United States from a complete disaster.

In a time of war a country needs strong leadership. Madison's leadership was not that of a strong leader. This is the first instance in our history in which the lack of good leadership became dangerous for the country. This inability to choose the best leader, particularly in times of crisis, left the future of the country in jeopardy, depending on luck to muddle through. Certainly Madison did the best he could, but his best was not enough.

A better leader would have avoided war altogether. Congress impetuously drove the country to war, and then, once war started, could only sit by and watch, hoping for the best. Congress wanted the War of 1812, but could not conduct the war, and so could argue that it was not responsible for the results. This irresponsibility only exacerbated the tensions between the North and the South and West.

By the end of Madison's two terms in office, he had accepted the need for a national bank and a standing army and navy, yet he was still inconsistently opposed to a strong central government. He supported the formation of the Second Bank of the United States in 1816, but at the end of his term, perhaps trying to make amends for his inconsistency, he vetoed a bill for internal improvements, contending that it was beyond the limited powers of the federal government to pay for such assistance to the states.

Despite the fact that Madison had signed several previous internal improvement bills, and that internal improvements were important to the conduct of the war, for the sake of his principles, he felt he could not approve of more such bills. Again, his weak and inconsistent actions were evident.

Fixing Boundaries

Following the early formative period of the new republic, much foreign policy was directed toward expanding and establishing the extent and boundaries of the country. Those presidents most involved in this effort were Jefferson, Monroe, Polk, and Theodore Roosevelt.

The President's almost unencumbered conduct of foreign policy begun by Washington continued with Jefferson. One of Jefferson's first acts was to dispatch a squadron of warships to the Mediterranean to fight the Barbary pirates. Fighting went on for years with the acquiescence of Congress—and without any formal declaration of war. This was the first instance in a long history of gunboat diplomacy by which the President can take the country to war, with congressional involvement only after the fact. As Remini remarks, "this war was a stunning example of executive encroachment on Congressional authority, and it only encouraged Jefferson to further efforts."[10]

The Louisiana Purchase was certainly the most important diplomatic measure of Jefferson's presidency. As the United States expanded westward, the port of New Orleans and access to it via the Mississippi became more and more vital. New Orleans had been a Spanish colony, but in 1802 Spain ceded the port of New Orleans and its surrounding territory to France—and closed the port to Americans. The United States immediately recognized this as a threat to their expansion. Congress appropriated $2 million for Jefferson to deal with the problem of New Orleans.

Jefferson sent Monroe to negotiate with the French; by the time he arrived, Napoleon had suffered a defeat in Haiti—and had given up his plans to revive the development of French colonies in the New World. He was thus willing to consider selling the entire Louisiana territory, and settled on a price of about $15 million. Monroe accepted this price and signed the treaty, even though it was much more than had been appropriated. Jefferson managed to persuade Congress to accept the purchase, just as Washington had gotten Congress to accept the Jay Treaty in 1794. Once again, the dominant President acted, and the subordinate Congress acquiesced.

When relations with Britain were deteriorating because of its war with France, Jefferson proposed and convinced Congress to support an embargo against British shipping. This had little effect on Britain, but was disastrous to American commerce, and was repealed—at Jefferson's suggestion—just before he left office.

Monroe, during his administration from 1817 to 1824, largely focused on establishing the boundaries of the U.S. territory, a process that eventually led to the Monroe Doctrine and manifest destiny. Monroe established the northern boundaries of the United States with the Rush-Bagot treaty with Britain, thereby beginning a long and fruitful period of cooperation.

He eventually acquired Florida from Spain, albeit only after incursions into Florida by Andrew Jackson as part of Jackson's impetuous and probably unauthorized efforts to eliminate the Indians from the southwest. These incursions, although not explicitly directed by the President, were used to put pressure on Spain to transfer Florida to the United States[11] Details of these events raise again the question of the extent to which the President can engage in war as a diplomatic tool without the approval of Congress.

Monroe also clarified the boundaries of the Louisiana Purchase in relation to Mexican territory, and prevented, with the cooperation of Britain, the involvement of Russia in the western hemisphere. He supported the independence of Latin American countries. These actions, orchestrated to a great extent by John Quincy Adams as Secretary of State, added up to the Monroe Doctrine, the declaration that the United States would be the dominant power in the New World and would resist the involvement of European powers in the western hemisphere.

President Polk devoted most of his term to completing the expansion of the United States to its continental borders, again with little input from Congress. He started a war with Mexico over Texas, and then forced Mexico, which had just achieved its independence from Spain and thus was weak, to give the United States California and New Mexico as well. Polk manipulated Congress into supporting the war, just as Monroe had done with the conflict over Florida, and Johnson and Bush were to do later. Domestically, the acquisition of Texas, California, and New

Mexico again raised the issue of allowing slavery in the new states of the union.

Theodore Roosevelt is not normally considered one of those involved in establishing the boundaries of the country. He came at the end of the process, when establishing boundaries was becoming more a process of establishing influence. Even before he was President, Teddy Roosevelt was very much involved in the Spanish-American War, by which Cuba gained independence from Spain. Congress and the President deliberately decided not to make Cuba part of the United States, but did acquire Puerto Rico and the Philippines from Spain. Congress could have made all three of these possessions part of the United States, but it did not, marking the end of its territorial expansion.

Roosevelt's predecessor, McKinley, recognized the growing importance of the United States in world affairs; he responded by proposing reciprocal trade agreements in place of the traditional tariffs by which the government funded itself. Roosevelt did not continue to push for these changes, and such agreements were not established until the 1930s, but Roosevelt was eager to assert U.S. authority in the world in other ways—and did so with input from Congress only after the fact.[12]

Roosevelt gave Cuba its independence, as the United States had promised to do at the start of the war, but he chose to fight the rebels in the Philippines. Expelling the Spanish from the Philippines was not a problem, but a group of indigenous rebels claimed the same right to independence as the Cubans. In the Philippines, Roosevelt chose to assert U.S. power and put down the rebellion. He did not believe the rebels had the authority to represent all the islands; racial prejudices also played a part. Congressional controversy over what Roosevelt was doing in the Philippines was not about whether the United States should be there, but about the atrocities committed by American troops.

Roosevelt's greatest triumph was finalizing the treaty by which the Panama Canal was built. The controversy here was whether the canal should be built in Nicaragua or in Panama. Roosevelt encouraged Panama to declare its independence from Colombia, and when it did so, Panama invited the United States to build its canal there. Roosevelt then persuaded the Senate to approve a treaty to build the canal across the continents in Panama rather than Nicaragua. This treaty ensured that the United States rather than some other western country would control commerce across the continents.

Roosevelt was active in other areas of foreign affairs: Without input from Congress, without even their knowledge, or that of even historians until recently, Roosevelt used gunboat diplomacy to dissuade the Germans from attempting to take over Venezuela. He mediated between the Russians and the Japanese in the Russo-Japanese War, and between the Germans and the French in the Tunisian affair. These activities in the international arena greatly enhanced the power and prestige of the United States, and of the President as the one in charge of foreign affairs.

The activities of these presidents in expanding and defining the extent of U.S. territory seem to have been done with the implicit consent of the majority of the population of the country. Their actions, however, established a practice and tradition that the President, alone with his advisors and free from the restraints of Congress, is the central actor in the conduct of international relations. To even question the validity of this tradition is to many inconceivable, an idea to be laughed at, and taken as proof of the questioner's naïveté about the real world. Yet in most other governments, especially those with a parliamentary form of government, the legislature is directly involved in the conduct of foreign affairs. Lack of constraints on the President has led to the rise in the twentieth century of the imperial presidency.

15

BECOMING A WORLD POWER

As long as the United States existed in its own separate world, apart from the affairs of Europe and the rest of the world, as it did in the nineteenth century, the Senate could focus on obstructing the efforts of the national government to assert its power over the states and over business. The twentieth century marked the end of this isolation, and the end of dominance by the states. The Spanish-American War was a turning point for the United States. It marked the achievement for the United States of the status of a world power, and shifted the focus of the federal government from its relation to the states, to its relation to the rest of the world.

The U.S. entry onto the world stage occurred between 1896 and 1908. McKinley had to deal with the dispute over Spanish control of Cuba, and in the course of what became the Spanish-American War, the United States became an empire. The dynamics of domestic political discourse changed as well. National issues could no longer be ignored, and the authority of the national government over the states and regional interests had to be recognized. The frontier had closed, and industries such as the railroads, oil, and steel were dominating the country and the government, and could only be dealt with at a national level.

Agitation against the power of monopolies and trusts was increasing, and business feared revolution. McKinley recognized that the world was changing, and that the United States needed to change as well. It was no longer possible to function with a weak, ineffective national government, one that looked inward through the Senate to the states for its cues. McKinley recognized that state parties could no longer be allowed to control the national government. He was the first President to campaign actively on his own behalf—and in opposition to his own party and the party "bosses."[13]

In his advocacy of reciprocal trade agreements, McKinley tried to educate Congress in its new responsibilities to the larger world. These early efforts did not succeed because of resistance in the Senate, and then McKinley was assassinated early in his second term, but the process had begun. The transition took time. The administrations of Taft, Harding, and Coolidge attempted to bring back the normalcy of previous times—normalcy that some still pine for[14]—but the change was inevitable.

Teddy Roosevelt was an activist President not only in foreign affairs, but also in domestic affairs. He greatly encouraged the professionalization of the civil service, which meant taking control of patronage from Congress and the parties and giving it to an executive agency, the Civil Service Commission. State party control of patronage diminished, and what patronage was left at the highest levels of government came increasingly under the President's control, thus consolidating his power.

Roosevelt also recognized the need to regulate business, and initiated litigation to rein in the monopolistic practices of the railway trusts in the Northern Securities case.[15] He managed to push the Hepburn bill through the Senate, revitalizing the Interstate Commerce Commission, making it a more effective regulator—but not without compromising with the Senate and accepting a weaker bill than he wanted.

One of Roosevelt's most lasting legacies was his conservation of forests and parks in the West through the establishment of a national park system, removing these lands from public land sales. (The sale of public lands was a major source of income for the government, and was a windfall for many businesses.) He took these actions using executive orders, acting without the consent of or input from Congress. Although they may have been well intentioned and are universally approved today, his designations of large areas of land as national parks and forests were excesses of presidential authority. Congress finally passed legislation ordering him to stop creating national reserves. He accepted the legislation, but did so only after defiantly designating thirteen final tracts just before he signed the bill. This defiance, together with Roosevelt's suspected use of the Secret Service to investigate members of Congress, made him very unpopular toward the end of his second term.[16]

Taft reverted to earlier Republican traditions. He agreed with the Republican position against government interference in business, and so was much less aggressive about asserting the power of the President, except in his control of the administration. He allowed the Senate to reestablish its preeminence.

Roosevelt was not involved in any major wars during his administration, and thus could not exercise the full extent of his powers. Wilson, whether he wanted it or not, was very much involved in making war; he was the first to realize the potential for the President in such circumstances. In domestic affairs, Wilson was a liberal, activist President in his first term; he broke a logjam of bills that had built up over the previous years of Republican dominance.

Wilson was more sympathetic and respectful of the role of Congress in government; with a Democratic majority in both houses in his first years in office, he was more able to cooperate with Congress and thus passed several major bills. Two constitutional amendments were passed, one to allow income tax, and the other for the direct election of senators. He created the Federal Trade Commission to further regulate business, and the Federal Reserve system to regulate finance.

With the coming of World War I, however, Wilson shifted his focus and eventually assumed almost dictatorial powers to control the economy in the name of mobilizing for war. This was necessary because there was no existing military structure with which to fight a war. As with Lincoln during the Civil War, Wilson had to take over and organize the production of military equipment and supplies. Wilson changed into a much more passionate but rigid and oppressive person, willing to suppress dissent, encourage suspicion, and even spy on Americans. He felt it necessary to suppress any opposition to his measures, all with the acquiescence of Congress. Wilson actively suppressed any pro-German or pro-socialist sentiment in the country, and even developed citizen networks to spy on suspected German sympathizers.[17]

Unfortunately, after the war ended and during the negotiations over reparations, Wilson suffered a stroke, and could no longer pursue his vision of post-war Europe, and moderate the vindictive attitudes of the victors toward the loser, Germany.

As was traditional after a war, the next administration under Harding removed many agencies and decrees Wilson had used to implement his war policies and reduced spending on the military. The Harding and Coolidge administrations again attempted to return the national government to its earlier role as a servant of local interests. Harding, however, was the President who finally put the budget making process solidly in the executive rather than the legislative branch.[18]

Harding's successor, Coolidge, was a minimalist President, doing little in his term. Herbert Hoover, his Secretary of Commerce and successor as President, was much more active and ambitious. Hoover envisioned creating a network of voluntary associations by which to deal with national problems.[19] He wanted to avoid dealing with Congress and work directly with private groups. "He suggested that the nation would be better off if Congress simply went home."[20] Thus the basic pattern of the President acting in opposition to Congress was well established even before Franklin D. Roosevelt. Hoover saw the government as providing only encouragement and assistance, not actually running or controlling his voluntary associations or the private economy.

The Depression

Our modern political world began with the Depression in 1929. Before then, the United States had maintained that it was not and did not need to be involved in the affairs of the rest of the world. It could trade with other countries and even lend a helping hand as it did in World War I, but it was primarily an observer of political and military events elsewhere. The dominant sentiment about foreign affairs was isolationism. The United States also pretended that the national government was not important in domestic affairs.

With the establishment of the Interstate Commerce Commission and the creation of the Federal Trade Commission and the Federal Reserve System in 1913, the role of the national government was increasing gradually, but the general bias continued to be that the federal government existed primarily only to set tariffs for the benefit of domestic industry, and give money to the states.

Politically the federal government was a government of competing sectional or regional interests vying to bring the most benefit to their different constituencies. Political parties, as they developed in the United States under Andrew Jackson and Martin van Buren, were never more than vehicles for the promotion of local interests.

National interest was thought of as only the victor in the competition among local interests. Meanwhile, the courts served to monitor the federal government to ensure that Congress and the President functioned under the constraints of a pro-business and pro-white South ideology.

The Depression changed everything. The United States finally had to admit that events in other parts of the world had influence at home, and that the national government had to deal with them, both internationally and domestically.

The causes of the Great Depression are fairly clear: according to a growing consensus, it was a function of the breakdown of the international adherence to the gold standard, and the failure of the Federal Reserve and other central banks to respond appropriately.[21] Problems with the gold standard had begun even before World War I. Countries wanted the gold standard, but they did not want to suffer the consequences of it when it meant economic contraction, deflation, and distress. If the contraction was short enough, it could be tolerated, but not if it persisted. Since currency rates were fixed against gold, a gradual adjustment of rates, as occurs with floating exchange rates, was not possible.

World War I further disrupted the gold standard; the combatants stopped trading with each other, and the world went off the standard. After the war, reparation payments and repayments of war debts to the United States complicated the adjustments. Germany could not pay reparations, and suffered hyperinflation in part because it was unwilling to go off the gold standard. Other countries such as Austria also suffered.

Britain wanted to return to the gold standard at the rate it had been before the war, but to do so it had to borrow from the United States. At the same time it and other countries in Europe were trying to repay their war debts to the United States. Its premature return to the gold standard in 1925 caused a recession in Great Britain, and did not resolve the monetary crisis. The British pound and the American dollar were reserve currencies for the rest of the world, and it was not until they both went off the gold standard in 1933 that world economies began to recover. Thus the Depression did not start in the United States, yet when it came, it was unexpected.

Most previous depressions had been sharp and painful but short, lasting no more than a year or so. The Great Depression lasted for at least ten years in the United States, from 1929 to 1939, and ended only with World War II. The length and severity of the Depression made it impossible for the government not to try to do something about it, even though many at its beginning felt the government should do nothing, that it would cure itself. Arguments continue over whether what the government did had any effect on the Depression, and whether it was positive or negative.[22]

The pressure to do something to help the country out of the Depression was tremendous. Many other countries were trying to handle their economies through government programs. Russia, Germany, Italy, Spain, and Japan were all in some way trying to manage their economies from the top down. Even Great Britain nationalized many industries. It is not surprising that the United

States also tried to solve its economic problems through the government.

In 1929 when the stock market crashed, Hoover had been President for less than a year. His initial reaction was to do nothing, expecting that the recession would cure itself in the next year or so, and life would go on. The worldwide extent of the crisis, and the insistence of many that it was necessary to adhere to the gold standard, prevented this. The United States had plenty of gold relative to other countries, but the worldwide demand for credit far exceeded the total amount of gold, resulting in a deflation in the value of currencies. It was not until the world went off the gold standard in 1933, a process not officially ratified until 1944, that the amount of currency available began to correspond to the demand for credit.

When it became evident that voluntary action was not going to cure the Depression, Hoover had no idea what to do. He was baffled and intimidated by the economic and international issues involved, and could not decide—or allow others to do so. Dealing with these problems was left largely to the Federal Reserve and to the private banks that controlled the Federal Reserve; conflicting pressures from Congress and the international community, especially the other central banks, hampered these efforts.[23]

Hoover's only direct reaction to the Depression was to get business to agree to maintain the level of wages, in hopes that this would encourage workers to spend, and so drive a recovery. This move was not effective because at the same time Hoover encouraged the passage of a tariff bill that raised the tariff on agricultural products. He hoped this would increase the income of farmers, who had been suffering even before the Depression.

Raising agricultural tariffs failed in its intent because other countries almost immediately raised their tariffs as well, nullifying the desired benefit to farmers, and causing everyone to suffer from higher prices. Hoover's final proposal was to raise taxes, in the belief that it was important for the federal government to have a balanced budget. Congress passed the Revenue Act of 1932, but it decreased the money available to the private sector to produce a recovery. Hoover vetoed measures to spend money on public works and the unemployed, believing these measures were only handouts to the undeserving.

Herbert Hoover was a gifted, successful administrator who organized people to deal with the Mississippi flood and with the refugee problem after World War I. When the Depression started in 1929, however, such organizational skills were not useful. No easily defined cause explained the failures of hundreds of banks and rising unemployment, and the solution was not obvious.

The required skills were not those of organizing people to attack a problem, but of knowing what the problem was in the first place. Hoover became paralyzed by his traditional political and economic ideas, indecisive on how to attack the credit crisis and deflation. The country had no alternative but to sit and wait for almost four more years before a leader with new ideas could take over.

The New Deal

For many people, Franklin Roosevelt was the first imperial President, given the way he took over the government during the Great Depression, and later during World War II.[24] It is not clear that the measures Franklin Roosevelt took to deal with the Depression were effective, but it is clear that he carried them out with the overwhelming support of his party and the people. Although a great deal of new legislation was passed through Congress, much of what Roosevelt did was done through executive orders and presidential fiat. His justification for closing the banks, for instance, involved the clever use of old, obscure, and not clearly relevant laws.[25]

The New Deal period is a good example of what government can do when the built-in tensions between Congress and the President are temporarily put aside. Unfortunately this was possible only by giving the President more power. When Roosevelt was elected in 1932 he was elected as a national leader, someone who would deal with national problems, not the parochial interests of whoever had sufficient influence. The people gave him an overwhelming majority of Democrats in both houses of Congress so there would be no question of whether he could accomplish his goals. Roosevelt was free to push through Congress whatever measures he thought would help resolve the economic crisis.

This was what the people wanted. As Remini comments, "... the depression had generated wild talk about the need for dictatorial direction of the government and the economy. 'A genial and lighthearted dictator might be a relief,' commented one publication, 'from the pompous futility of such a Congress as we have recently had.'"[26]

Roosevelt's election and an overwhelmingly Democratic Congress gave one political party the ability to enact the legislation the party had promised. The result was the famous hundred days in which numerous bills to relieve the Depression were enacted.[27] Roosevelt declared a bank holiday as a way to reassure the country; he reduced federal salaries to bring them in line with the deflation others had suffered; and he repealed the Prohibition Amendment. Roosevelt created the Agricultural Adjustment Act, the first in a long line of agricultural subsidy measures; and he acted to protect farmers and homeowners from foreclosure.

Roosevelt created the Civilian Conservation Corp (CCC), the Public Works Agency (PWA), the Works Progress Administration was created in 1935 (renamed the Work Projects Administration in 1938), and numerous other programs designed to provide relief to workers by giving them government jobs. He went off the gold standard and created the Securities and Exchange Commission (SEC) to regulate the stock market. With the Tennessee Valley Authority, FDR began the promotion of public utilities; with the National Industrial Recovery Act (NIRA), he tried to revive business through regulation. All this was done in the first hundred days of Roosevelt's administration. It was as if the dam of governmental inertia had broken, and a flood of pent-up change had engulfed the old order.

The NIRA was later, in 1935, ruled unconstitutional, and the program was dropped, but most of the other changes survived. The Agricultural Adjustment Act (AAA) was also judged unconstitutional, but it was revived in later legislation. Social

Security legislation was passed, and the National Labor Relations Act was passed. The Reciprocal Trade Agreement was passed, giving the President the authority to set tariff rates, thereby removing one of the last major roles of Congress, setting tariffs.

The most important point about these developments is that they were possible only when the President had an overwhelming majority of his party in Congress, i.e., more than a two-thirds majority in both houses. This meant that Roosevelt, as the leader of the Democratic party, passed legislation without considering the positions of the minority Republican party. The Democrats had more than the two-thirds majority necessary to make it impossible for the Republicans to block the legislation in the Senate.

Only with such a supermajority can the majority party in Congress coordinate policy with the executive, and get its programs passed. In comparison, the British parliament needs only a simple majority to do the same thing. The American government, in other words, needs an extraordinary set of circumstances for a party to see its program—its platform—realized. With such a supermajority, however, the American government also puts itself in the odd position of having a dictatorial government.

The President, to be sure, has to maintain good relationships with his party in Congress, but as the leader of his party and the leader of the country, the pressure is on members of his party to follow his direction, to subordinate their interests to their leader. Under such circumstances, the President is the dominant power, akin to the British Prime Minister without the constraints of being a part of the legislature.

Such special circumstances did not last long. By 1935, when the Supreme Court invalidated the NIRA and the AAA, members of Congress started to resent the President's dominance over the legislative process. Relations between the President and Congress frayed. Tension and distrust between the executive and the legislative branches reasserted itself, and members of Congress, even within the President's own party, placed obstacles in the way of implementing the party program. The chairman of the rules committee in the House resented the President's tendency to ignore his committee, and resisted the President's initiatives because of what he saw as violations of proper procedures.

The House rules committee chairman was unpopular even within his own party, but seniority had placed him in this powerful position, and allowed him to control the flow of legislation according to his own prejudices. Using seniority as the criterion for leadership positions suggests the low importance of the agenda of the party in choosing committee leaders. Seniority and lack of real party discipline became a problem in 1937 when a coalition of southern Democrats and northern Republicans put roadblocks in the path of legislation. Congress increased its "principled" opposition to the "intrusions" of the President into congressional business.

In the special session in November 1937, the conservative coalition of both Democrats and Republicans on the rules committee "pretty much brought House action on a number of administration bills to a near complete halt."[28] Action on a wages and hours bill was barred, and a measure that would have allowed the President to reorganize executive departments was defeated. Roosevelt had to negotiate and bargain with members of his own party to get bills passed in the next year.

The point is not whether the President was being arrogant and overreaching—he may have been—but that the executive and the legislative branches were at odds with each other. This has been a constant in U.S. history, and reappeared soon after the euphoria of the New Deal had subsided. The President and the Congress were set up to be independent of each other, but this is not the way it has to be or should be—or is for most governments most of the time.

Such a presumption of opposition and distrust, of jockeying back and forth for control, has been a pervasive characteristic of U.S. government, especially since Roosevelt and the tremendous increase in the power of the executive. The Depression was not the beginning of the shift of power from Congress to the President that has been characteristic of the modern age, but the transition was most drastic in and after the Depression.

According to Smith,[29] Roosevelt made three mistakes in his administration during the New Deal period: The first was his attempt to change the number of Supreme Court justices. It was an action he took without consulting his party, and without their support. He could not push his measure through Congress and lost credibility in the process. The second mistake was to reduce spending on the relief programs he had created. Doing so was a cause of the "depression within a depression" in 1937, and again lost him support. Finally Roosevelt's 1938 attempt to influence local elections to purge Congress of members who opposed his programs backfired.

These "mistakes" provide insight into the dynamics between the President and Congress. Roosevelt's frustrations with the Supreme Court were similar to the difficulties Jefferson had had with the Supreme Court in the early years of the nation. Jefferson was upset that a small group of men, and in particular Marshall, could assert themselves between him and Congress, and judge the validity of actions he took. Jefferson was against Marshall's assertion of the power and reach of the federal government, believing instead that the individual states were meant to be the dominant force. Jefferson lost that battle, and the Supreme Court established itself as a third branch of government.

Few Presidents have been happy with the existence of a third policy making body in the national government—except when the courts rule in their favor. Since Jefferson most have found the Supreme Court useful in their fights against Congress. Jackson simply ignored the courts with respect to the treatment of the Indians, and was not challenged about his banking veto.

After the Civil War, Congress did nothing to undo the damage the Supreme Court did to the blacks in the South, in its support of white dominance, nor in its misinterpretation of the 14th and 15th Amendments to protect business from government oversight and control. The rest of government used the Court as a cover for their support of white dominance and business freedom.

Roosevelt was the first President since Jackson to find the Court opposed to the actions he was taking. He did not like being second-guessed in his decisions about what the country needed by a group of men he felt were out of touch with what was going on. For him they were judging his political decision making, and he resented their interference.

To some extent the Supreme Court's judgments were more about how the legislation they objected to was written than with its content.[30] Normally, writing legislation is the responsibility of the individual legislators in Congress and their staffs. They have the expertise to make sure legislation is written correctly. In the rush to get something done, and with clear majorities, Roosevelt bypassed normal procedures, allowing poorly written legislation to get through.

Roosevelt wanted to act directly with Congress, without worrying about the courts second guessing his judgments. He, like Jefferson, did not want a third party, the Supreme Court, interfering with this process. In his reelection campaign in 1936, "Roosevelt saw the election as a referendum. 'There is one issue in this campaign. It is myself, and the people must be either for me or against me.'"[31]

He identified himself with Andrew Jackson, as one fighting for the little people against the powerful and wealthy. Given that Roosevelt was himself one of the wealthy, this translates into the assertion that he and he alone is better at representing the poor than other wealthy people. This is demagogic talk, and the people loved it, but it is not the expression of democracy.

The Supreme Court was not as reactionary as has been thought. Even before 1937 when Roosevelt started his effort against the Court, the Justices had started approving of his actions. "Historians are fond of saying that Roosevelt lost the battle but won the war. But the war was won when Roberts joined Hughes, Brandeis, Cardozo, and Stone in December 1936."[32] The tendency of the President to act independently, especially in times of crisis, is built into our system, given that the President is considered independent of Congress. It is thus natural that the President tries to make his job easier by reducing the power of other players, such as the Supreme Court.

Roosevelt's second mistake, according to Smith, was to reduce funding for the relief programs he had created before the Depression was over. Roosevelt was committed to experimenting with whatever worked in solving the problems of the Depression; he was *not* committed to any one measure or method. When Roosevelt decided an experiment had gone on long enough, he was not averse to ending it. Deep down he still believed in a balanced budget; evidence seemed to indicate that the country was recovering from the Depression.

Smith[33] attributes much of the "Depression within a Depression" to Roosevelt's cuts in the relief programs, but there were other factors: taxes for Social Security started, and the Federal Reserve increased the reserve requirements for banks by fifty percent. Shlaes,[34] without mentioning cuts in the relief programs, blames the downturn on these other factors, and adds that business in general had developed a feeling of insecurity and distrust about what the government was going to do next, making it unwilling to invest. She points to the undistributed profits tax that had reduced the ability of corporations to invest in new projects.

Roosevelt acted without consulting his party, perhaps knowing that there was more than enough support in Congress for cutting these programs, especially among minority Republicans. At the least, Roosevelt's actions suggest a lack of sensitivity to economic processes, but this is what happens when a President can act on his own biases rather than on the basis of his party's positions.

Roosevelt's third mistake was to try to control the composition of Congress by attempting to prevent the election of individuals in his own party that did not support his programs. This effort is revealing about political parties in the United States. On the one hand, it would seem desirable for a party to punish members who do not support the party's program. Such discipline is an intrinsic part of the political process in Britain. This is not how parties function in the United States, and could be considered a weakness of American parties. There is no way even now for the party to force a member to adhere to the party platform. It was natural for Roosevelt, as leader of his party, to try to punish those members who did not support his programs.

It was equally natural for Congress, given the structure of the government, to see Roosevelt's efforts as a threat to Congress' independence. If the President can control whom his party nominates to Congress then he controls Congress, the separation between the President and Congress set up by the Founders is gone.

On this point Roosevelt lost the support of his own party. Congress has a justifiable fear of being overwhelmed by the President, but the solution the Founders proposed—of separating Congress from the executive—has never worked very well. Roosevelt's actions were only an escalation of the underlying conflict between the President and Congress; an escalation that can only really be resolved when Congress, specifically the House of Representatives, asserts its control over the President. The President as CEO in a democracy has to be directly responsible to Congress.

For Smith these were Roosevelt's "mistakes"; the system worked in that the errors were prevented or corrected, and life went on. Any large complex system is going to continue to function in spite of occasional mistakes, simply because it is so large. Its own momentum and inertia will incline it toward ignoring its mistakes, attributing them to transient circumstances. If the mistakes are repeated over and over, however, maybe they should not be ignored.

16

WAR: HOT, COLD, AND FOREVER

War and the threat of war motivates countries and governments to put aside partisan disagreement to unite behind a common enemy. When there is a real threat to the country from an external enemy, this is appropriate and necessary. When, however, a government creates the threat of war, or goes to war to unite the country behind its policies and preserve its power, it is not so clear that it is appropriate or patriotic to unite behind that government. The line between these two reasons for war is not clear and distinct. The series of wars the United States has fought since World War II raises the question of whether war has become a device by which government, and in particular the President, accumulates power.

World War II

The late 1930s were overshadowed by events in Europe. By 1938 attention was shifting to Europe and Asia, and the role the United States was going to play in these events. The prevailing attitude was isolationism or neutrality, even after World War I. Given the diverse ethnic origins of people in the United States, the government did not want to take sides in what was seen as a European dispute.

As events unfolded, however, Roosevelt became more and more committed to defending Britain and France against Germany, Italy, and Japan. As the war came closer, Roosevelt made even more use of his executive powers to evade the express restrictions of Congress, such as in the Lend-Lease program. After the war started, he invoked his role as commander in chief to create a plethora of agencies and programs to carry out the war, often without clear congressional authority. He managed to find ways to evade the Neutrality Act of 1937 and assist Britain in its fight against Germany. The navy was built up, and the Selective Service was established to draft men into the army.

When Japan attacked Hawaii on December 7, 1941, the President was given the powers he needed through the War Powers Acts—more power than a President had ever wielded. He imposed rationing and price controls, and interned citizens of Japanese descent. His spending for defense was tremendous, and Congress ended many of the New Deal programs to help pay for these increases; nevertheless, income tax rates went up. The people accepted these measures because, for the first time in over 100 years, an external force had attacked the United States.

Roosevelt was no longer acting as the leader of his party, but as the leader of the country—the United States had a President who was acting on his own, independent of his party. Though nominally a Democrat, Roosevelt governed with whatever coalition served his purposes at the time, disregarding party ties. His support came from the coalition of northern Republicans and southern conservative Democrats—a coalition that was to continue until the 1960s.

The Cold War

Almost immediately after the end of World War II, the United States turned from war against fascism to war against communism. Unlike the period after World War I, during which the United States tried to return to isolationism from the rest of the world, after World War II the country accepted that it was now the leader of the free world, and was integral in managing world affairs. Russia, in the form of the U.S.S.R., was the primary rival to U.S. leadership; its behavior became the focus of U.S. attention.

Russia's domination of the eastern European countries, and its attempts to reunify Germany on its terms, leading to the Berlin Blockade in 1948, created difficulties for the United States and

Europe, resulting in the North Atlantic Treaty and the formation of the North Atlantic Treaty Organisation (NATO). On the other side of the world, the communists took over China under Mao Tse Tung and the North Koreans under Kim Il Sung tried to unify Korea, leading to the Korean War from 1950 to 1953.

These events created the perception in the United States that war with the U.S.S.R. was a real possibility—and that it would involve nuclear weapons. There were already fears of communism; what became the House Un-American Activities Committee had been established even before World War II. Truman responded to these new perceived threats by choosing to maintain rather than dismantle the military establishment created during the war.

He felt empowered to use the military, on his own, to enter the Korean War, without congressional authorization. He set up the National Security Council and the Central Intelligence Agency. He developed the Marshall Plan for the reconstruction of Europe, and he supported the establishment of the United Nations as a part of the struggle against communism. Spending on the military saw a huge increase.

Truman's actions continued the development of the imperial presidency, with the assertion of the almost unlimited power of the President to carry out foreign and military activities—even in the absence of a declared war. Although Truman's attempt to take over the steel industry was blocked, the idea that the President could act on his own was becoming accepted. The crisis atmosphere created by the threat of communism enhanced the power of the presidency as leader of the country and the free world. Eisenhower, for example, quietly asserted presidential authority even more strongly over the federal bureaucracy, using executive orders to reorganize it.

From this point, until the 1990s, American foreign policy was conducted through the prism of the communist menace. The Marshall Plan, by which the United States gave aid to Europe to rebuild its economies, was justified at least in part as a way to protect western Europe and the United States from the threat of communism. When Cuba became communist in 1959, Eisenhower supported measures to invade Cuba, quite outside the purview of the legislature.

The United States had previously overthrown a Guatemalan government that it did not like, and thought that it could do the same with Cuba. The resulting Bay of Pigs invasion, planned in the Eisenhower administration but carried out in the new Kennedy administration, was a fiasco—but there was never any question of whether the President could make such policy decisions. The invasion failed miserably in part because Kennedy was ambivalent about it, but also because Castro was well prepared for an invasion.

This failure led to the Cuban Missile Crisis, in which Khrushchev began to place missiles in Cuba. When Kennedy found out, the threat of a nuclear war became all too real. Kennedy has the distinction of having resolved the Cuban Missile Crisis, again entirely on his own, without any effective assistance from Congress, but the result was that Cuba was allowed to remain communist, and became a continuing irritant to the United States. To an extent, the presence of communist Cuba just off U.S. shores was used to justify the fight against communism even after the immediate fear of war with the U.S.S.R. diminished.

Kennedy's successor, Lyndon Johnson, seduced Congress into supporting the Vietnam War, much as Polk had done earlier in the Mexican War. The conflict in Vietnam was the next instance of our reaction to the threat of communism. The Vietnamese were initially trying to overthrow the French colonial government, just as many other third world countries had after World War II. Unlike other countries, such as India and Indonesia, the French resisted decolonization, and the United States supported France, because communists led the Vietnamese.

When the French gave up the fight, the United States chose to continue it, for no better reason than to prevent communism from spreading to other countries, as if communism were a disease. In reality the Vietnamese communists were more nationalists than communists, just as Cuba was more concerned with their economic development than spreading Marxist theory to other countries. Vietnam was the last battle of the Cold War, although the war lingered on until 1989, when the U.S.S.R dissolved and the Berlin Wall was brought down.

Each of these military adventures further cemented not only the role of the United States as the leader of the world, but also the authority of the President as commander in chief. Congress became even more irrelevant and subordinate in forming foreign policy.

The Post Cold War Period

In the forty years from 1930 to 1970 the nature of U.S. government changed in ways that would have been inconceivable to the Founders. The centralized military power we have today was precisely what the Founders feared most. These changes are, however, only the culmination of a long process in which the power of the President, as the chief executive and leader of the country, has gradually increased and the influence of Congress has gradually and correspondingly decreased. Congress, for the President, has become just an obstacle to be overcome in implementing his policies.

The accumulation of power in the presidency was muted after Jackson and Lincoln, with the dominance of the states, but burst forth again in the early twentieth century with Teddy Roosevelt and Wilson, and then FDR and Truman. Only in the last forty years, though, has the weakness of Congress given the President the license to act in opposition to Congress in the name of national security.

Three events from 1968 to the present have shaped this new attitude toward dealing with Congress: the Watergate scandal, the Iran-Contra scandal, and the aftermath of 9/11. In each case the President chose to defy the will of Congress. The reactions of Congress and the people to the President's defiance differed.

Richard Nixon was at war with the Democratic Congress almost from the day he was elected. He did not agree with the legislation they passed, and when forced to accept it, he made every effort to subvert it by such measures as impounding funds and hiring people for positions who were strongly against the programs for which they were hired. He asserted his authority to control the selection of officers in charge of programs to kill or at least delay the programs' implementation. Nixon could arguably be accused of violating his oath of office to "faithfully execute the laws," but his attitude toward governing was accepted and has continued.

All this was considered within the range of normal politics, given the structure of our government.[35] In 1972 Nixon stepped over the line of what was then normal, when he or his staff arranged to have burglars break into the Democratic party headquarters to spy on their activities. When this crime was exposed, the nation was appalled—and then enthralled for several months by the special congressional hearings. Nixon was forced to resign under threat of impeachment.

Nixon set a precedent for presidential defiance of Congress and the will of the people, but the threat of impeachment and his resignation was not for his defiance of Congress, and little was done to prevent such actions in the future. Congress believed Nixon's resignation ended the problems he presented, and nothing further needed to be done.

The illusion that Watergate would not repeat itself was shattered in 1986 with the revelations of the Iran-Contra affair. Reagan had directed or allowed (we will never fully know which) his subordinates to engage in deals in which the U.S. government would sell arms to Iran, at that time at war with Iraq, without congressional approval; the proceeds from these sales would then be used to fund operations in support of opposition to the Sandinistas in El Salvador—support that Congress expressly forbid.

Once again the President was acting in defiance of Congress, pursuing his own policies because, as President, he felt he knew better than Congress—and because he could. Again Congress rose up and held hearings, and a few people were charged with crimes; some even went to jail, but in this case the President himself was not threatened. Congress rationalized the affair as a mere foreign policy disagreement, and went on with its routines. The boundaries of normal politics and presidential power expanded—and Congress just accepted it.

President George W. Bush used the excuse of the 9/11 attacks to induce Congress to approve waging an unnecessary, unprovoked war in Iraq that lost the respect of the rest of the world for the United States as champions of democracy and freedom. His supplemental spending on the war—not counted as part of the regular budget—along with his tax cuts, devastated the economy. The deficit ballooned so much that at the end of his term an international credit crisis threatened the world. Bush claimed the right to interpret laws and treaties as he saw fit: He violated legislatively enacted policies on wiretapping, torture, and the Geneva Conventions in the name of national security, his role as commander in chief, and the so-called unitary executive.

President Bush felt justified in politicizing the Justice Department, then refused to cooperate with Congress in its investigations of these issues, asserting executive privilege to maintain secrecy about presidential activities. He pursued his policies by manipulating the public, and stonewalling Congress. Beginning with the refusal of Vice President Cheney to provide information about his discussions with oil executives about energy policy, Bush used executive privilege to conceal presidential activities from the oversight of Congress.

His secrecy and refusal to communicate with Congress, or allow other members of his executive to explain their actions has further undermined the power of Congress, and reduced people's respect for both legislative bodies. Bush's defiance of Congress is the legacy he leaves to future presidents, following in the footsteps of Nixon and Reagan.

Presidents since Washington have used presidential prerogative, but it is only in the last fifty or so years that it has been used aggressively. The claim of executive privilege or presidential prerogative is a consequence of setting up the President as an independent power similar to the King in Britain. Just as the royal prerogative was claimed by kings in the days before Britain had a parliamentary system, so the President claims presidential prerogative.

The King's use of the royal prerogative was a major part of what led to the British Revolution of 1688 and the explicit dominance of parliament over the king. The royal prerogative is no longer an issue in Britain, but it continues in the United States. To allow a President to withhold information from Congress on the basis of executive privilege or presidential prerogative is to admit that Congress really has little power to control the executive branch.

Congressional requests for information become not just polite ways of requiring information—they are requests the executive can choose to grant or ignore as it wishes. The consequences of ignoring Congress are slow to come, and can be delayed almost indefinitely. Meanwhile, contempt for Congress grows within the executive—and in the general population.

Congress puts itself in the position of begging for information. Appeals to the Supreme Court only delay the process further, and place Congress in the position of supplicant, unable to manage its own affairs. When Congress admits that it must depend on a third party, a party that may side with the President, it further diminishes itself.

The futility of Congress going to the Court to get information from the executive in the face of presidential refusals was shown in the lawsuit brought by the House of Representatives against Harriet Miers, President Bush's executive secretary: She refused, on the advice of the President, to testify before the House. The issue was whether the President can refuse to cooperate with Congress in its investigations and can instruct other people to refuse on the basis of presidential prerogative.

Historically these disputes have been dealt with by negotiations between Congress and the President, with ultimately some resolution. In this case, the President argued that this dispute should be dealt with in the same way, but without any indication that he would cooperate. The courts usually refuse to be involved in disputes between the executive and the legislative.

The crucial question is, what happens if the President simply refuses to cooperate or negotiate with Congress? If the courts refuse to get involved, or if the President refuses to recognize their jurisdiction, "then Congress would have little choice but to make war against the President when it was denied access to information that it believed it needs to carry out its Constitutional duties."[36] Or it could do what it has historically always done: acquiesce to the President. The reality is that Congress has little capacity to overrule the President.

This dispute never reached the point at which the issue had to be decided. Time ran out, President Bush's term in office expired, and with a new President the issue disappeared—swept under the rug for future generations to deal with. The issue of whether the President can withhold information from Congress still exists, but Americans can now pretend it does not.

Congress has also been powerless in its supposed responsibility for declaring war. Although technically the Constitution gave the power to declare war explicitly to Congress, it also designated the President as the commander in chief of the army and navy of the United States. The resulting ambiguity has been a problem since the founding of the United States. In 1973 Congress passed a War Powers Act in an attempt to clarify the issues involved in war making without an official declaration of war. The War Powers Act has never been invoked, and Presidents have considered it unconstitutional.

Recently James Baker and Warren Christopher, former secretaries of state, have made some suggestions for improving the 1973 War Powers Act: Require that the President consult more with Congress in making war decisions. Baker and Christopher want Congress to be more actively involved, but as Lithwick states, "Congress is always too deferential, too credulous, and too timid to check a strong President in wartime, and only ever speaks out after the war has become unpopular."[37] It is no wonder the President has accumulated power.

The lesson from the last forty years is that when national security is invoked, the President can do pretty much what he wants, and it is all too easy to invoke national security, to have war forever. The acquiescence of Congress to the executive is shown also in its passage of the Electronic Surveillance Act in 2007; Congress tried to define, clarify, and restrain the executive in its intelligence gathering—and ended up giving the President essentially what he wanted.

President Bush is only the latest in a line of presidents who have progressively claimed more and more power, especially since World War II,[38] with the assent of Congress. The problem is one of the basic structure or Constitution of our government, namely the weakness of Congress, rather than the strength of the President. At the end of the nineteenth century, the national government became more central, and the weaknesses in the design of the U.S. government became evident. The President accumulated power, and Congress became weaker.

Mann and Ornstein[39] describe the 2006 Congress as suffering from a decline in institutional identity, a disappearance of oversight, a tolerance of executive secrecy, a decline in adequate deliberation of legislation, a failure to object to violations of the rules of procedure, an explosion of earmarks, a collapse of ethical standards, and a pervasive influence of lobbying and fundraising. This disarray in Congress further contributes to the crisis in the essential relationship between the executive and the legislative.

The dysfunction of Congress in 2006, before the Democrats gained power, may be extreme, but it is not new.[40] As Congress has become more confused, the President has stepped in to fill the vacuum. The balance of power has always been in favor of the President: disarray in Congress has been more the rule than the exception.

Under Bush, urgent issues such as the reform of Social Security, Medicare and the entire health care system, deficit spending, and global warming were not addressed. President Bush was just not interested in dealing with these issues, or could not appreciate their importance, and Congress did not initiate measures on its own. Deference to the President, or alternatively the necessity of fighting with the President to get his cooperation, made it impossible for Congress to initiate and take action on issues the President did not favor. Even the basic appropriations process was regularly delayed until the last minute, then covered up with continuing resolutions.

Unfortunately the boundaries of what is considered normal politics were stretched to such an extent under the Bush administration that it appears Congress will again do nothing about what Bush did, implicitly and passively letting the world and the citizens of the United States know it considers his actions normal politics.

Congress and we the people can only hang on to the forlorn hope that future presidents will not use Bush as an example. Bush and his administration are now part of history, and we can thankfully return to pretending that nothing is wrong, that Bush was only an exception to the proper functioning of our perfect system. Congress will once again ignore warnings such as that by Savage, that

> The expansive Presidential powers claimed and exercised by the Bush-Cheney White House are now an immutable part of American history—not controversies, but facts. The importance of such precedents is difficult to overstate. As Supreme Court Justice Robert Jackson once warned, any new claim of executive power, once validated into precedent, "lies about like a loaded weapon ready for the hand of any authority that can bring forward a plausible claim of an urgent need. Every repetition imbeds that principle more deeply in our law and thinking and expands it to new purposes." Sooner or later, there will always be another urgent need.[41]

These conflicts between the President and Congress only encourage the President to take on even more of the power and responsibility that belongs properly to Congress. With the 2008 economic crisis that has frozen credit markets and threatens to produce a wave of worldwide deflation similar to the 1929 Depression, should we not be concerned that as Justice Jackson said, the tools of power are still lying about, ready to be used?

V

TOWARD A MORE COMPLETE
DEMOCRACY

17

STRUCTURE OF THE U.S. GOVERNMENT

Our government was formed in a different time, with a very different understanding of what government should be. Fortunately, the structure of the government formed then has been sufficient until now, at least in terms of preserving and providing stability to our country. It has not been perfect however, and the stresses it is now facing require substantial change if it is to continue to function. If the United States is to become the democracy we think it is, then we must make some fundamental changes to our government.

The preceding review of our history suggests some of the deficiencies of the government:

1. The U.S. government is undemocratic. This is not even controversial for anyone who has given a serious look at the Constitution and U.S. history. The Founders deliberately designed the government so that it is not democratic. This was a function of the particular historical circumstances of the late eighteenth century. The Founders had little firsthand experience with democracy—and what they knew made them cautious and fearful of it. Democratic Republican government in particular did not exist anywhere except in books on Greek and Roman history. The models of successful governments the Founders were most familiar with were monarchies, not democracies. They can be forgiven, therefore, for failing to design a truly democratic government in modern terms—but

we cannot be forgiven for adhering to their tentative and half-hearted attempt to move toward democracy. Over our history we have increased the range of those who can vote in elections, and in this sense the country has become more representative, but the undemocratic structure of government has limited the effects of this increase in representation. To the extent that we believe that our Founders produced the best government that could be designed, we have also become afraid of real democracy. The Founders were afraid of democracy, and their apprehensions drove their construction of the government we have. We need to rise above the veneration of our Founders, and produce a better government than what they gave us. We need to consider that the model of a democratic government for most of the rest of the world is not the U.S. government: it is British parliamentary government.

2. The separation of powers doctrine is a myth. It is without empirical or historical foundation, and interferes with the natural functioning of the government. The separation of powers is based on an erroneous and misguided description of the British government by Montesquieu, who was largely unacquainted with the real nature of the British government at the time he wrote. Montesquieu based his account of the British government on the writings of those who wrote in the 1600s, before the Glorious Revolution of 1688 that fundamentally changed it. These writings accepted the monarchy as the status quo. The separation of powers doctrine became the façade behind which the Founders created a government more similar to the monarchies they knew than to the democracy they feared.

The primary defect of the separation of powers is that it places the functions of government in opposition to each other, encouraging conflicts among them; a well-run organization needs these functions working *with* rather than against each other. To assume and institutionalize them in opposition to each other only serves to make government inefficient and wasteful. It does not prevent excessive concentration of power. It prevents timely, responsive attention to issues.

3. Judicial supremacy has served to preserve an essentially dysfunctional system. It has served as a mediator between the state governments and the federal government, and as the judge of legislative action. In the process it has encouraged the passive acceptance of rule by just nine individuals. The judiciary in a well-run government is a minor, essentially housekeeping part of government that applies the law to particular cases according to rules and precedents. It does not make policy; most judges do not want to be involved in making policy. The judicial role in government also exists in the many agencies that apply regulations to businesses such as the Federal Trade Commission or the Federal Drug Administration.

To elevate the judiciary to a policy making role deprives the true policy makers, Congress, of their proper role. Congress makes a law, but then abdicates its right and responsibility to say what it means. Congress gives directions to the executive or to the people, but in the American system, the judiciary has also been given the right to say what the directions mean when there is a dispute. The result is that Congress' role in policymaking is further diminished. Giving the courts interpretive powers is just another way to render the House subordinate to the rest of government.

Having nine individuals, appointed for life terms, has meant that major policy changes occur only at the glacial pace of generations, as the Supreme Court slowly turns over. The Court's restraints on political change provide only a false sense of stability—at the cost of a Civil War, race riots, credit crises, and cries for revolution. The Court has helped discourage Congress from acting in a timely manner on issues, for fear of their adverse interpretations of the laws. Pressures build up to explosive levels as a result. For example, federal regulation of business practices was delayed for decades by the Supreme Court's rejection of legislation regulating corporations.

4. The anti-party bias of many in government has distorted communication between the people and the government, making the government unresponsive to the majority will. Initially, our leaders tried to run a government without parties; when parties were inevitably recognized with the election of Jackson in 1828, they were incomplete, state parties masquerading as national parties, meeting every four years only to select presidential candidates on the basis of popularity.

American political parties, unlike parties in any other country, are not national parties that set national priorities and possess the discipline to see that those priorities are realized in the policies and legislation of the national government. American political parties are rather local and state organizations that get together only every four years to elect a President. Outside this brief period, their orientation is toward the local districts and states. For most of our history, selection of national representatives was a secondary concern of the state parties, with selection primarily based on what the representatives could do for the state or district.

The national interest was seldom a concern for parties. It was and still is left to the individual representatives to define what is in the national interest, often with little guidance from their parties. The result was and is that congressmen are too easily influenced by special interests outside the party system, and often go against their own party. Such individualism is held up as a virtue, even though it weakens the power of the party to enact its programs. When such parties were justly criticized starting in the late nineteenth century, the resulting effort to eliminate money and its influence from politics succeeded only in making the development of truly national parties more difficult. Campaign finance laws have consistently weakened parties' ability to reflect the will of the people without noticeably reducing the influence of money. Money flows to campaigns in a fragmented, incoherent process, but still it flows.

The other part of the effort to eliminate party influence in government, the part that is more justifiable and has been common to all modern democracies, has been incomplete in the United States. Politics has been taken out of the bureaucracy in that Congress now has little patronage power. Instead Congress has shifted patronage to the President, as has been evident in the efforts of Presidents such as Reagan, Nixon, and Bush to politicize appointments to the heads of agencies such as the Civil Rights Office of the Justice Department and the Environmental Protection Agency. Complete professionalization of the bureaucracy would make even the heads of the departments subject to the rules and standards of the civil service. This same professionalization would deprive the President of much of his power, and require that the House exercise real leadership of the departments.

5   The House of Representatives has been subordinated and rendered weak and ineffective, incapable of producing timely and decisive legislation. The House itself gave the President the authority to hire and fire heads of departments. In doing so, the House surrendered control over what the executive does in implementing the laws Congress passes. In recommending policies to Congress, the President also became the policymaking organ of the government, with the legislature only approving or disapproving of the policies. Congressional oversight hearings on executive activities have become merely forums for congressmen to rant and rave about the executive, with little power to change executive policies and procedures without the President's agreement.

The arrogation to the Senate of the right of the minority to block the will of the people completed the subordination of the House. The Senate, through the device of allowing unlimited debate—filibuster—and unrestricted amendments, made it possible for a minority in the Senate to stall or even defeat measures supported by the majority. Thus the Senate maintained its status as the upper, more superior chamber—at the cost of making the government unresponsive to the will of the majority of the people. The House was and is constantly accommodating the minority in the Senate to avoid prevention of progress. The result has been Congresses that at best muddle through crises, and at worst give up power to the President. The long drawn-out efforts to eliminate slavery and then to establish social and economic justice are prime examples of the weakness of Congress.

6 Presidents have been encouraged to become more and more the focus of power in their relations with the rest of government and with the people. Almost inevitably, power comes to be concentrated in the presidency. The President already has almost complete freedom to conduct foreign policy, and as chief policymaker, power focuses on the President in all areas. The U.S. government functions best only when power is concentrated in the President, as with Jackson, Lincoln, Wilson, and FDR.

The aggrandizement of power began with Jefferson in his war with the Barbary pirates in North Africa. Monroe used the reckless actions of Jackson to pressure Spain to give up Florida; Polk sent troops into Texas to provoke the Mexicans to attack the United States. McKinley, egged on by Teddy Roosevelt, used the pretext of the sinking of an American ship in a Cuban harbor to go to war against Spain. The use of pretexts to justify going to war is not a new, twentieth-century phenomenon, with Truman in the Korean War, Lyndon Johnson in the Vietnam War, and Bush in the Iraq War. This feature is endemic to the form of the government we have, one not likely to change through legislation.

More recent assertions of presidential power in the name of national security (Nixon, Reagan, and George W. Bush) have been more disturbing: They are employed more as an excuse to accumulate presidential power than as an appropriate response to threats. Such assertions threaten to increase the oppression and manipulation of the people; the sort of measures that lead to dictatorships. Although technically the President is constrained by Congress in declaring war, it is all too evident that he can create the circumstances for going to war, and thus override the clause in the Constitution that specifies that Congress is the body to declare war.

Even without war, the President can use his veto power to run a minority government. Jackson derailed and delayed the natural expansion of the federal government through his veto of the Bank Act—in spite of the will of the majority in Congress. In so doing he encouraged the advocates of states' rights to oppose the federal government, ultimately secede from the union, and provoke the Civil War. Subsequent Presidents may not have used this power as blatantly, but it has continued, and became especially important recently. The mere threat of a veto along with the threat of a Senate filibuster forces the House to weaken, dilute, and distort legislation that the majority of the people desire.

Our government as it is structured is often inefficient, unresponsive, and too rigid to respond to the will of the majority of the population as circumstances change. We can muddle along, as we have for the last 220 years, or we can consider changes that will allow a more democratic and efficient system to emerge.

Amending the Constitution

The traditional response to criticism of the government is to say we need constitutional amendments that would correct its defects. There is a long tradition of writing on constitutional reform going back at least to Woodrow Wilson.[1] Most suggestions do no more than make marginal changes, with little substantive change in the government itself. Sanford Levinson's recent book[2] is representative of this tradition; it provides a detailed account of some of the defects in the U.S. Constitution, ranging from the electoral college to the composition of the Senate; it describes primarily defects in representation, yet provides no specific suggestions for change other than calling for a constitutional convention. This does not really further a debate; without specific proposals there is nothing to debate.

Larry Sabato's book[3] has numerous specific suggestions, and also calls for a constitutional convention to implement them. Unfortunately none of his proposals would make any fundamental change in government structure. Further, neither author has created very much of a groundswell for a constitutional convention. Both books emphasize how the present governmental structure is not *representative* of the American people, as if that were the major defect in the government.

Other aspects of the governmental structure are more in need of discussion than how representative it is. For instance, several previous authors of books on constitutional change,[4] most notably Wilson (1880), suggest that the prohibition on making members of Congress executive officers should be relaxed, allowing members of Congress to serve as department heads. This could lead to a real structural change in the government, but there has been little discussion of it recently, and as with all the other propositions, nothing has come of it.

There are so far twenty-seven amendments to the Constitution. The first ten amendments, the original Bill of Rights, were enacted because it was universally expected that they would be enacted as a condition of ratification of the Constitution. The Bill of Rights consists of either restrictions on the federal government or statements of individual rights, depending on one's point of view. Madison selected nineteen such amendments from a collection of hundreds that had been suggested. Through debate and discussion in the House and Senate, they were further reduced to the ten we now have. Interestingly, some opposition to these amendments emanated from those who wanted a new constitutional convention.

Their fear, which turned out to be fully justified, was that these amendments would reduce the pressure for such a convention by assuaging the fears some had about the federal government.

The remaining seventeen amendments can be grouped in several ways. Eight of the amendments relate to voting. Four are concerned with who can vote: African-Americans (no. 15), women (no. 19), 18-year-olds (no. 26), and residents of the District of Columbia (no. 23). The other four are concerned with how voting is to be conducted with regard to the vice president (no. 12), senators (no. 17), the number of terms for the President (no. 20), and the prohibition of the poll tax and other restrictions on voting (no. 24). Thus the majority of amendments to the Constitution have addressed individual rights and representation—not the structure of the government.

The two prohibition amendments (nos. 18 and 21) cancel each other out. The remaining amendments can be grouped into rules for the larger society: the amendments abolishing slavery (no. 13), and granting citizenship to all residents regardless of race (nos. 14 and 15); and five housekeeping amendments that address minor aspects of how the government operates. These describe the jurisdiction of federal courts over suits against states (no. 11); the income tax (no. 16); the starting dates of terms of office for Congress and the President (no. 20); the order of succession for the President in case of death or disability (no. 25); and how Congress can increase its own pay (no. 27). None of these amendments involve any substantial change in the structural relationships between the parts of the government. These amendments may be seen as evidence of how little our government needs changing or improving—or alternatively, as an indication of how difficult it is to make any real changes.

These amendments could also be divided in terms of those that were effective and those that failed. The prohibition amendment is most clearly a failure; this was recognized when it was repealed. The other failures were associated with the Civil War, and failed because they were amendments the winners tried to impose on the losers of the war. Slavery was abolished as the result of the war, but the amendments giving citizenship and voting rights to the former slaves failed because there was no consensus for the change, and Congress was too weak to fulfill its objectives with the rebellious states. Instead it allowed the Supreme Court to misinterpret the amendments to maintain the status quo.

This review of the amendments to the Constitution[5] suggests that most were enacted only *after* the changes they address had already gained consensus among the people. In the cases in which such a consensus did not exist, the amendments were ineffective. Amendments require two-thirds of the members of Congress, then three-quarters of the states. The substantial effort to gain such a vote was not attempted unless a consensus already existed.

It may be that it is impossible to change the Constitution unless the change is non-controversial, or a general consensus for the change has already developed among the people. Without this consensus, even a constitutional amendment will not produce any effective change.

The Constitution, then, will change only when changes in the culture and government have taken place. Changes in governance come first, and changes in the formal Constitution follow as a ratification of the changes. It does not help to suggest changes in the Constitution without first considering whether substantive changes in government or society have already taken place that need to be ratified by amendments.

Changes in government and society do not necessarily require constitutional change. In the period of the Great Depression and the New Deal changes were made without a change in the Constitution. It was clear at that time that major changes were needed in how the government operated and related to its citizens. The crisis was great enough that a veto-proof majority was elected in Congress, ready to try new approaches. Several measures were enacted that were at the time considered unconstitutional. If the Supreme Court had not changed its judgments about the constitutionality of these measures, there would undoubtedly have been constitutional amendments allowing them, but such amendments were not necessary. The government changed without a change in the Constitution.[6]

The difficulty of changing the Constitution has resulted in an approach that resembles religious approaches to sacred texts. The Supreme Court is considered the supreme authority for the interpretation of the text, and an entire area of legal and judicial scholarship has developed devoted to constitutional interpretation, just as Christian scholars interpret the Bible, Jews interpret the Torah, and Muslims interpret the Quran. In each case, the sacred text has become more important than the world to which it refers. Constitutional scholars, like other religious scholars, have gained a vested interest in preserving the text—and resisting attempts to change it—since it is their reason for being. The only allowed operation on the text is its interpretation.

18

CHANGING THE GOVERNMENT

To make the national government more democratic we need to change the government, not the Constitution. The problem is that the House of Representatives, the democratic part of government, has been subordinated to the President, the Senate, and the Supreme Court. The solution to improving the functioning of our government is to enhance the role of the House of Representatives. This is the most direct way to make the government more responsive to the will of the people. The House is the truly representative part of our government, and the part that operates by majority rule—the democratic part. The House needs to dominate the operation of government, as Madison had thought it would and as it did in fact,[7] in the first Congress.

Subordinating the Senate

The disastrous consequences of congressional gridlock have become more and more evident, especially in recent years, as the filibuster or threat of filibuster has been used more and more frequently as a way to prevent timely legislation, or at least to weaken and distort the intent of the legislation. More people now recognize that the source of this problem is in the procedures of the Senate, where debate is unlimited, and any Senator can hold up the proceedings, allowing the minority to obstruct the process.

Reducing the power of the minority to block the majority involves either the Senate giving up its obstructive powers, the filibuster, the threat of filibuster, and the ability of individual Senators to place holds on legislation, or the House making the Senate minority irrelevant to the overall process.

The Senate, at the beginning of a session, could revise its rules of procedure so that they include the ability of a member of the Senate to call for the question, a parliamentary procedure that cuts off debate and forces a vote on the matter under discussion. This is the rule that was dropped in 1806, and could simply be reinstated.

In reality, however, ending the filibuster is only a half measure, and in fact may even be irrelevant to solving the problem of congressional gridlock. The minority uses the filibuster to prevent or delay legislation when both the Senate and the House have majorities of the same party.

When the two chambers have majorities of different parties, the party with the majority in the Senate is able to prevent legislation from the House from becoming law, and gridlock continues. In fact, according to current legislative procedures even when both chambers have the same majority party, the Senate is able to have ultimate control over the final form of the legislation, since without its approval the legislation dies. This was the situation in the late 1800s and early 1900s. The Senate, the unrepresentative, undisciplined body that allows minority obstruction, is the body that dominates the House, the representative, disciplined body that operates by majority rule.

At this point in most discussions of the federal government, the conclusion is that nothing can be done, that it is just the way the government is, and we must work around it. For most people a change in the relation between the House and the Senate is inconceivable. It is possible to suggest a way out of this impasse, however.

The House could make a rule that it will no longer consider legislation initiated in the Senate; this would more completely demote the Senate and make it clearly subordinate to the House. The Senate would be limited to suggesting amendments to House bills, to be accepted or rejected by the House, with a definite time limit for the return of suggested amendments.

If the Senate did not act on legislation submitted to it within the time limit, the House would assume that the Senate had no objections, and consider the measure passed. If the Senate proposed amendments, the House would accept or reject them, and the bill would be considered passed and go on to the President.

In some ways this is not so different from current procedures, except that the final approval of legislation would be in the hands of the House, not the Senate. That is, the Senate could propose amendments, including entire new bills, but if the House did not accept these amendments, the Senate would have no further recourse. The House would have the final authority over the legislation.

This was actually how the Senate operated in the first years of the U.S. government[8]—the role of the Senate was to "propose or concur with Amendments" (Article I, Section 7). The Senate should be returned to this limited role. With the adoption of this internal House rule, the House would simply be forcing the Senate to return to the intent of the Constitution. No constitutional obstacle prevents the House from taking this step. The Constitution explicitly states that "Each House may determine the Rules of its Proceedings" (Article I, Section 5).

This move would be a declaration of war against the Senate as it is now, and would not be accepted easily. The most likely response is that this is something that the House would never do even if it could, and so the whole idea is simply not serious. To be taken seriously, the House would have to show that it is determined to make the change, and be willing to endure the debate that would follow.

A great deal of preliminary debate and consideration of the implications of the change for the future operation of the government would have to take place both in and outside of the House. It would require a strong movement in the country supporting such a move, strong enough to cause at least one of the parties to adopt it as part of its platform. Then, if that party gained the majority in the House, it would be committed to implementing the change, a political, not a constitutional, change.

The first step in creating such a movement would be to take the idea seriously, to accept that the House could indeed make such a change in its rules, and that doing so would be beneficial for the country. The Senate, of course, and those who benefit from having the Senate the way it is now, would produce a series of strong arguments against making such a change.

Debate over the pros and cons of such an assertion of authority by the House would be extensive and involved, and would take an extended period of time. The discipline and determination of the people supporting the change, and of the parties representing them, would be crucial to the success of the change. Some of the immediate implications of the change can be anticipated.

With the clear subordination of the Senate to the House, it would no longer matter whether the Senate allowed unlimited debate or minority obstruction. The House of Representatives, the chamber more representative of the people and in control of the purse would be in charge of legislation. The Senate would be no more than an advisor to the House.

The Senate, more than any other body, holds up the virtue of bipartisan cooperation on bills; bipartisanship has been raised to an article of faith. Bipartisanship, though it sounds good, is no more than a device for blocking legislation, or forcing compromises with the minority that counter the purpose of the legislation.

Partisanship, the expression of the partisan majority, is what is needed for a government to function without gridlock. The lack of partisanship because of the supposed virtue of "bipartisanship" is what has produced the lack of accountability of the parties, and the consequent loss of respect of the people. If voters cannot count on the party to do what it promises, why should they respect the party? With real party discipline, the game of bipartisanship can be terminated.

The Ascendance of the House

As the power of the Senate to obstruct legislation diminishes, the parties in the House would no longer have to look over their shoulders at what the Senate might do, and would be able

Changing the Government

to focus more clearly on getting their programs for the country realized when they are in the majority.

Power would shift significantly to the House, specifically to the House majority leader who would have authority parallel to the prime minister in Britain. This person and his/her advisors, who are now chairmen of the various committees, would come to have more direct authority over the heads of the departments.

If these executives come to have civil service status, as seems reasonable, the House leaders would expect their cooperation in the formulation of legislation. The House could easily revise the laws creating the departments to make it clear that the secretaries of the departments should also be subject to the rules and requirements of the civil service.

This is what has happened in Britain: The secretaries of the departments are required by law to follow the guidance of the respective ministers in parliament. The secretaries, executive heads of the departments, administer their departments according to professional standards, but are responsible to their respective ministers for policy guidance.

Similarly, the political aspects of the management of the departments would be taken over by the leaders of the House. The executive bureaucracy would work automatically with the majority party in the House as soon as the majority changes.

Theoretically this would mean that the direction of the government could change every two years, with each new election to the House, but in fact such frequent changes are not likely. If it did become a problem, then a constitutional amendment could be passed to change the frequency of elections, or make them more a function of the confidence of the House in its leaders, as in Britain.

The organization of the House would change along with its increase in control. Standing committees, made up of members of both parties, would become less important as the authority of each committee chairman over the corresponding executive department increases, and the influence of the minority party decreases. House organization would take the form of making specific individuals in the House responsible for the affairs of each executive department.

The representative responsible for each department would take on more the role of a minister, and less that of a committee chairman. He would be chosen on the basis of expertise. The ranking minority members of the committees would form a shadow government, ready to take over when the majority of the House changed.

As the role of the parties and their leaders in the House become more a matter of governing, not just legislating, the government as a whole would be more directly and transparently accountable to the people. Party positions and platforms would become more central to the determination of how the voter votes.

With the role of the parties increased, they would be more organized and involved in selecting candidates for the representatives to the House. Politically ambitious individuals would gravitate to the House rather than to the Senate or the presidency. Party candidates would be much more tied to the policies and programs of their party.

Leadership of the party would be based on who could best realize party goals as decided in a general party conference. The federal bureaucracy would no longer face the dilemma of having to serve two masters, the President and Congress.

To assist in promoting party discipline, campaign finance rules could be changed so they support parties rather than individual candidates. Requiring that all funding of political campaigns be through the parties—and only through the parties, individual candidates would have no role in raising funds. They would be unable to solicit or accept contributions directly from individuals or corporations, including unions. This would leave them free of the demands of holding fundraising dinners and rallies. Their role in a campaign would only be to talk to voters about the issues.

This approach is a complete reversal of the standard view of the problem of campaign finance, that parties are corrupted by too much money. Given the failure of 100 years of attempts at reform under this view, it is time to reconsider its assumptions.

The debate over campaign financing is not and cannot be whether or not corporations, labor unions, and other organizations should influence elections. They do and should influence elections and party policy. The issue is rather *how* they exert this influence. Influencing individual candidates and members of Congress is corruption and properly should be illegal. Influencing a *party* is a normal, natural, essential part of the political process. Parties exist to evaluate and coordinate these different influences and arrive at a coherent political program by which they can achieve a majority at the polls. The voters are and should be the final judge of the party program.

Making campaign fundraising solely the job of the party and not of the candidate may not solve all the issues in fundraising, but it would impose a buffer between the candidate and the special interests giving the money—a buffer that does not exist at present—thus attenuating the influence on the individual candidate. Fear that a corporation or a union could buy the votes of an individual congressman would evaporate. The fear that a single corporation or union or industry could 'buy' an entire party is absurd.

Implications of the recent Supreme Court decision (*Citizens United v. FEC*, 2010) on campaign financing are not clear and will not be for some time. It ruled specifically that laws limiting the ability of corporations to produce material directed at a presidential candidate were unconstitutional, an abridgment of the corporation's right to free speech. More generally, it ruled that any limitation on a corporation's ability to produce political statements is an abridgment of the corporation's right to free speech.

If this ruling means Congress can no longer limit in any way a corporation's contribution to any political organization, then Congress could not say that contributions can be made only to political parties. By contributing to the campaign funds of individual candidates, a corporation could "buy" that candidate. An energized House, of course, could simply overrule the Supreme Court.

If Congress could still control how contributions are made, it would be possible to limit contributions to individual candidates. If Congress made a law that individual candidates can accept and solicit funds only from their identified political parties, this would not infringe on the ability of corporations to produce political material and contribute to campaigns.

Corporations, labor unions, and nonprofit organizations could contribute as much as they wanted to campaigns, but only through the parties. If a corporation wanted to produce its own campaign material, and could prove the material was not a covert contribution to an individual candidate, and had the approval of the party, it could do so. Such proof would be difficult.

Whatever the effects of this recent ruling on campaigns and their financing, a primary reason for financing campaigns only through the parties is to give the party more influence over the conduct of the members when they get to Congress. Only then will the party be able to realize its objectives.

Presidential Acquiescence

As the majority party in the House more clearly determines the policy for the government, the President would be forced to cooperate with the leaders of the House. The heads of departments would either become civil service positions, or would be selected by the House party leaders.

The President would be subordinate to the leaders of the majority party in the House, and would have to appoint the people that the House leadership wants as heads of executive offices, the heads of the various departments, or accept the status of the heads as civil service officers. These officers would be responsible to the House first, and the President only secondarily. The President would have no choice but to accede to this arrangement.

The President's power and influence would be drastically reduced. He would be at best a super administrator working in cooperation with Congress to coordinate the activities of the different departments. In British terms, he would be the head of state, but not the head of government.

The President's political party affiliation would come to be irrelevant. He or she would have no choice but to go along with the policies of the House majority party. Other governments would seek out and negotiate with the House majority leader, not the President. The majority leader would have the authority of representing the majority of the country. The executive would no longer be fighting with the legislature over the implementation of policy. Executive officers would have a clear understanding of their duties and responsibilities, without receiving mixed signals from the President and Congress.

Reverberations

Much of the bureaucracy developed in recent years could disappear. The huge staff in the office of the President would no longer be necessary because the role of the President would have diminished. The office of the President grew as presidents tried to gain control over the executive departments; since the President would no longer have control of these departments, the office would be unnecessary.

Congress has also hired huge staffs, in both the offices of individual congressmen and the congressional committees. This was a desperate attempt to reproduce the executive departments, and thus to exert some influence over them. These excessive staffs would no longer be necessary because Congress would have direct control over the executive departments; members of these departments would do much of what is now done by congressional staff. A drastic reduction in the bureaucracy necessary to run the federal government could be expected.

The issue of how fair the electoral college is would lose importance because, with the President having little actual power, it would no longer matter as much how he is chosen. We could avoid all the expense and hoopla of the current presidential elections, since the President would no longer be so central to the government.

The unrepresentative character of the Senate would no longer be debated because, with the power shifting to the House, the Senate would be unable to meaningfully interfere with the legislative process in the House. The Senate would be a secondary body, a group of advisors valuable for their experience and wisdom.

The possibility of a divided government would disappear, and those who tout its virtues would be forced to seek other ways to reach their ends. The so-called supporters of divided government are primarily those who prefer that the government achieve as little as possible. Nowadays this means primarily business interests, who use the system to prevent undesired regulation, while allowing the government to do it favors.

Presented with the idea of giving more power to the House of Representatives, most Americans would immediately and vigorously reject it. The perception of the House is that it is the most irresponsible, fractious, and inefficient branch of government, so to give it more power would be seen as a disaster.

This attitude was an explicit reason the designers of our government made it the way it is. They had no faith in the ability of the majority of representatives of the people to govern responsibly. They built in structures that would monitor and restrain the expected excesses of the majority.

They expected the majority to be irresponsible, impetuous, and irrational. "Adult" supervision was necessary, so they added the Senate and the President. Even this was not enough, and eventually the Supreme Court became another source of adult supervision.

The problem with designing such a system is that one tends to get what one expects. If you expect representatives to be irresponsible and impetuous, they will be. If you expect them to be responsible and prudent, they will be. The government was designed to expect that the representatives of the people will be irresponsible, and so they have been.

Given the character of the House as it is now, few would expect it to govern our country well. But our representatives are not, by nature, irresponsible. They are responsible adults who are able, given the chance, to make responsible, prudent decisions about policy. If the people expect our representatives to act with wisdom, they will.

It is time for Americans to begin treating elected representatives as adults, to start trusting that they will govern well. The example of Britain and many other parliamentary governments shows that representatives of the people can be trusted to govern by themselves, without supervision by a president, a court, or a superfluous upper chamber.

Changing the Government

This proposal of how a change in the government could occur—without any constitutional amendments or revolutionary confrontation—is well within the scope of ordinary political development. The result would be revolutionary.

CONCLUSION

As Huntington[9] pointed out, our government is one in which sovereignty is divided and fragmented, similar in many striking ways to the medieval government of Elizabeth I. As the result of the economic and political changes in the late seventeenth century, Britain developed a system in which sovereignty was centralized and concentrated in the House of Commons. The fragmentation of sovereignty does not allow the expressed will of the majority to rule. Far from suffering from the excesses of majority rule, which our Founders feared, and which we have been taught to be afraid of ever since, the problems we have had, and continue to have, are due to the lack of rule by the majority.

The problems the United States has had in its history, congressional gridlock and paralysis, and presidential imperialism, come down to the fragmentation of sovereignty. Our government needs to move toward a more parliamentary form, one in which power is concentrated in the House of Representatives. Anything less will fail in the goal of achieving a more democratic, efficient government. Eliminating the President's veto power, or trying to clarify the President's war powers—efforts that have already been tried—do not attack the fundamental issue of who is in charge of our government. The only real and durable solution is to have the House of Representatives control the executive.

The Founders of our government may have had good reasons to form the government they did. The sensitivities of the individual states, each with its own established government, were certainly factors. Asking them to subordinate themselves to a national government was not easy, and required compromise. The fight over states' rights, however, has been resolved: We now have a national government with the states subordinate. It is time our government also became a fully democratic government.

The ideas presented in this book will not be accepted easily. They go against fundamental assumptions about the U.S. government. There has, for instance, been a long tradition that the nomination and appointment of major officers to the executive is the President's power alone. Corwin[10] documents this history, and Wood[11] shows that giving the power of appointment to the President was also an aspect of the revisions of the original state constitutions, part of the effort to make government less democratic.

As Congress becomes more and more obviously incapable of governing effectively, and as the President continues to claim more power, it may eventually become obvious that change is vital.

It is possible to achieve the dominance of the House of Representatives through a gradual, non-disruptive pathway, starting with a movement to subordinate the Senate. Such a path will take time and will not be easy, but it is within the bounds of normal politics. Ultimately there may be revolutionary moments in which the House simply defies the President or the Senate, and forces them to accede to its demands, but such moments could be accomplished peacefully.

Many will reject the idea that we need a revolution. Our country has survived for 220 years, and it may continue to muddle through with the government we have for an indefinite period. We may acclimate to alternating between congressional gridlock in which nothing gets done, and the assertion of more and more presidential power. But, if we want a better, more efficient and responsive, more democratic government, then we must undertake changes that will, ultimately, be revolutionary.

APPENDIX

GREEK DEMOCRACY

Modern scholarship has developed a deeper understanding of the Athenian government, revealing that it was distinctively different from modern governments. In the Athenian government that Aristotle used as the best model of a polity, all the citizens of the state were nominally members of the assembly, the ultimate authority in the state. The government required at least 6,000 of its citizens (out of a total population of approximately 250,000) to be present for business to be conducted in the assembly. Meetings were held at least 40 times a year, meaning they met about once a week with 12 weeks off, probably for religious ceremonies, festivals, and athletic competitions.[12] Each meeting lasted for only a day, and involved making many major decisions. The assembly thus had little involvement in formulating the issues to be voted on; it only gave a final yes or no to each issue.

Athenian governance assumed that every citizen participated or should participate in the assembly's deliberations. Dahl's criteria of what is required for a democracy nicely defines what this means for the citizen:

1. Effective Participation—Citizens must be involved in the process of debating policies.
2. Equality in Voting—Citizens must vote on the policies.
3. Enlightened Understanding—Citizens must become informed about the policies.

4. Final control over the Agenda—Citizens must be involved in setting the agenda.
5. Inclusion—All competent citizens must be included.

Not all the citizens were actually involved in the assembly. Aristotle admitted that there were frequent problems getting citizens to attend the assembly, and suggested paying the poorer citizens to attend—and fining the richer citizens for not attending. These challenges suggest that even in small city-states over 2000 years ago, distinctions arose between those who wanted to be involved in government, and those who did not.

Perhaps the most distinctive aspect of the Athenian government was the Council of 500, which was really the most important part of its government.[13] This body was made up of 50 members from each of 10 tribes, into which the population of Athens and its territory were divided. These tribes were not groups of individuals related by tradition to a common family, as tribes are usually thought of. Rather they were deliberately constructed groups of towns and districts (demes in Greek). They were joined so each tribe consisted of demes from the city, from the coastal area, and from the inland area. Thus each tribe contained within itself all the diversity of the entire population. In that sense, each tribe was representative of the whole of Athens.

The 50 members of each tribe were chosen by lot from the members of each tribe for a term of one year; they were not chosen through an election to represent the tribe, but they did represent the tribes in the Council of 500. Any adult male citizen of the tribe could be a member of the Council of 500, and over his lifetime he had a good expectation that he would be a member. Over the years almost all the citizens were members.

Such an arrangement forced every citizen to be strongly involved in actually running the government. The assumption was that every citizen had an equal ability to run the government. The details and procedures of the Council of 500 could be learned on the job during the year of service, along with learning from the experience of predecessors. Citizens did not have a choice in whether to be involved in government; it was a requirement. This is the most distinctive aspect of the Athenian government.

Many other offices of the government were similarly filled through choice by lot of the citizens of Athens. There were people's courts, judicial magistrates, magistrates in charge of accountability, treasurers, and so on. Only a few offices, such as the generals in charge of war making, were elected. Thus over a lifetime a citizen was likely to be involved, either on the Council of 500 or as a magistrate of some kind, in the actual operation of the government, just as jury duty is required of everyone today.

The Council of 500 was in charge of setting the agenda for the assembly meetings, and it "had the responsibility for the day-to-day administration of state affairs, including meeting foreign delegations and reviewing the performance of outgoing Athenian magistrates."[14] Each set of 50 members from each tribe presided over the activities of the Council as a committee of 50 for one-tenth of the year. It was thus a combined executive, legislative, and judicial body, but with the final legislative and judicial decisions left to the larger assembly or to the people's courts, and other executive and judicial roles left to the groups of magistrates.

Thus the Athenian government was unique in the degree to which it forced all its citizens to be involved in all three functions of government, not just the legislative role. It was a successful government, maintaining its participatory character for about 180 years, despite brief periods of oligarchy. It was the most successful and prosperous Greek city-state. Nevertheless, it could not survive the overwhelming force of nation-states like Macedonia and Rome. Athens was not able—or did not want—to move beyond the rule of its own citizens to the rule of territory and people outside its own community.

NOTES

1. Abraham Lincoln, "The Perpetuation of Our Political Institutions: Address to the Young Men's Lyceum of Springfield, Illinois, 1838," in Abraham Lincoln, *Speeches and Writings: 1832-1858*, ed. Don Fehrenbacher (New York: Library of America, 1989), pp. 32–33.
2. Bradford Plumer, "The Revisionaries: The Tea Party's Goofy Fetish for Amending the Constitution," *The New Republic* (September 23, 2010), pp. 16–21.
3. Eric Lane, and Michael Oreskes, *The Genius of America: How the Constitution Saved Our Country and Why It Can Again* (New York: Bloomsbury USA, 2007).
4. Robert Remini, *The House: The History of the House of Representatives* (New York: HarperCollins Publishers, 2006), p. 311.
5. Louis Fisher, *Constitutional Conflicts between Congress and the President* (Lawrence: University Press of Kansas, 2007).
6. See Stephen Skowronek, *Building a New American State: The Extension of National Administrative Capacities, 1877-1920* (Cambridge: Cambridge University Press, 1982); Raymond J. La Raja, *Small Change: Money, Political Parties, and Campaign Finance Reform* (Ann Arbor: University of Michigan Press, 2008).
7. E. S. Corwin, *The President: Office and Powers* (New York: New York University Press, 1957).
8. Arthur M. Schlesinger, *The Imperial Presidency* (Boston: Houghton Mifflin, 1973).
9. Charlie Savage, *Takeover: The Return of the Imperial Presidency and the Subversion of American Democracy* (New York: Little, Brown and Company, 2007).

10. Sanford Levinson, *Our Undemocratic Constitution* (New York: Oxford University Press, 2006); Larry Sabato, *A More Perfect Constitution* (New York: Walker Press, 2006).
11. Bruce Ackerman, *We the People: Foundations* (Cambridge, Mass.: Belknap Press, 1991); Bruce Ackerman, *We the People: Transformations* (Cambridge, Mass.: Belknap Press, 1998); Bruce Ackerman, *The Failure of the Founding Fathers: Jefferson, Marshall, and the Rise of Presidential* (Cambridge, Mass. Belknap Press, 2005).
12. Thomas Mann and Norman Ornstein, *The Broken Branch: How Congress is Failing America and How to Get It Back on Track* (New York: Oxford University Press, 2006).
13. Sheldon Wolin, *Democracy Incorporated: Managed Democracy and the Specter of Inverted Totalitarianism* (Princeton: Princeton University Press, 2008).
14. John Dean, *Conservatives without Conscience* (New York: Penguin Group, 2006).
15. Savage, *Takeover*.
16. Arend Lijphart, *Parliamentary versus Presidential Government* (Oxford: Oxford University Press, 1992).

I: Creating an Undemocratic Government

1. Don Cook, *The Long Fuse: How England Lost the American Colonies, 1760–1785* (New York: Atlantic Monthly Press, 1995).
2. Charles Beard, *An Economic Interpretation of the Constitution of the United States* (New York: Macmillan Publishing Company, 1913).
3. John F. Manley and Kenneth M. Dolbeare, *The Case against the Constitution: From the Antifederalists to the Present* (New York: M. E. Sharpe, 1987).
4. Terry Bouton, *Taming Democracy* (New York: Oxford University Press, 2007).
5. Woody Holton, *Unruly Americans and the Origins of the Constitution* (New York: Hill and Wang, 2007); Woody Holton, *Forced Founders: Indians, Debtors, Slaves, and the Making of the American Revolution in Virginia* (Chapel Hill: University of North Carolina Press, 1999).
6. Bouton, *Taming Democracy*.
7. Baron de Montesquieu, *The Spirit of Laws* (Chicago: Encyclopedia Britannica, 1952).
8. Donald S. Lutz, *Popular Consent and Popular Control: Whig Political Theory in the Early State Constitutions* (Baton Rouge and London: Louisiana State University Press, 1980).

9. Holton, *Unruly Americans*.
10. Bouton, *Taming Democracy*.
11. Remini, *History of the House of Representatives*.
12. Lutz, *Popular Consent*; Gordon S. Wood, *The Creation of the American Republic 1776–1787* (Chapel Hill and London: University of North Carolina Press, 1969).
13. Wood, *Creation of the American Republic*.
14. In the records of the Federal Convention, 1787, quoted in Bouton, *Taming Democracy*.
15. Holton, *Unruly Americans*.
16. Levinson, *Our Undemocratic Constitution*; Larry Sabato, *A More Perfect Constitution*.
17. Tony Wright (ed.), *The British Political Process* (London and New York: Routledge, 2000).
18. Max M. Edling, *A Revolution in Favor of Government: Origins of the U.S. Constitution and the Making of the American State* (New York: Oxford University Press, 2003).
19. Wood, *Creation of the American Republic*, p. 562.
20. Holton, *Unruly Americans*.
21. Edward L. Rubin, *Beyond Camelot: Rethinking Politics and Law for the Modern State* (Princeton: Princeton University Press, 2005).
22. James Madison, *Federalist Paper No 10*, 1787.
23. Edling, *A Revolution in Favor of Government*, p. 200.
24. Holton, *Unruly Americans*.
25. Dahl, Robert. *A Preface to Democratic Theory*, expanded edition (Chicago: University of Chicago Press, 2006), p. xiv.
26. Wood, *Creation of the American Republic*, p. 502.
27. Gordon S. Wood, *Revolutionary Characters: What Made the Founders Different* (New York: The Penguin Press, 2006).
28. Rubin, *Beyond Camelot*.
29. See J. R. Pole, *Political Representation in England and the Origins of the American Republic* (London: Macmillan, 1966) for an extended discussion of this issue.
30. For a review of theories, see David Held, *Models of Democracy* (Stanford, California: Stanford University Press, 2006).
31. Rubin, *Beyond Camelot*, p. 121.
32. Wood, *Creation of the American Republic*.
33. Lijphart, *Parliamentary versus Presidential Government*.

34. Przeworski, Adam, Michael Alvarez, Jose Antonio Cheibub, and Fernando Limongi. "What Makes Democracies Endure?" *Journal of Democracy* 7, no. 1 (1996), pp. 39–55.
35. Rubin, *Beyond Camelot*, ch. 5.
36. Held, *Models of Democracy*, p. 155.
37. Robert Dahl, *Democracy and its Critics* (New Haven and London: Yale University Press, 1989), p. 162.
38. Dahl, *Democracy and its Critics*, p. 162.
39. Ibid.
40. Ackerman, *We the People: Foundations*, pp. 251–259.
41. Ibid., pp. 255–256.
42. Ibid.
43. Levinson, *Our Undemocratic Constitution*.
44. Ibid., p. 33.
45. Ibid.
46. Wright (ed.), *British Political Process*.
47. Bradshaw, Kenneth and David Pring, *Parliament and Congress* (London: Quartet Books, 1982), p. 11.
48. Even in other countries with bicameral legislatures, one house is usually subordinate to the other. Having both houses with almost equal power is unique to the presidential system. See Levinson, *Our Undemocratic Constitution*.

II: Perpetuating an Undemocratic Government

1. Montesquieu, *Spirit of Laws*.
2. John Locke, *Two Treatises of Government*, 1689/90.
3. Lutz, *Popular Consent*; Remini, *The House*.
4. Lutz, *Popular Consent*.
5. Ibid. Edling, *A Revolution*.
6. Brendan McConville, *The King's Three Faces: The Rise and Fall of Royal America, 1688–1776* (Chapel Hill: University of North Carolina Press, 2006).
7. Wood, *Creation of the American Republic*.
8. Samuel P. Huntington, *Political Order in Changing Societies* (New Haven and London: Yale University Press, 1968).
9. Wood, *Creation of the American Republic*, p. 15.
10. Daniel Lazare, *The Frozen Republic: How the Constitution is Paralyzing Democracy* (New York: Harcourt, Brace & Company, 1996), p. 27.
11. Wood, *Creation of the American Republic*, p. 15.

12. Elaine K. Swift, *The Making of an American Senate* (Ann Arbor: University of Michigan Press, 2002).
13. Swift, *Making of an American Senate*, p. 81.
14. Gregory J. Wawro and Eric Schickler, *Filibuster* (Princeton: Princeton University Press, 2006).
15. Remini, *The House*, p. 27. To get some idea of how these pay rates compare to amounts in current dollars, a time series of production worker compensation provided on measuringworth.com was used. According to it, $6/day would translate into about $7,210/day in 2010 dollars, or, assuming the congressman worked 100 days, $72,100/year. In these terms, the pay of congressmen has gone up since 1790. The President's salary of $20,000/year would translate into $24,000,000/year, comparable to the compensation of current corporate CEOs, but much more than what the president now receives.
16. Remini, *The House*, pp. 27–28.
17. Ralph Ketcham, *James Madison: A Biography* (Charlottesville and London: University of Virginia Press, 1971), p. 288; Fisher, *Constitutional Conflicts*.
18. Remini, *The House*, p. 28.
19. Max Farrand, *The Framing of the Constitution of the United States* (New Haven: Yale University Press, 1913).
20. See Ralph Volney Harlow, *The History of Legislative Methods in the Period before 1825* (New Haven: Yale University Press, 1917) for a detailed account of standing committees in America.
21. Eric Redman, *The Dance of Legislation* (Seattle: University of Washington Press, 2001).
22. Remini, *The House*, pp. 40–41.
23. Ackerman, *Failure of the Founding Fathers*.
24. Sean Wilentz, *The Rise of American Democracy* (New York: W. W. Norton & Company, 2005).
25. Daniel Walker Howe, *What Hath God Wrought: The Transformation of America, 1815–1848* (New York: Oxford University Press, 2007).
26. Remini, *The House*, p. 75.
27. Ibid., p. 76.
28. Skowronek, *Building a New American State*.
29. Louis Fisher, *The Politics of Shared Power: Congress and the Executive* (College Station: Texas A&M University Press, 1998).
30. Keith E. Whittington, *Political Foundations of Judicial Supremacy* (Princeton and Oxford: Princeton University Press, 2007).
31. Whittington, *Political Foundations*, p. 245

32. Jean Edward Smith, *John Marshall: Definer of a Nation* (New York: Henry Holt and Company, 1996).
33. Smith, *John Marshall*.
34. Ackerman, *Failure of the Founding Fathers*.
35. Jack Beatty, *The Age of Betrayal* (New York: Alfred A. Knopf, 2007).
36. Beatty, *Age of Betrayal*, p. 135, quoting the Supreme Court decision.
37. Beatty, *Age of Betrayal*.
38. Ibid.
39. Ibid., ch. 6.
40. Whittington, *Political Foundations*, p. 256.
41. Ibid.
42. Ibid., p. 263
43. Quoted in Whittington, *Political Foundations*, p. 262
44. Beatty, *Age of Betrayal*.
45. David R. Mayhew, *Parties and Policies: How the American Government Works* (New Haven: Yale University Press, 2008); Keith Krehbiel, *Information and Legislative Organization* (Ann Arbor: University of Michigan Press, 1992).
46. Skowronek, *Building a New American State*, p. 31.
47. Quoted in George Will, "The Final Repudiation," *Newsweek*, November 17, 2008.
48. Anne Appelbaum, "No Job for Mr. Nice Guy," *Washington Post*, June 24, 2008.
49. Bruce Bower, "Simpleminded Voters," *Science News* 174, no. 3, pp. 22–25.
50. Howe, *What Hath God Wrought*.
51. Wilentz, *Rise of American Democracy*.
52. Howe, *What Hath God Wrought*, p. 360.
53. Lewis L. Gould, *Four Hats in the Ring: The 1912 Election and the Birth of Modern American Politics* (Lawrence: University Press of Kansas, 2008), p. 23.
54. The following account relies primarily on La Raja, *Small Change*.
55. La Raja, *Small Change*, p. 106.
56. Bruce Ackerman and Ian Ayres, *Voting with Dollars: A New Paradigm for Campaign Finance* (New Haven: Yale University Press, 2002).
57. La Raja, *Small Change*.
58. Ibid.
59. Ibid., p. 201.
60. Mayhew, *Parties and Policies*; Krehbiel, *Information and Legislative Organization*.
61. La Raja, *Small Change*.

62. Skowronek, *Building a New American State*, p. 49.
63. Ibid., p. 44.
64. Ibid.
65. Ibid., p. 48.
66. Ibid., p. 61.
67. Ibid., p. 181.
68. Ibid., p. 189.
69. Ibid., p. 192.
70. John Brewer, *The Sinews of Power: War, Money and the English State 1688–1783* (Cambridge, Mass.: Harvard University Press, 1988).
71. Skowronek, *Building a New American State*.
72. Beatty, *Age of Betrayal*.

III: Congressional Gridlock

1. Remini, *The House*, p. 106.
2. Howe, *What Hath God Wrought*.
3. Wilentz, *Rise of American Democracy*.
4. Ibid., p. 327.
5. Remini, *The House*.
6. Ibid., p. 188.
7. Michael W. Fitzgerald, *Splendid Failure: Postwar Reconstruction in the American South* (Chicago: Ivan R. Dee 2007), p. 20.
8. Ibid., p. 35.
9. Ibid., p. 40.
10. Ibid., p. 45.
11. Holton, *Forced Founders*.
12. Charles Sellers, *Market Revolution: Jacksonian America, 1815–1846* (New York: Oxford University Press, 1991).
13. Wilentz, *Rise of American Democracy*, p. 206.
14. Harry L. Watson, *Liberty and Power* (New York: Hill and Wang, 2006); Sellers, *Market Revolution*.
15. Wilentz, *Rise of American Democracy*, p. 206.
16. Watson, *Liberty and Power*.
17. Gerard N. Magliocca, *Andrew Jackson and the Constitution: The Rise and Fall of Generational Regimes* (Lawrence: University Press of Kansas, 2007).
18. Howe, *What Hath God Wrought*, p. 380.
19. Robert Wright and David J. Cowen, *Financial Founding Fathers: The Men who Made America Rich* (Chicago: University of Chicago Press, 2006).

20. Howe, *What Hath God Wrought*; Magliocca, *Andrew Jackson*; Watson, *Liberty and Power*.
21. Remini, *The House*, p. 250.
22. Lewis L. Gould, *The Most Exclusive Club: A History of the Modern United States Senate* (New York: Basic Books, 2005), pp. 5–6.
23. Gould, *Most Exclusive Club*, p. 38.
24. Skowronek, *Building a New American State*, p. 142.
25. Scott James, *Presidents, Parties, and the State: A Party System Perspective on Democratic Regulatory Choice, 1884–1936* (New York: Cambridge University Press, 2000).
26. Edling, *Revolution*.
27. Skowronek, *Building a New American State*, p. 6.

IV: Imperial Presidents

1. Remini, *The House*.
2. Ibid., p. 57.
3. Ketcham, *James Madison*.
4. Remini, *The House*, p. 89.
5. Ibid., p. 90.
6. Ibid.
7. Ibid., p. 91.
8. Ketcham, *James Madison*.
9. Ibid., A. J. Langguth, *Union 1812: The Americans who Fought the Second War of Independence* (New York: Simon And Schuster, 2006).
10. Remini, *The House*, p. 77.
11. Howe, *What Hath God Wrought*.
12. Edmund Morris, *Theodore Rex* (New York: Random House, 2001).
13. Crenson and Ginsberg, *Presidential Power*, p. 114.
14. E.g., Gene Healy, *The Cult of the Presidency: America's Dangerous Devotion to Executive Power* (Washington, D.C.: CATO Institute, 2008).
15. Morris, *Theodore Rex*.
16. Skowronek, *Building a New American State*, p. 185.
17. Healy, *Cult of the Presidency*.
18. Crenson and Ginsberg, *Presidential Power*, pp. 20-21.
19. Ibid., p. 148.
20. Gould, *Most Exclusive Club*, p. 114.
21. Gene Smiley, *Rethinking the Great Depression* (Chicago: Ivan R. Dee, 2002); Amity Shlaes, *The Forgotten Man* (New York: Harper Collins, 2007).
22. E.g., Shlaes, *Forgotten Man*.

23. Liaquat Ahamed, *Lords of Finance: The Bankers who Broke the World* (New York: The Penguin Press, 2009).
24. Other candidates for first Imperial President are Andrew Jackson, Abraham Lincoln, Teddy Roosevelt, and Woodrow Wilson. See Schlesinger, *Imperial Presidency*.
25. Crenson and Ginsberg, *Presidential Power*; Jean Edward Smith, *FDR* (New York: Random House, 2007).
26. Remini, *The House*, p. 311.
27. Smith, *FDR*.
28. Remini, *The House*, p. 320.
29. Smith, *FDR*, p. 409.
30. Ibid.
31. Ibid., p. 360.
32. Ibid., p. 388.
33. Ibid., p. 396.
34. Shlaes, *Forgotten Man*.
35. Whittington, *Political Foundations*; Savage, *Takeover*.
36. Alan B. Morrison, "Can the President Ignore Congress?" *New Republic*, June 26, 2008.
37. Dahlia Lithwick, "Wrestling over War Powers," *Newsweek*, July 12, 2008.
38. Schlesinger, *Imperial Presidency*; Savage, *Takeover*.
39. Mann and Ornstein, *Broken Branch*.
40. Remini, *The House*.
41. Savage, *Takeover*, p. 330.

V: Toward a More Complete Democracy

1. John R. Vile, *Rewriting the United States Constitution: An Examination of Proposals from Reconstruction to the Present* (New York: Praeger, 1991).
2. Levinson, *Our Undemocratic Constitution*.
3. Sabato, *A More Perfect Constitution*.
4. Vile, *Rewriting the United States Constitution*.
5. Akhil Reed Amar, *America's Constitution: A Biography* (New York: Random House, New York, 2005).
6. Ackerman, *We the People: Transformations*.
7. Remini, *The House*
8. Sarah A. Binder, *Stalemate: Causes and Consequences of Legislative Gridlock* (Washington, D.C.: Brookings Institution Press, 2003).
9. Huntington, *Political Order*.
10. Corwin, *The President*.
11. Wood, *Creation of the American Republic*.

12. Held, *Models of Democracy*, p. 18.
13. Josiah Ober, *Democracy and Knowledge: Innovation and Learning in Classical Athens* (Princeton and Oxford: Princeton University Press, 2008).
14. Ibid., p. 142.
15. In the introduction to Mayhew, *Parties and Policies*.

BIBLIOGRAPHY

Ackerman, Bruce. *The Failure of the Founding Fathers: Jefferson, Marshall, and the Rise of Presidential Democracy*. Cambridge, Mass.: Belknap Press, 2005.
———. *We the People: Foundations*. Cambridge, Mass.: Belknap Press, 1991.
———. *We the People: Transformations*. Cambridge, Mass.: Belknap Press, 1998.
Ackerman, Bruce & Ian Ayres. *Voting with Dollars: A New Paradigm for Campaign Finance*. New Haven: Yale University Press, 2002.
Ahamed, Liaquat. *Lords of Finance: The Bankers who Broke the World*. New York: Penguin, 2009.
Amar, Akhil Reed. *America's Constitution: A Biography*. New York: Random House, 2005.
Appelbaum, Anne. "No Job for Mr. Nice Guy" *Washington Post*, June 24, 2008.
Beard, Charles. *An Economic Interpretation of the Constitution of the United States*. New York: Macmillan, 1913.
Beatty, Jack. *The Age of Betrayal*. New York: Alfred A. Knopf, 2007.
Binder, Sarah A. *Stalemate: Causes and Consequences of Legislative Gridlock*. Washington, D.C.: Brookings Institution Press, 2003.
Bouton, Terry. *Taming Democracy*. New York: Oxford University Press, 2007.
Bower, Bruce. "Simpleminded Voters." *Science News* 174, no 3 (July 5, 2008): 22–25.
Bradshaw, Kenneth and David Pring. *Parliament and Congress*. London: Quartet Books, 1982.
Brewer, John. *Party Ideology and Popular Politics at the Accession of George III*. London: Cambridge University Press, 1976.
———. *The Sinews of Power: War, Money and the English State 1688-1783*. Cambridge, Mass.: Harvard University Press, 1988.
Broder, David. "Dumbing Down the Presidency." *Washington Post*, June 29, 2008.

Bibliography

Cook, Don. *The Long Fuse: How England Lost the American Colonies, 1760-1785.* New York: Atlantic Monthly Press, 1995.

Corwin, E. S. *The President: Office and Powers.* New York: New York University Press, 1957.

Crenson, Matthew and Benjamin Ginsberg. *Presidential Power.* New York: W. W. Norton, 2007.

Dahl, Robert. *Democracy and its Critics.* New Haven and London: Yale University Press, 1989.

———. *Dilemmas of Pluralist Democracy.* New Haven and London: Yale University Press, 1982.

———. *A Preface to Democratic Theory.* Chicago: University of Chicago Press, 2006.

Dean, John. *Conservatives without Conscience.* New York: Penguin, 2006.

Edling, Max M. A. *Revolution in Favor of Government: Origins of the U.S. Constitution and the Making of the American State.* New York: Oxford University Press, 2003.

Farrand, Max. *The Framing of the Constitution of the United States.* New Haven: Yale University Press, 1913.

Fisher, Louis. *Constitutional Conflicts between Congress and the President.* Lawrence: University Press of Kansas, 2007.

———. *The Politics of Shared Power: Congress and the Executive.* College Station: Texas A&M University Press, 1998.

Fitzgerald, Michael W. *Splendid Failure: Postwar Reconstruction in the American South.* Chicago: Ivan R. Dee, 2007.

Gaddis, John Lewis. *We Know Now: Rethinking Cold War History.* Oxford: Clarendon Press, 1997.

Gould, Lewis L. *Four Hats in the Ring: The 1912 Election and the Birth of Modern American Politics.* Lawrence: University Press of Kansas, 2008.

———. *The Most Exclusive Club: A History of the Modern United States Senate.* New York: Basic Books, 2005.

———. *The Presidency of William McKinley.* Lawrence: University Press of Kansas, 1980.

Harlow, Ralph Volney. *The History of Legislative Methods in the Period before 1825.* New Haven: Yale University Press, 1917.

Healy, Gene. *The Cult of the Presidency: America's Dangerous Devotion to Executive Power.* Washington, D.C.: CATO Institute, 2008.

Held, David. *Models of Democracy.* Stanford, Calif.: Stanford University Press, 2006.

Hill, Christopher. *The Century of Revolution: 1603-1714.* Edinburgh: Thomas Nelson and Sons, 1961.

Holton, Woody. *Forced Founders: Indians, Debtors, Slaves, and the Making of the American Revolution in Virginia*. Chapel Hill: University of North Carolina Press, 1999.

———. *Unruly Americans and the Origins of the Constitution*. New York: Hill and Wang, 2007.

Howe, Daniel Walker. *What Hath God Wrought: The Transformation of America, 1815–1848*. New York: Oxford University Press, 2007.

Huntington, Samuel P. *Political Order in Changing Societies*. New Haven and London: Yale University Press, 1968.

James, Scott. *Presidents, Parties, and the State: A Party System Perspective on Democratic Regulatory Choice, 1884–1936*. New York: Cambridge University Press, 2000.

Ketcham, Ralph. *James Madison: A Biography*. Charlottesville and London: University of Virginia Press, 1971.

Krehbiel, Keith. *Information and Legislative Organization*. Ann Arbor: University of Michigan Press, 1992.

La Raja, Raymond J. *Small Change: Money, Political Parties, and Campaign Finance Reform*. Ann Arbor: University of Michigan Press, 2008.

Lane, Eric and Michael Oreskes. *The Genius of America: How the Constitution Saved Our Country and Why It Can Again*. New York: Bloomsbury USA, 2007.

Langguth, A. J. *Union 1812: The Americans who Fought the Second War of Independence*. New York: Simon and Schuster, 2006.

Lapidus, Ira M. *A History of Islamic Societies*. Cambridge: Cambridge University Press, 1988.

Lazare, Daniel. *The Frozen Republic: How the Constitution is Paralyzing Democracy*. New York: Harcourt, Brace & Company, 1996.

Levinson, Sanford. *Our Undemocratic Constitution*. New York: Oxford University Press, 2006.

Light, Paul C. "Can't Do Government." *Washington Post*, June 25, 2008.

Lijphart, Arend. *Parliamentary versus Presidential Government*. Oxford: Oxford University Press, 1992.

Lincoln, Abraham. "The Perpetuation of Our Political Institutions: Address to the Young Men's Lyceum of Springfield, Illinois, 1838." In Abraham Lincoln, *Speeches and Writings: 1832–1858*, edited by Don Fehrenbacher, pp. 32–33. New York: Library of America, 1989.

Lithwick, Dahlia. "Wrestling over War Powers." *Newsweek*, July 12, 2008.

Locke, John. *Two Treatises of Government*, 1689/90.

Lutz, Donald S. *Popular Consent and Popular Control: Whig Political Theory in the Early State Constitutions*. Baton Rouge and London: Louisiana State University Press, 1980.

Madison, James. *Federalist Paper No 10*.

Magliocca, Gerard N. *Andrew Jackson and the Constitution: The Rise and Fall of Generational Regimes*. Lawrence: University Press of Kansas, 2007.

Manley, John F. and Kenneth M. Dolbeare. *The Case against the Constitution: From the Antifederalists to the Present*. New York: M. E. Sharpe, 1987.

Mann, Thomas and Norman Ornstein. *The Broken Branch: How Congress is Failing America and How to Get It Back on Track*. New York: Oxford University Press, 2006.

Mayhew, David R. *Parties and Policies: How the American Government Works*. New Haven: Yale University Press, 2008.

McConville, Brendan. *The King's Three Faces: The Rise and Fall of Royal America, 1688–1776*. Chapel Hill: University of North Carolina Press, 2006.

Montesquieu, Baron de. *The Spirit of Laws*. Chicago: Encyclopedia Brittanica, 1952.

Montgomery, Lori and Jeffrey H. Birnbaum. "Political Maneuvers Delay Bill After Bill in Senate." *Washington Post*, June 28, 2008.

Morris, Edmund. *Theodore Rex*. New York: Random House, 2001.

Morrison, Alan B. "Can the President Ignore Congress?" *New Republic*, June 26, 2008.

Ober, Josiah. *Democracy and Knowledge: Innovation and Learning in Classical Athens*. Princeton and Oxford: Princeton University Press, 2008.

Plumer, Bradford. "The Revisionaries: The Tea Party's Goofy Fetish for Amending the Constitution." *New Republic* (September 23, 2010): 16–21.

Pole, J. R. *Political Representation in England and the Origins of the American Republic*. London: Macmillan, 1966.

Pollard, A. F. *The Evolution of Parliament*. London: Longmans, Green and Co., 1926.

Przeworski, Adam, Michael Alvarez, Jose Antonio Cheibub, and Fernando Limongi. "What Makes Democracies Endure?" *Journal of Democracy* 7, no. 1 (1996): 39–55.

Purkiss, Diane. *The English Civil War: Papists, Gentlewomen, Soldiers, and Witchfinders in the Birth of Modern Britain*. New York: Basic Books, 2006.

Redman, Eric. *The Dance of Legislation*. Seattle: University of Washington Press, 2001.

Remini, Robert. *The House: The History of the House of Representatives*. New York: HarperCollins, 2006.

Robertson, Geoffrey. *The Tyrannicide Brief*. New York: Pantheon Books, 2005.

Rosen, James. *The Strong Man: John Mitchell and the Secrets of Watergate*. New York: Doubleday, 2008.

Rowse, A. L. *The England of Elizabeth: The Structure of Society*. London: Macmillan, 1951.

Rubin, Edward L. *Beyond Camelot: Rethinking Politics and Law for the Modern State*. Princeton: Princeton University Press, 2005.

Sabato, Larry. *A More Perfect Constitution*. New York: Walker Press, 2007.

Savage, Charlie. *Takeover: The Return of the Imperial Presidency and the Subversion of American Democracy*. New York: Little, Brown and Company, 2007.

Schlesinger, Arthur M. *The Imperial Presidency*. Boston: Houghton Mifflin, 1973.

Scott, Jonathan. *England's Troubles: Seventeenth Century English Political Instability in European Context*. Cambridge: Cambridge University Press, 2000.

Sellers, Charles. *Market Revolution: Jacksonian America, 1815–1846*. New York: Oxford University Press, 1991.

Shlaes, Amity. *The Forgotten Man*. New York: HarperCollins, 2007.

Skowronek, Stephen. *Building a New American State: The Extension of National Administrative Capacities, 1877–1920*. Cambridge: Cambridge University Press, 1982.

Smiley, Gene. *Rethinking the Great Depression*. Chicago: Ivan R. Dee, 2002.

Smith, Jean Edward. *FDR*. New York: Random House, 2007.

———. *John Marshall: Definer of a Nation*. New York: Henry Holt and Company, 1996.

Swift, Elaine K. *The Making of an American Senate*. Ann Arbor: University of Michigan Press, 2002.

Verney, Douglas. *The Analysis of Political Systems*. London: Routledge and Kegan Paul, 1965.

Vile, John R. *Rewriting the United States Constitution: An Examination of Proposals from Reconstruction to the Present*. New York: Praeger, 1991.

Watson, Harry L. *Liberty and Power*. New York: Hill and Wang, 2006.

Wawro, Gregory J and Eric Schickler. *Filibuster*. Princeton: Princeton University Press, 2006.

Whittington, Keith E. *Political Foundations of Judicial Supremacy*. Princeton and Oxford: Princeton University Press, 2007.

Wicks, Elizabeth. *The Evolution of a Constitution: Eight Key Moments in British Constitutional History*. Oxford and Portland, Ore.: Hart Publishing, 2006.

Wilentz, Sean. *The Rise of American Democracy*. New York: W. W. Norton, 2005.

Will, George. "The Final Repudiation." *Newsweek*. November 17, 2008.

Bibliography

Wolin, Sheldon. *Democracy Incorporated: Managed Democracy and the Specter of Inverted Totalitarianism*. Princeton: Princeton University Press, 2008.

Wood, Gordon S. *The Creation of the American Republic 1776–1787*. Chapel Hill and London: University of North Carolina Press, 1969.

———. *Revolutionary Characters: What Made the Founders Different*. New York: Penguin, 2006.

Wright, Robert. *Hamilton Unbound: Finance and the Creation of the American Republic*. Westport, Conn. and London: Greenwood Press, 2002.

Wright, Robert and David J. Cowen. *Financial Founding Fathers: The Men who Made America Rich*. Chicago: University of Chicago Press, 2006.

Wright, Tony (ed.). *The British Political Process*. London and New York: Routledge, 2000.

INDEX

9/11, 211, 212
13th Amendment, 105, 150
14th Amendment, 105, 106, 107, 108, 109, 122, 150, 151, 154, 202
15th Amendment, 105, 107, 122, 151, 154, 156, 202

A

Ackerman, Bruce, 6, 49, 50, 89, 103
Adams, John, 15, 18, 38, 70, 85, 88, 182
Adams, John Quincy, 85, 115, 143, 144, 145, 161, 162, 187
African-Americans, 106, 109, 154
Agricultural Adjustment Act (AAA), 199, 200
Alien and Sedition Acts, 100, 101, 182
amendments, constitutional, 153, 227, 228, 229, 230
American Revolution, 11, 12, 14, 16, 30, 31, 33, 71, 180
"American System", 160. *See also* Clay, Henry
anti-democratic, 24
    Federalists as, 89
anti-federalists, 29, 31, 84, 173
anti-party position/attitude, 114, 129, 131, 224
Appelbaum, Anne, 117
appropriations, 92, 94, 184, 216
aristocracy, 18, 35, 73
Aristotle, 35, 36, 37, 40, 41, 247, 248
army, 134, 135, 136. *See also* military
    integration of, 155
    standing, 29, 84, 134, 185
Articles of Confederation, 16, 20, 21, 27
assassination, vii, 132, 149, 155, 192
Athens, 35, 36, 37, 38, 39, 248, 249
    government of, 26, 247

B

balanced government, 18, 38, 71
balance of power, 216
banking/banks, 166
    Bank of North America, 16
    Bank of the United States, 163, 165, 183
    Bank War, 163
    First Bank of the United States, 158, 159
    National Bank of the United States, 162

266

Index

Second Bank of the United
  States, 159, 160, 184, 185
state banks, 162, 165
Barbary pirates, 186, 226
Bay of Pigs, 210
Beard, Charles, 12, 14
Beatty, Jack, 108
Berlin Wall, 208, 211
Biddle, Nicholas, 163
Bill of Rights, 48, 57, 83, 228
bills. *See* legislation/legislative
Bipartisan Campaign Reform Act,
  125
bipartisanship, 8, 75, 236
Black Codes, 150
Boland Amendment, 97
Bolingbroke, Lord, 70, 71
Bouton, Terry, 12
Brewer, John, 134
Britain/British, 16, 19, 20, 33, 67, 87,
  134, 158, 187, 196, 237
  –American relations, 11, 14, 15,
    67, 159, 179, 180, 182, 183, 185,
    186, 207
  changes after 1688, 15, 26,
    63, 68–70, 81, 213. *See
    also* Glorious Revolution (of
    1688)
  civil service in, 55, 77, 131
  development of government,
    62, 63, 65, 69
  France and, 12, 180
  money and, 12, 13, 14
  role of Parliament, 8, 62, 181,
    200
  role of parties in, 113, 114, 122
  system of government, 15, 18, 24,
    25, 26, 29, 42, 45, 47, 49, 50, 53,
    54, 55, 56, 57, 61, 63, 65, 73, 81,
    86, 94, 98, 222, 237, 245
  vs. U.S. government, 49, 50, 56,
    242

Budget and Impoundment Act, 93
budget/budgeting, 2, 80, 90, 91, 92,
  93, 94, 95, 98, 194, 197, 204, 213
Budgeting and Accounting Act, 93
Bureau of the Budget, 3, 93, 94
Burr, Aaron, 104
Bush, George H. W., 226
Bush, G. W., 4, 5, 97, 98, 187, 212, 213,
  214, 215, 216, 217, 225, 227
business, 111, 122, 123, 124, 127, 166,
  167, 172, 174, 193, 195, 197, 242. *See
  also* corporations
  regulation of, 168, 192, 199, 224

C

Calhoun, John, 143
California, 108, 146, 187
campaign finance, 114, 123, 124, 125,
  126, 127, 128, 225, 238, 239
Canada, 184
candidates
  parties and, 121, 127
  presidential, 118, 121
  selection of, 114, 115, 116, 119,
    122, 238
Cannon, Joseph, 169
capitalism, 110
Castro, Fidel, 210
Catholicism, 64, 70
caucuses, 116, 117
Ceaser, James, 117
Central Intelligence Agency, 209
checks and balances, 3, 7, 8, 61
Cheney, Dick, 6, 213
Cherokee, 144, 145
China, 209
citizens/citizenry, 35, 37, 39, 41, 49
Civilian Conservation Corp (CCC),
  199
civil rights, 111, 150, 151, 153, 155, 156
  legislation, 97, 154, 155
  movement, vii, 57, 139, 156, 168

267

Civil Rights Act, 107, 155
    Office of the Justice
    Department, 225
civil service, 55, 64, 77, 92, 129, 130,
    131, 132, 133, 168, 192, 225, 237, 240
Civil Service Commission (CSC),
    130, 132, 133, 192
Civil War, 4, 91, 95, 105, 120, 121, 134,
    135, 139, 141, 146, 147, 148, 154, 156,
    162, 166, 167, 168, 193, 202, 223, 227,
    229
Clay, Henry, 121, 143, 144, 160, 161,
    183, 184
Cleveland, Grover, 166, 172
Clinton, William, 97
cloture, 76, 174
Cold War, 210
Colombia, 188
commander in chief, 208, 211, 213, 215
commerce. *See* trade and commerce
Commission on Economy and
    Efficiency, 92
committees, 82, 83, 90
    congressional, 81, 92, 147, 169,
    201
communism, 208, 209, 210
Compromise of 1790, 87
Compromise of 1850, 146
Confederacy, 150
Congress, vii, 2, 20, 23, 26, 28, 62, 76,
    77, 78, 86, 94, 96, 105, 109, 110, 119,
    123, 133, 136, 143, 150, 154, 168, 186,
    189, 197, 200, 202, 204, 226
    budget/funding, 90, 91, 92, 93,
    200
    on civil service, 132, 192
    control over federal agencies,
    3, 82, 133
    executive/President and, 3, 5, 7,
    25, 29, 62, 81, 86, 88, 92, 96,
    118, 129, 152, 153, 180, 186, 187,
    192, 194, 198, 200, 202, 203,
    208, 213, 214, 217
    first, 32, 73, 76, 78, 83, 84, 86,
    139, 233
    legislation and interpretation,
    82, 100, 203, 223
    role of parties, 126, 127
    salary of, 77
    seniority in, 168, 169
    on slavery, 139, 145
    southern states and, 150, 152
    subordination of, 6, 80, 86, 91,
    139, 165, 181, 194, 211, 214, 215
    war, declaring and prosecuting,
    98, 147, 179, 180, 184, 185, 186,
    215, 227
Congressional Budget Office
    (CBO), 93
consensus, 33, 47, 51, 56, 230
Conservative party, 64
Constitution, 16, 23, 24, 25, 27, 29, 36,
    37, 57, 58, 74, 77, 79, 85, 88, 106, 145
    amendments to, 107, 154, 228,
    229, 230, 231
    creation of, 12, 29, 30, 33
    executive authority and, 28, 78,
    163, 179
    idealization of, 1–2, 25
    interpretation of, 99, 102, 103,
    108
Constitutional Convention, 6, 14,
    20, 21, 24, 27, 33, 85, 228
contributions. *See* campaign finance
conventions, national, 116, 117, 119,
    121
Coolidge, Calvin, 110, 192, 194
corporations, 109, 111, 172. *See
    also* business
Corwin, E. S., 4, 246
courts/court system, 83, 101, 104. *See
    also* judiciary/judicial system;
    Supreme Court

268

Index

slavery, 76, 104, 105, 107, 130, 139, 140, 141, 142, 143, 144, 145, 146, 148, 149, 150, 153, 154, 167, 173, 188, 226, 229
slave states/free states, 140, 141, 146, 188
Smith-Connally Act, 125
Smith, Jean, 102, 103, 201
Social Security, 175, 199, 204, 216
South Carolina, 143, 144, 162
Southern Pacific Railroad, 108
South/southern, 108, 167
    blacks, 57, 153
    Democrats, 124, 132, 201, 208
    independence of, 134, 135, 145
    minority, vii, 57, 104, 105, 141
    Rebel debt, 150
    reconstruction of, 149
    resistance to federal government, 107, 135, 144, 145, 147, 154, 155
    states, 95, 105, 107, 108, 141, 144, 147, 150, 151, 152, 154, 156, 162
    way of life, 107, 139, 140, 141, 143, 152, 160
    whites, 153, 155
sovereignty, 143, 245
Spain, 187, 188
Spanish-American War, 92, 135, 136, 188, 191
Speaker of the House, 55, 183
special interests, 1, 4, 121, 224, 239
spoils system, 120, 162
standing committees, 80, 81, 82, 237
State Department, 82
state(s), 110
    constitutions, 17, 18, 19, 20
    debt, 87, 157
    militias, 84, 134, 135, 179, 184
    relation to federal government, 100, 101, 102, 104, 148, 158
    states' rights, 103, 104, 140, 143, 167, 173, 174, 227, 246

viability of governments, 16, 17, 20
stock market, 197, 199
Stuarts, 70
suffrage, 151
supermajority, 28, 47, 51, 56, 200
Supreme Court, 62, 98, 99, 104, 145, 203, 223
    as interpreter of laws, 100, 101, 102, 109, 153, 154, 203, 231
    justices, 202
    President and, 6, 202, 203, 214

T

Taft-Hartley Act, 125
Taft, William Howard, 92, 133, 192, 193
Tallmadge, James, 141
Tammany Hall, 167
tariffs, 83, 91, 143, 144, 160, 173, 188, 195, 197, 200
taxation, 11, 69, 83, 84, 108, 197
    direct, 29
    indirect, 83, 122
    rates, 208
Tea Party, 1
Tennessee Valley Authority, 199
Tenure of Office Act, 151
Texas, 187, 226
Tillman Act, 124, 125, 126
Tory party/Tories, 64, 65, 70, 71, 115
trade and commerce, 157, 160, 183, 187, 192
    regulation of, 172, 173
Trail of Tears, 145
Treasury Department, 79, 91
Truman, Harry, 93, 155, 209, 211, 226
Tyler, John, 154, 164, 165
tyranny, 35, 37, 38, 57, 79
    of the majority, 16, 23, 57

U

unemployment, 198
unions, 124, 125, 132. *See also* labor
United Nations, 209

V

van Buren, Martin, 142, 164, 165, 195
veto, 163, 227
   executive/presidential, 23, 28, 56, 120, 146, 148
   royal, 25
   at state level, 15, 17
Vice President, role of, 149, 154
Vietnam War, vii, 210, 226
Virginia, 15, 65
Virginia Plan, 79
voting, 40, 229
Voting Rights Act, 155

W

war, 69, 179, 180, 183, 184, 185, 186, 187, 193, 207, 209, 213, 215, 226, 227, 229
   funding of, 159, 183, 184, 193, 213
War Department, 79, 147
War of 1812, 134, 144, 159, 161, 182, 184, 185
war powers, 95, 98
   Congress and, 98
War Powers Act, 208, 215
Washington, D.C., 120
   nation's capitol, 87
Washington, George, 78–79, 79, 85, 86, 87, 88, 97, 115, 181, 186, 213
Watergate, 96, 211, 212
Whigs, 63, 64, 65, 115, 116, 165
   Country Whigs, 64, 70
white dominance/supremacists, 153, 202
Whittington, Keith, 100, 101, 109
Wilentz, Sean, 89, 121, 144, 145
Wilson, Woodrow, 133, 136, 166, 167, 193, 194, 211, 226, 227, 228
Wolin, Sheldon, 6
Wood, Gordon S., 30, 32, 246
Works Progress/Projects Administration, 199
World War I, 135, 136, 193, 195, 196, 198, 207, 208
World War II, 124, 136, 155, 196, 198, 207, 208, 209, 210, 216

X

XYZ affair, 182

ABOUT THE AUTHOR

Gary Y. Larsen is a retired psychologist who has had a continuing interest in and concern about our government for many years, having grown up in the Washington, D.C. area. Not being a lawyer, historian, political scientist, or politician, he has no vested interest in upholding the status quo, in describing things only as they are. He is more interested in what could be and should be. He wants to explore ways to make government more effective and responsive to its citizens. For more information, visit www.demosphobia.com. The author can be reached by email: gary.larsen@demosphobia.com.

COLOPHON

The main text was set in 11/14 Adobe Caslon Pro designed by Carol Twombly for the Adobe Corporation. William Caslon released his first typefaces in 1722. Caslon's types were based on seventeenth-century Dutch old style designs, which were then used extensively in England. Because of their remarkable practicality, Caslon's designs met with instant success. Caslon's types became popular throughout Europe and the American colonies; printer Benjamin Franklin hardly used any other typeface. The first printings of the American Declaration of Independence and the Constitution were set in Caslon. For her Caslon revival, designer Carol Twombly studied specimen pages printed by William Caslon between 1734 and 1770.

This book was published by Boyd Street Press, a small, independent publishing house specializing in scholarly works that are timely and thought provoking. See our website for more information: www.boydstreetpress.com.

This book was printed in the United States by the Hamilton Printing Company of Castleton-on-Hudson, New York, on 50# Hamilton offset 92 (500 ppi) with a four color 10 point CIS cover stock.